Write m

ALSO BY RACHEL MCALPINE

Books about writing
Nine Winning Habits of Successful Authors
Web Word Wizardry
The Passionate Pen
Global English for Global Business
Real Writing
Song in the Satchel

Fiction
Scarlet Heels: 26 stories about sex
Humming
Farewell Speech
Running Away from Home
The Limits of Green
Maria in the Middle (for children)

Poetry
A for Blog
Another 100 New Zealand Poems for Children (Editor)
Tourist in Kyoto
Selected Poems
Thirteen Waves
Recording Angel
House Poems
Fancy Dress
Stay at the Dinner Party
Lament for Ariadne

Plays
The Dazzling Night: A Noh play in English
Driftwood
Peace Offering
Power Play
The Stationary Sixth Form Poetry Trip

Textbooks for ESL students
The Great New Zealand Study Trip
Katherine Mansfield in New Zealand
Masako in New Zealand
The Secret Life of New Zealand

Rachel McAlpine is an expert in writing online content—in other words, business writing in the electronic era. Founder-director and curriculum developer for Contented Enterprises, Rachel lives in Mt Victoria, Wellington, New Zealand, and is also known as a poet, playwright and novelist.
Web site: www.contented.com

Write me a web page, Elsie!

*How to write fresh, findable content
for web sites, intranets and social media*

Rachel McAlpine

Published by CC Press
PO Box 19184
Wellington 6149
New Zealand
info@ccpress.info

© Copyright Rachel McAlpine Trust 2008
This reprint © copyright Rachel McAlpine Trust 2011

The moral rights of the author have been asserted.
Printed and bound in New Zealand by Astra Print.

Notice of rights
All rights reserved. This book is protected by international copyright laws, and the Rachel McAlpine Trust owns the intellectual property. Except for the purposes of fair reviewing, no part of this publication may be reproduced, stored or transmitted in any form or by any means, electronic, digital or mechanical, including CD, CD-ROM, DVD, e-book, PDF, photocopying, recording, or by any means via the Internet, World Wide Web or an intranet, or by any other means, without the prior permission of the Rachel McAlpine Trust. Infringers of copyright are liable to be prosecuted. To ask permission for reprints and excerpts, contact CC Press.

Notice of liability
The information in this book is distributed on an "As is" basis, without warranty. While every precaution has been taken in the preparation of this book, neither the author, nor CC Press, nor the Rachel McAlpine Trust shall have any liability to any person or entity with respect to any loss or damage caused or alleged to be caused directly or indirectly by the instructions contained in this book.

ISBN 978-0-473-14042-7

For you, and thanks to you

This book is dedicated to...

Everyone who ever wrote an advertisement, agenda, annual report, chart, discussion document, form, graph, instruction, law, letter, memo, manual, marketing document, newsletter, mission statement, news releases, news story, pamphlet, policy statement, procedure, promotion, proposal, presentation, report, RTF, schedule or specification.

And then the boss said, 'We've decided to put this on the intranet.' (Or web site ... or Facebook page ...)

Thanks to...

Many thanks to Alice Hearnshaw, my brilliant partner at Contented Enterprises. And thanks to Miraz Jordan, Mary Barr, and all our Contented clients, learners and supporters. I learn something new every day from journalists, bloggers, researchers and teachers tweeting and blogging about a huge range of topics—thank you.

The 2011 reprint

Some chapters have been lightly revised because of developments in technology, culture, social media, search—in the world, in fact.

Any book about online content is out of date the moment it's printed, because communication culture, technology, channels, hardware and software change with dizzying speed.

By now, most of my web examples, good or bad, have changed or disappeared. Don't worry when you see screenshots from a few years back: they demonstrate points that are still relevant, and the principles of good online writing remain the same.

Table of Contents

1.	21st century business writing	1
2.	Why the dream seems impossible	13
3.	Not your usual reader	19
4.	Plain language online	26
5.	F-headlines: flying the flag	33
6.	F-summaries: do or die	44
7.	F-links and cuff-links	54
8.	The feng shui of online content	66
9.	Function and dysfunction	76
10.	Focused, freestanding content	85
11.	Fresh and factual content	102
12.	Photos, figs, Flash and audio	111
13.	Findable content	128
14.	Web Me-Too and what else is new	145
15.	Standard pages need a brain	157
16.	The secret life of intranets	180
17.	E-government: because you must	196
18.	Commercial content: trust me	215
19.	Academic content: practise what you preach	230
20.	International content	245
21.	Culture change: getting contented	253
	Endnotes	267
	Index	281

1.

21st century business writing

Here's the dream: that all business documents are useful and easy to understand, regardless of where they are read—on paper, or on a web site or intranet. Here's the reality: much business writing is a struggle to read, and misses its goal by a mile. Consequently, although plenty of web sites are well designed and functional, they fail because of poor content. Here's the crunch: nothing will change until everyday business documents are routinely web-proofed before they leave the desk.

Strange to say, that's not necessarily very complicated or expensive.

Churning, chipping and tipping

Historically, salaried staff have churned out business documents that were never going to be published. Instead, they were destined for the eyes of a few select readers. Much was forgiven in this environment: readers made an effort to understand documents despite wordiness, jumbled thoughts and errors. With the rise of the web and intranets, a high proportion of these very documents are now destined for publication online.

Publication means made public: the documents, now renamed *content*, are exposed to the entire world. (Or the entire organisation, in the case of an intranet.) As soon as everyday documents are published online, all their inherent shortcomings become apparent. Worse, even fairly OK documents seem to lose their shine: writing web content, it seems, requires some special skills.

In general, management has responded by chipping away at the problem. The usual pattern has been to label a small number of staff members *content authors*, and train them. Trouble is, the problem is far too big to remove one chip at a time. The problem of useless online content needs an organisation-wide solution. 21st century business writing should be the norm, not the exception. That means writing that works both on paper and in a browser window—F-writing. (All will be explained.)

How Little Things Can Make a Big Difference is the subtitle of Malcolm Gladwell's book *The Tipping Point*.[1] Let's follow his advice and think of the necessary mind-shift as an epidemic. The whole writing culture of an organisation can improve when many staff members make a few small changes. Not every staff member needs to be converted, because the changes escalate when a tipping point is reached. We don't know what that tipping point will be—perhaps it will be a fixed number such as 200, perhaps a percentage of staff such as 30%.

How come? Well, say Mary-Jane is a hold-out: no way does she intend to change her old habits and adopt this new thing called F-writing. Mary-Jane writes an article for the staff newsletter in the bad old style. But the newsletter editor is an F-writer, so the article is changed accordingly. And when her article appears in the newsletter, it's the odd one out, the least interesting, and even Mary-Jane can see the difference. At this point, quietly, without fanfare, she begins to change her ways by choice, not because she is told to.

When a certain number of Mary-Janes begin to accept the idea, the epidemic is underway.

A crisis of communication

Government agencies, universities and businesses have a communication crisis. It's not the familiar story of overspending on IT projects. It's a story of colossal waste as people attempt to read material that was written for paper and is now published on an intranet or web site.

They stare at a screen trying to figure what the page is about. They unwittingly read the wrong version of a document. They read a page three or four times before getting the message. Or they don't get the message at all, and waste everybody's time inquiring about a routine procedure.

Many employers realise they have a crisis on their hands. The penny drops when a site is redesigned or a new content management system or publishing tool is purchased. With the technology finally under control, they are obliged to confront the obvious: their sites have far too much content, and much of it is awfully bad.

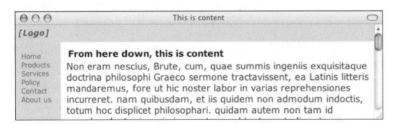

The screenshot above is the simplest illustration of what I mean by *content*. But the next one is also a screenshot of content, because Word documents and PDFs abound on web sites and especially intranets.

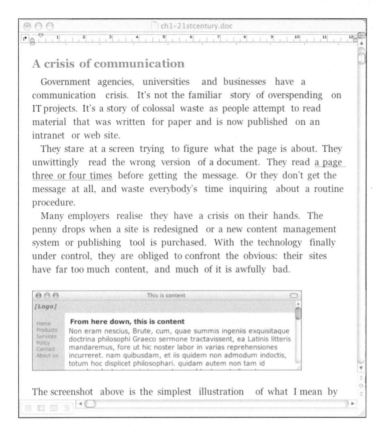

It's all content now

The crisis is magnified because web content matters more than ever before. Content doesn't merely document the business or promote the business: content *is* the business. Gerry McGovern explains as follows.[2]

> The Web has changed the role of content. Content can now make the sale, deliver the service and build the brand. Slowly, organizations are beginning to realize that content is a business asset. [...] This is the age of the Web. This is the age of content. If commerce is selling with people, then ecommerce is selling with content. If government is serving with people, then egovernment is serving with content.

The web is the reason that content is—or should be—finally in the spotlight. The shortcomings of content are horrifyingly obvious when seen on a web site.

However, it's high time we started regarding all business documents as content. That's what they are, the moment they are stored on a company hard drive or in a document management system. Company documents and applications are a major asset of any organisation. They store data, they record data, they process data, they are data.

They are contained in a system of some sort, and so they are content.

Don't blame the writers—train the writers

Strangely, nearly everyone can recognise bad content at ten paces. Faced with a page that's impenetrable, illogical or unusable, people react instantly. They get annoyed. They abandon the site within seconds. They go back to Google and try again.

But if you ask the same people to improve the content, they can't do it. Often they know what's wrong, but they don't know how to fix it.

I have the utmost sympathy for anyone who writes online content, whether intentionally, incidentally or accidentally. Some are communication experts such as journalists or professional writers, but many are simply people who happen to write as part of their job. Suddenly, much to their surprise, their writing is published online. They are obliged to do a hard job, an unwanted job, an annoying job, an extra job— with little or no guidance. Some struggle to comprehend why their years of experience are of little avail when documents go online.

Content writers deserve much more attention and guidance and support. Their efforts are often treated as an afterthought, yet they are crucial to the success of any web site.

Don't believe me? In August 2006, Next Communications surveyed digital agencies about their priorities:[3]

- Priorities cited for website projects were design (75%), development (55%) and search engine optimisation (65%), with only 10% of agencies questioned saying website content was top of their agenda.
- When asked what caused website launches to be delayed, 55% cited 'content not ready' or 'content not suited to web pages' as key reasons.
- Delays ranged from one to three months, with associated costs of between £25,000 and £100,000.

An exasperated James Robertson of StepTwo Design let rip in a forum: [4]

> I have seen sites delay going live for over 12 months because no one was capable of writing the "about us" page! [...]

> In EVERY single instance where I have left a company with a perfect, working CMS and also a trained internal member of staff to do the updates I have had to come back in and do the updates myself. No internal staff get given the job as a priority - - they never get any recognition, time or extra pay to do this extra work, so even if they do the first update they never do the second. [...] Companies ALWAYS mistake content creation as a technical task and not as a marketing / online copy writing task; they ALWAYS find it impossible to add new content - and NEVER delete old or out of date content.

It is still remarkably common for content to be perceived as a responsibility for IT. As if they haven't got enough to do! And when did the IT team become writing experts?

Web sites and intranets can only succeed with strenuous team work. It's essential for content managers, web developers, HR and Corp Comms to join forces if they want to improve content quality.

Most content writers I meet are employed by large organisations. Without support from managers, staff writers can't even undertake training, let alone implement their new knowledge. And even when every officially designated content author has been trained, the job is hardly started—because at least half of what goes online was written by other people.

Mammoth in the meeting room

So, what to do about the problem of bad content? It's a mammoth in the meeting room. You know the story. The web team huddles in a corner of the room. They're addressing issues as hard as they can go. They may discuss governance, design, business analysis, information architecture, customer relationships, content management, applications, workflow, timeframes, coffee breaks, usability, focus groups, you name it, and a hundred other things.

They huddle in a corner because most of the meeting room is occupied by a mammoth: content, not the management thereof but the quality thereof. But the mammoth is not on the agenda. Managers can hardly be blamed for averting their eyes, for it seems that to deal with the mammoth, they'll have to demolish the building.

The problem is so enormous, so intractable, that by tacit agreement everybody dodges the topic. It's just too scary.

They all know the intranet or web site has too much content, much of it useless. They have set up systems for all content to be reviewed regularly—but too often, even the new content is useless.

Naturally they all dream of a site where all content is useful and usable. They've tried using outside writers—but that's expensive, and anyway, their own staff are the subject experts. They've provided standards and a style guide—but these are mysteriously ignored. They've trained more staff every year—but the benefit evaporates within weeks. As fast as they weed out redundant, outdated and trivial content (ROT), more springs up in its place.

What do people want?

What do people want when they visit your web site or intranet? Most of the time, they want information or applications—content. Naturally, they also want great design and functionality, but that's not why they visit the site. They want content.

Technology can't fix content. Content management systems do help us to manage information and even to structure pages–but they can't do the writing. Automatic metataggers have their limitations. Search engines produce useless results if content writers don't understand the conventions. An elegant, well oiled web site or intranet is pointless if the content is hard to understand, irrelevant, inaccessible, inaccurate, trivial or out of date.

The fact is, without high quality content, you have nothing. Or worse than nothing: frustrated customers, and increased pressure as staff find work-arounds to compensate for the site's shortcomings.

As with every crisis, this one presents an opportunity. No one pretends that all their paper documents are uniformly well written. Luckily, when you improve the writing of online documents, you improve all business documents.

What more do people want?

Visitors to your site want information but they also want action, achievement and power. They want facts and sometimes analysis. They want stories, but even more, they want to be part of the story. They want involvement, sharing, a sense of community. They want to be heard.

They want pages that generate truthful, sensible search results, and match what they see in search results.

They want content to be more than merely usable (although goodness knows, that alone would be fantastic). They want the online experience to be a pleasure.

Great content doesn't necessarily win accolades: more often, it is barely noticed. People rarely stop to tell their neighbour, 'Hey, what a great page!' When content shines, they complete a task so quickly that it never crosses their mind.

Once upon a time, the quality of content was hardly an issue. We talked about *surfing the web* as if it were a sport or a kind of tourism. Remember those good old, bad old days? For the site owner, it was prestigious just to have a web site, never mind the content. And people actually had time to explore the web, going online just to check the action.

That does still happen, especially on social sites such as YouTube. But during working hours, idle surfing is an unthinkable luxury for most people. When they open a browser nowadays, they usually have a goal–for example, booking a flight with frequent flyer points.

When people achieve their online goals, they feel satisfied and capable, because they have improved their skills and taken control. Achieving online goals with ease is so rare that a happy customer is inclined to love the site and trust the owner.

Great content is easy to find, easy to read, and easy to use. Great content makes people feel contented.

What content turns people off?

Visitors do not want puffery, gobbledegook or sweet talk. They do not want information of the we-know-best, shut-up-and-listen variety. They don't want to be treated like ninnies.

They don't want long pages of dense prose. They don't want messy, ugly pages that are hard to scan.

They don't want ROT.

They don't want long-winded, saggy-baggy content.

They don't want chaotic, confusing content.

But how do you know if you have written great content? The following tests are relevant to almost all web content. They are all the responsibility of the writer.

The 10 tests for quality web and intranet content

1. **The 3-second test**[5]

   Can people get the gist of this page in 3 seconds, without scrolling or reading every word?

2. **The serenity test**

   Does the content of the page look well organized, calm and orderly?

3. **The tip-top test**

   Is the essential information at the top of the page, in the headline and first paragraph? Does the first paragraph contain a summary, description or key message of the page?

4. **The identity test**

   Is it obvious who owns this content? Is the owner's location obvious in the content (not just in the logo or banner)?

5. **The plain language test**

   Are the words familiar and easily understood? Are sentences 20 words or fewer? Are paragraphs 65 words or fewer?

6. **The *so what?* test**

   Can your target readers instantly see the relevance of the content to their own needs and situation? Does content use the word *you*, speaking directly to the reader?

7. **The action test**

   Can readers quickly see how to take the next logical action online? Are links useful to the reader? Are links conveniently placed?

8. **The accessibility test**

   Can all readers get the information from this page, regardless of their physical abilities, computer, browser or systems? Are all images clear, well-sized, and useful? Do all images have ALT-text? Do complex images have a text equivalent?

9. **The *yeah, right!* test**
   Will readers trust this information? Is it obviously up to date? Does the content seem expert and reliable? Is it easy to contact the owners?
10. **The free-standing test**
    Does the content of this page make sense out of context? Does it make sense even if it is the first page on a site that a person visits? Does it make sense without the logo? Would the headline and first paragraph make good sense in search results?

C for Cinderella

Web site development has streaked ahead this century. But at present, content is poor little Cinderella, technology the prince.

If an organisation is to see a return on dollars spent on web sites and intranets, they need good content. Without it, the sites bleed cash from every link. And speaking of cash, budgets speak loudly about the value an organisation places on content.

Take the intranet redevelopment budget of an imaginary company, Telepop Limited. Telepop has 1,000 employees.

Software purchase	$200,000
Software installation & customisation	$150,000
Business analysis	$30,000
Content audit	$8,000
Template design	$30,000
IA, usability tests, extra functionality	$30,000
TOTAL	$480,000

Contrast this with Telepop's investment in content writers:

Training 20 writers (one day)	$5,000

After spending a mere $5,000, Telepop's CEO assumes the issue of content quality is done and dusted. In a telling contrast, managers take it for granted that the CMS will require an annual licence fee plus ongoing upgrades and maintenance.

As time goes by, the initial content grows stale and dated, and new content is written by untrained staff. Telepop's intranet content degrades, and the dream of usable content fades to pale.

The next chapter looks at why usable content seems like an impossible dream to many organisations. But don't panic—the dream is achievable.

The 96:4 rule

What skills do all content writers need? This book contains at least 96 tips that are useful for writers, but you can't teach hundreds of busy people 96 tips and expect them to apply them all.

It's far more effective to train 96 employees in 4 skills than to train 4 employees in 96 skills. Just choose the 4 skills with maximum impact. Together, they add up to F-writing.

From criteria to skills

Long ago in 1997, John Morkes and Jakob Nielsen took us halfway by identifying three criteria for usable content.[6] They said content must be:

- concise
- scannable
- objective.

They and others have repeatedly proven that when content meets these three criteria, the usability of a web site doubles.

Wow! Say again? By merely editing the content you can double the usability of a web site or intranet? That's amazing!

Alas, criteria alone are not enough. Sure, trained journalists may need no more than those three clues. Just utter the magic words, *concise, scannable* and *objective*, and professional writers will click their heels and make it happen. The trouble is, non-professional staff writers don't know how. *Concise, scannable* and *objective* are just adjectives to them. Anyway, Mary-Jane already believes her business writing is *concise, scannable and objective*. What she needs is skills.

F-writing makes business documents web-worthy

F-writing corresponds to the way people skim-read web pages. Typically, readers focus briefly on patches of text that stand out, and as their eyes flick rapidly over the page, they usually track the approximate shape of an F.

Since 2004, thousands of eyetracking studies by numerous companies and universities have confirmed F-reading as the dominant pattern of online readers.

Three heatmaps from a large study in 2006 by Nielsen Norman illustrate the syndrome.[7]

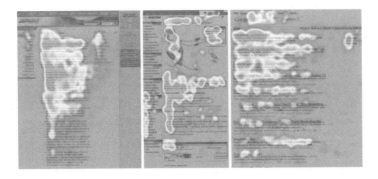

The heatmaps are computer-mapped records of where readers' eyes rested briefly on three different web pages as they performed certain common tasks. Certain areas stand out from background grey (and blue, if you can see the colours). On each heatmap, a sort of F-pattern emerges, showing that many people look at headlines. After that, they also look at words on the left hand side of the main content. The words they read form a flagpole on the left, flying one or more flags across the page. They read more at the top and less at the bottom of the page. You'll also notice considerable chunks of writing that nobody even glanced at during the test.

That's F-reading. And F-writing is necessary because online, people F-read.

The basic formula for writing business documents that work on the web and on the screen is this simple:

Plain language + F-headlines + F-summaries + F-links = F-language.

Here's how it works:
- plain language is concise, and
- F-headlines, F-summaries and F-links are scannable and objective.

The 4 rock-bottom essential rules for content writing are explained in Chapters 4-7. When staff writers know, understand, and apply the rules in those chapters, the usability of intranets and web sites takes a mighty leap forward, and all business writing improves.

When you web-proof, you screen-proof

Of course, not all business documents are bound for publication on a web site or intranet. However, the vast majority will be read on a computer monitor, which is automatically more difficult than reading text on paper.

This is a fact that may elude top managers. Their executive assistants helpfully print out important documents and present them for perusal on easy-peasy paper. Thus the CEO is frequently spared the everyday hassle of reading on the screen, and doesn't have a fair chance of understanding the problems of bad content.

The differences between web content and ordinary business documents are not as extreme as you might think. Non-web documents, just like web content:
- are usually read from a hard, dazzling, blurry screen
- can be deposited in a database (a document management system) and indexed
- should be searchable
- can be optimised for search engines
- can contain bookmarks
- can have hyperlinks to and from web sites.

As we know, those common or garden documents in Word and PDF are very likely to be available on intranets and web sites. In that case, they are not just *like* web content: they *are* web content. That's one reason why the rules for writing web content are so appropriate and so helpful for ordinary business documents.

F is for F-reading, F-writing, and the number 4

But wait, there's more!

F is for favourite pages.

And F is for other fine factors of quality business documents and web content: free-standing, front-loaded, focused, forceful, functional, factual, fast, fresh, friendly and findable.

F is for fabulous, fantastic, formidable, and futuristic. Fair enough: this all points to better business writing and great web content.

Remember the end of the fairy tale? Cinderella Content wants to marry Prince IT. It's high time he proposed—the ugly sisters have had their day.

Let's just call it writing

Many web developers, designers and content managers avoid the verb *to write* when discussing online content. Instead they talk about *creating* and *authoring* and *producing* and *modelling* content.

I don't know how this habit originated. Maybe it happened because technical people dislike writing (they're not alone), so they invented new labels to sweeten the task. Trouble is, the alternative words can be even more intimidating to a reluctant writer.

Or maybe they thought writing web content was a more technical, specialised activity than mere business writing, needing its own rarified verbs. Perhaps they had in mind content such as applications, games and movies. Certainly, content does consist of more than words. It's essential for the writer to think in a dynamic, webby sort of way—to consider non-text things like links, interactivity, images, sound and forms. Also, writing may seem almost like a different process when you are using templates.

So perhaps words like *create* and *author* are intended to warn writers that special skills are needed for web content. That's true, but only because so much common old business writing is sub-standard to begin with. It turns out that exactly the same skills are needed to upgrade paper documents.

Anyway, I'm going to call writing *writing*. For people at work, generating content usually consists first and foremost of writing and editing. All those fancy verbs perpetuate a phony distinction between paper writing and print writing. Why must I *write* an article for a paper newsletter, but *author* it for the intranet? It's absurd.

Instead, mutter this mantra.

Web writing is business writing.
Business writing is web writing.
Web writing
is business writing
is web writing
is business writing.

2.

Why the dream seems impossible

Experts have improved web sites and intranets beyond all expectations over the last ten years. So why should content be the sticking point? Let's examine the barriers to achieving the dream of usable content. Only by fearlessly confronting the mammoth can we turn it into a pussycat. The barriers are:
- the sheer size of the problem
- the number of staff involved
- poor business writing
- cost of traditional training
- blurred areas of responsibility.

1. The sheer size of the problem

Mountains—no, mountain ranges—of paper documents are already online, and they build up and up. Intranets with 50,000+ pages are common. The Nielsen Norman Group's shortlist of ten 'best' intranets in 2007 had on average 6 million pages![8]

Size brings trouble: the large number of pages means that staff cannot find information, so they publish new versions without removing the originals. The new versions are redundant and inconsistent, wrecking credibility. Or as Bob Boiko, author of the *Content Management Bible*, puts it:[9]

> Web managers face real challenges: their sites are being deluged by content that is out of control and of dubious value.

Large web sites can turn content into a hydra-headed monster. No sooner do you lop off one hissing head than two more grow in its place. You cull the dross from your intranet, and before you can blink, staff are publishing more bad content.

In the last few years, the amount of material written at work has increased exponentially.
- People at work write memos, manuals, policy, procedures, instructions, discussion documents and legislation. They write forms, charts, presentations, minutes, specifications, newsletters, news releases, calendar entries and schedules. They write reports, mission statements, proposals and marketing material.

- In a government organisation, everything gets documented. What has happened, could happen, should happen, will happen and won't happen, who does what and how and why—it's all documented. Then government bodies audit their documents, and document the audit process.
- Academic institutions produce vast quantities of documents for their students, teachers and the public. Teachers from kindergarten to university are writing course material, teacher resources, lessons, timetables, reports and academic articles.

Nowadays, a high proportion of these documents is published online, often without editing or discrimination.

Once web sites were just glorified company brochures, and the intranet was primarily a staff directory. Now we have mass online publishing.

Massachusetts Institute of Technology (MIT) is a famously ambitious and idealistic example.[10] MIT OpenCourseWare is a large-scale, web-based publication of the educational materials from virtually all of MIT faculties. MIT intends putting 1,800 courses online. That's quite a lot of pages. And how do you control the writing of 1,800 professors?

MIT OpenCourseWare | Master Course List

Departments

- Aeronautics and Astronautics
- Anthropology
- Architecture
- Athletics, Physical Education and Recreation
- Biological Engineering
- Biology
- Brain and Cognitive Sciences
- Chemical Engineering
- Chemistry
- Civil and Environmental Engineering
- Comparative Media Studies
- Earth, Atmospheric, and Planetary Sciences
- Economics
- Electrical Engineering and Computer Science
- Engineering Systems Division
- Experimental Study Group
- Foreign Languages and Literatures
- Health Sciences and Technology
- History
- Linguistics and Philosophy
- Literature
- Materials Science and Engineering
- Mathematics
- Mechanical Engineering
- Media Arts and Sciences
- Music and Theater Arts
- Nuclear Science and Engineering
- Physics
- Political Science
- Science, Technology, and Society
- Sloan School of Management
- Special Programs
- Urban Studies and Planning
- Women's Studies
- Writing and Humanistic Studies

Aeronautics and Astronautics

- 16.00 Introduction to Aerospace Engineering and Design, Spring 2003
- 16.01 Unified Engineering I, II, III, & IV, Fall 2005 - Spring 2006
- 16.02 Unified Engineering I, II, III, & IV, Fall 2005 - Spring 2006

Much content is garbage

Can any organisation mass-produce first-rate content? Some of these paper mountains are garbage mountains. For example, web content expert Gerry McGovern was working on the 100,000 page intranet of a large non-governmental organisation. He deleted 60,000 pages and nobody even noticed: there was not one single enquiry for the deleted pages.[11]

How redundant is that?

I suspect this is the norm for intranets: they may have valuable information and tools, but far too much content is unnecessary, unusable, unfound, unwanted, unnoticed and unloved.

2. The number of staff involved

When a content management system is adopted, a licence is usually purchased for every writer. That's when the fact must be faced: many employees will be writing and publishing their own content. That's the trend, and publishing tools make it easy.

It is commonly believed that online content is written, edited, or at least controlled by a small group of experts in HR, the web team, and the marketing and Corp Comms departments. That may have been true ten years ago, but not now. True, on small sites, a handful of professional writers can still control the quality of all content, and some organisations use contractors to produce all the content on their public web sites. But nowadays subject experts, not writing experts, produce most of the content for intranets and government and academic web sites.

Centralised control just doesn't work with high volume intranet content. The system breaks down. Swamped with work, your little team of expert web editors haven't got a dog's show of fixing every web page—they don't even try, because:

- the number of pages is overwhelming
- many documents are copyright and must not be changed
- some documents are so badly structured they cannot be fixed
- some writers take offence if their document is edited.

So let's assume that:

- about two thirds of salaried staff write as part of their job[12]
- writing web content is a mainstream skill
- all writers in an organisation should meet the same standards—not just official content authors.

On this basis, a majority of salaried staff need to at least understand the basic rules for writing content. That's daunting.

3. Poor business writing

On public sector and academic sites, most content essentially consists of regular business writing, which in general is far from perfect. When it goes online, the imperfections are brutally exposed for all to see. Documents that would pass-with-a-push on paper often seem incoherent on a web site. Not only do they look horrible on the screen, but their clumsy structure and confusing style suddenly become obvious to vast numbers of the general public.

Many people imagine online writing is a specialised technical activity, quite different from ordinary business writing. But that's not true. Online writing is mainstream business writing, because:

- intranets are primary work tools
- staff publish their own documents online
- government sites are legally obliged to publish a great deal of information online.

Fortunately, whatever you do to improve online content will also improve your paper documents. A document written expressly for the web will usually work successfully on paper, but not vice versa.

General writing skills are crucial for a majority of salaried workers. In September 2004 the US National Commission on Writing published the results of a survey of business leaders.[13] Among their findings:

- 2/3 of salaried employees in large American companies have some writing responsibilities
- poor writers are not hired and rarely last long enough in a job to be promoted
- there is a great deal of corporate interest in how changing forms of communications such as email, PowerPoint, web sites and intranets modify writing demands
- businesses spend US$3.1 billion per year training employees in remedial writing; approximately one third of their employees need some training.

Later, the Commission found that for state government agencies, writing skills were even more crucial, and that training their employees to write better costs US taxpayers nearly a quarter of a billion dollars annually.[14] The Commission called for a writing revolution, stating:[15]

> Writing, education's second "R," has become the neglected element of American school reform.

So an awful lot of people in the workforce, people with at least a high school education, still need to be trained how to write, and not only in the US.

Writing: the neglected "R"

Writing is an area where New Zealand students could do better.

So said the Ministry of Education in the *Student Outcome Overview 2001-2005*, a report that combined and analysed results from a number of studies.[16] Writing was seen as the main problem area, whereas in reading and mathematics New Zealand students achieve at a high level compared to other countries.

It's not as if writing were particularly well taught in the past. Before the 1970s, teachers stressed the minutiae of handwriting, grammar, spelling, and punctuation. At school, we were never taught *how* to write: we were told *what* to write.

Today, even five-year-olds are supposedly taught to think first, then draft, write, edit, and publish, in that order. By contrast, many adults:

- don't know what they don't know
- fear grammar
- assume their first draft should be perfect
- assume they should regurgitate the jargon of their organisation
- have never heard of plain language.

4. Cost of traditional training

At this point, eyeballs are rolling. OK, let's say the directors of Telepop Limited accept that among their 1,000 employees, at least 300 need training in web content writing. That the business depends on it. That without mass training, their IT spend is wasted.

In the US, employers estimated that about one third of employees would each require eight hours' training at US$400 each, just to bring their business writing up to scratch. Hm, let's see: that's $120,000 per year, and we haven't even approached critical mass.

Let's say Telepop accepts the fact that there's no chance of making usable web content the norm unless a majority of staff is trained to write it, including managers (who can undo good work if they don't understand the new rules). Hm, training 600 people: that's US$240,000 per year. Yeah, right—fat chance!

Conclusion: a much more economical way of training staff writers is desperately required. After spending ten years training groups in workshops, I reluctantly concluded that face-to-face seminars are for personal development, not organisational development. Individuals benefit, but long term, the organisation does not.

As an affordable alternative, some kind of e-learning is a logical starting point. The initial cost of mass training your staff is obviously higher than the cost of doing nothing. But in the long run, failing to train content writers is far more expensive. What's the cost of training compared with the cost of unused, unpopular web sites and intranets? This is a serious question, which needs to be answered when assessing the return on investment from training staff writers.

5. Blurred areas of responsibility

Whose job is it to raise standards of content? Nobody's. Whose budget pays for training staff content writers? Nobody's.

I exaggerate: of course many organisations do have a governance group responsible for web standards, and presumably they ensure someone enforces those standards—for example, their Corp Comms team. But do they allocate sufficient resources? That would be extremely unusual.

Content writing is the least sexy aspect of web development. People tend to nod off if you mention the subject. The strange use of the word *content* betrays the fact that this is widely regarded as boring stuff to put inside a shiny bright container. After the developers do the hard work, it's a case of *just add content*... if only.

Few web site owners budget realistically for content. Nowadays most web developers know exactly how important content is, but they can have a hard time convincing clients to take it seriously. They should build it in to their quotes as an annual cost—but who will be first to do so, and risk losing contracts?

Everybody's job is nobody's job. Web sites require extraordinary feats of cooperation, so it's not surprising if content writing slips through the cracks.

- Writers see content as the domain of geeks.
- IT people see content as something for Corp Comms.
- Developers see content as the site owner's responsibility.
- Site owners expect the developer to wave a magic wand and convert all paper documents into useful content.
- Content managers expect to manage content, not edit it.
- Staff see web content as a specialist area for the chosen few.
- Managers see content development as a once-only task within a specific project.

Within any organisation, the budget and responsibility for content should be shared between those with a stake in the outcome. For example:

- IT is responsible for the success of web sites.
- Corp Comms is responsible for maintaining the quality of corporate documents including those online.
- HR is responsible for ensuring staff develop core competencies such as writing, essential for their careers.

In real life, thrashing out issues of ownership and budget is tough. This may be the only real barrier to raising the standard of corporate web and intranet content. And it is one problem I can't solve for you. But don't be deceived: all the other barriers can be overcome—and so can this one. Where there's a will there's a way.

3.

Not your usual reader

Write for your reader.

This is hardly a new thought: it's the first rule of plain language. Whenever you write as part of your job, you should write with a target reader in mind. So why bother even mentioning a standard plain language guideline?

For one thing, this cardinal rule is frequently ignored. Even when writing for print, people tend to be vague about purpose and audience. They often get away with it, because print documents are comparatively easy to read.

There's a second reason for re-examining the reader-rule: your online reader is not your usual reader. People behave quite differently when reading a document on a web site or intranet. There are many reasons for the difference—physiological, psychological and technical.

Consider the way you yourself read online, and you'll soon see why it's necessary to rethink the way you structure, write and format documents that are published on web sites or intranets.

A pain in the neck

Your online readers are uncomfortable. They are stuck in front of a computer, staring at a hard, vertical, dazzling screen, trying to decipher fuzzy dots of light instead of crisp print on flexible paper. Simply reading text on a computer monitor screen is said to be 25% more difficult than reading on paper. You know that, or you wouldn't print out so many web pages, would you?

Your readers may have occupational overuse syndrome (OOS), also known as repetitive strain injury (RSI). Look around: your colleagues are hunched over the keyboard, with heads poked forward like vultures, neck tendons like hawsers and shoulder muscles like rocks. Using a computer literally gives you a pain in the neck.

As they try to read your web pages, readers may have other frustrations: computer crashes, server problems, a slow modem or other accessibility barriers. You know what it's like.

So the writer has to take more care: think harder, say less and structure more strictly. Consider it a miracle that anyone is willing to read a fraction of what you write.

On a screen, documents appear in landscape layout, not the more familiar portrait layout; and only the top of the page can be seen. Therefore what you write at the top of the page is utterly crucial: get that wrong, and your readers won't bother scrolling to the rest of the page. Formatting issues arise: for example, italics are difficult—sometimes impossible—to read, and footnotes inappropriate.

Your readers make your darling pages morph

When a document is printed, it remains pretty much the same until shredded. The text looks the same, the font looks the same, the pages stay the same size and the images stay where you put them.

Not so with web and intranet copy. Your beloved text design is a mere toy for others to play with. Readers can hide your images. They frequently change the font size and face. They can easily change the shape of the document by making a browser window larger or smaller. They can change the colour of the text and background. They can shut their eyes and listen to the text being read aloud by a voice programme. They can read it on their cell phone screen.

Granted that people can and will take such shocking liberties with your web pages, what's a poor writer to do?

With experience and knowledge, you can compensate by cannily, cunningly, craftily structuring every document. Font, size, colour, images—they are mere frills. Get the bones of your document right, and the surface does not matter. Readers cannot tinker with the bones.

Your readers are on a quest

Your readers have a goal. They are searching for specific information, and it's not an easy task.

Think of a web site as a publication, similar to a book, magazine, journal or corporate publication in a non-print medium. A web page is like one chapter or article within that publication.

Now compare the way we search for information in real life and online.

In the physical world, if you want some information you phone the librarian or go to the library. Searching is an orderly check of a limited number of publications. The article you want will be in a book or journal on a specific shelf known to the librarian. It's either there, or not. It doesn't take long to find out.

Online, your readers probably spend about 75% of their time searching for information. Searching can be stressful. Directories imitate libraries, grouping web pages according to category—but within a category, there may be thousands or millions of items to consider. Search engines have enormous databases of web pages, and attempt to rank results according to the searcher's query.

Need I go on? You know the frustration of trying page after page after page, changing your search terms, knowing there are truckloads of other web pages—and the right page may be just one click away. You skim-read the top of each page at lightning speed before moving back to Google results.

The search factor has major repercussions for on-the-job writers.

Your readers are in a steaming hurry

Sore neck, searching, skim-reading—for these reasons alone, your readers are in a very big hurry to find the information they want. So don't torture them!

Thanks to the wonders of eye-tracking experiments, we now know exactly how much time people spend looking at a web page: a few seconds at most. In 2005, repeated experiments showed that people reading search results had an incredibly short attention span.[17] Nobody studies every single search result on a page, of course, and when they do decide to focus on a listing, two thirds of consumers spend only 0.7 seconds. Not even one second!

As people are in search-click mode for about 75% of their time online, clearly their impatience should influence the way online content is written.

Your readers don't trust you

In the real world, simply getting published is a pretty sure sign that a manuscript has been selected, checked, edited and proofread. Roughly 95 manuscripts are rejected for every one that is accepted for mainstream publication. Half-written, unedited, amateurish articles and stories rarely appear in hard copy. Copyright laws are respected and enforced. Quality is controlled. Date of publication is obvious and credible.

Online, anyone can publish anything. So your readers wonder, 'Who wrote this? When? Who published it? Can I trust the information? Can I trust the publisher?'

Gaining the trust of your readers starts with the web design and the reputation of the company. If a site looks good and works well, and visitors know the brand, then they start from a position of trust. Easy navigation and perfect functionality are also very important.

Beyond those factors, retaining trust is largely up to the writers. They need to demonstrate expertise, trustworthiness and accuracy with high quality content. A web page, like a novel or play, must persuade people to suspend their disbelief. ROT destroys a site's credibility. Professional proofreading is a must. A typo like the one in the screenshot below can shake your faith in an entire site.[18]

Your readers long to click

Web content without interactivity can seem curiously boring. People expect your web pages to link to others, and to enable them to instantly complete forms, send email messages, check accounts, book tickets and purchase goods.

Your readers (like you) have an overwhelming urge to click. That forefinger sits on the mouse button, just itching for a chance to visit another page or just make something happen. People often want to do more than read a page: they want to use it.

It's very different with words on paper. Readers have very few ways of instantly interacting with paper. They can choose to read it, ignore it, write on it, post it or toss it in the garbage. Generally, to respond to a paper business document, people have to grab a phone or a pen... or go online. But the online reader can click.

So when writing web content, you need to think, 'What can people do with this page apart from just reading it? What do people really want to do after reading this page, and can I make that happen online?'

Clicking is only a symptom of people's desire for mastery or reciprocal communication. They get considerable satisfaction from achieving a task, mastering something new, moving on to the next stage. Another joy online is joining in: posting comments on a blog, contributing to a forum, having a review published on Amazon, correcting an entry on Wikipaedia. Writers can give readers a sense of accomplishment and community by keeping these needs in mind.

Your readers are easily lost

People reading paper documents usually know what they are reading, because they can instantly look at the cover, title, author and table of contents. In any substantial printed document, pages are usually numbered and bound, stapled or folded together in sections.

The same is not true on a web site. Web pages don't have numbers, and it is usually impossible to tell how large the web site is. Sometimes it is not clear who the publisher or owner is. A good logo is clear and readable, but a logo is not enough.

Never assume that people will always enter a site through the home page. They can and do enter web sites through any page, just by following search results. In fact, that's the purpose of search engines: to direct people not just to a suitable site but to the exact page they need.

People don't read web pages in any sequence you might consider logical. They'll click one link after another, and read only the information they need.

For this reason, every single page of a web site or intranet must make sense alone. Every single web page must make sense in isolation, even if people never read another page on your site. Every page must be credible, and its purpose and subject obvious. That's a monstrous change when you're used to writing for paper! It's the writer's job to create self-sufficient, self-explanatory content, and to provide context through words alone.

Your readers notice technology only when it fails

People who read your web content will usually be unaware of technical factors… until technology fails. Once in a while, this is the responsibility of the writer, not the technical team.

21st century business writers do need to know a little bit about web technology. They don't need to be experts; they don't even need to write HTML. But they need to understand the reasons behind certain standards and guidelines.

Luckily, as internet users, most on-the-job writers have a basis of understanding on which to build.

Your readers are diverse

Once your writing goes on a web site, your potential audience is far larger and more diverse than it would be for the same document on paper. By definition, web pages are open to the whole world. That includes millions of people in other countries, from different cultures. It includes people who speak different languages, people of all ages and nationalities. It includes people hard of hearing, sight impaired or blind, ill or disabled in various other ways, whether temporarily or permanently.

You cannot cater for every possible reader, and you should be clear about who your intended audience is. However, the diversity of your audience has many implications for the way you write, structure and format any documents including online content.

Even an intranet audience may be far larger and more varied than you might assume. And if you work for a large company, government agency, or university, your intranet pages may be visited by employees from many different departments and countries.

Your readers decide in a blink

I've saved the most significant feature until last. You are writing for people who make lightning decisions based on minimal information: online readers.

Online reading is a perfect example of the phenomenon celebrated and analysed by

Malcolm Gladwell in *Blink*.¹⁹ Experienced web-users know in a flash whether a web page is going to be worth the effort of reading. They know without knowing why they know. They know without thinking. They can instantly filter out pages that are off-topic, confusing, badly written or generally unsatisfying—without thinking—without *reading* a word in the conventional sense.

Their first impression is right on the button; when they glance at a page, their adaptive unconscious clicks on. They make a snap decision based on the sum total effect of many factors discussed in this book.

- They see layout, headlines, and links, and make deductions about how well organised the page is.
- In a split second they will see the proportion of long words and full stops, deducing the level of readability.
- They'll recognise the pattern of too many tiny words that signifies space-wasting chit-chat.
- The word *you* will jump off the page and give an impression of friendliness.
- They'll look for keywords and spot them if they're in the right position.
- All this in less than a second. All this without any conscious thought.

Online readers shift gears often, even while reading a single page. As a writer, you have to capture target readers who just flick their eyes at the page for a millisecond. You also need to satisfy those who stay and read in depth.

First gear: finding

Typically, people start an online episode by shopping around for the right site and the right page, often using Google or Yahoo! (On an intranet, people may use the navigation system, links in the content, or the on-site search engine.)

In first gear, people will click on a search result in full knowledge that they have other options. Just one click away are another ten pages, and another, and any of those pages may be the one they really want. That's what puts pressure on the writer. People are not committed at this stage. They are window-shopping in a monster mall. They are not reading, in fact they are barely even skim-reading. They are just glancing at your page.

Second gear: F-reading

After your readers land on your web page, do they read it? No: at first they F-read. They flick their eyes rapidly over the surface, grabbing at fragments of content that might tell them what the page is about. They're still thinking, 'Is this the page I want?' So they make an instant judgement on the basis of a quick glance at your headlines, images or links—and anything else that grabs their attention.

Initially, many people don't bother looking at the menu or logo. They have tunnel vision. They zoom into the centre top of the page, the start of the real content, and ignore everything else. Will they scroll down? In your dreams!

They skim-read, focusing briefly on stand-out text in particular spots, which generally form a kind of F-pattern. To satisfy people at the F-reading stage, content needs to be expertly written. They're going to F-read, so you have to F-write.

But if your headlines are vague, if your link-text is *click here*, if your images are generic—your potential readers leave within seconds. They're too smart to waste time on a page that might be irrelevant.

Third gear: studying or using the page

Now and then, people decide they are looking at a good page, the right page, the page they want. Then they read it (partially or wholly) or they use it.

Got the message?

All business documents should be written in full knowledge that:
- the document may be published on the intranet or web site
- for 10 reasons, online readers are in another zone.

This may all be old news to you. But the facts about online reading are persuasive when you are explaining to other busy people why business writing needs to be updated for the 21st century.

4.

Plain language online

The flight deck box in the cockpit of a Boeing 737 aircraft houses 12-15 manuals. If each manual was 20% lighter, the weight of flight deck box would be reduced by about 4-5 kg. A 5kg fuel saving over thousands of flights per year = big dollars.[20]

The return on investment for plain language is obvious when you look at the sheer volume of communication thundering down upon us, whether on paper or online. Plain language is concise and easy to understand. Surely that's got to be good?

Is any other justification required for plain language? Consider the reading level of different audiences. We know how most people read web content: they scan in a kind of F-shape, and the next few chapters explain exactly how to satisfy those F-readers.

But how about the silent minority, those who can read but have lower literacy skills? According to Jakob Nielsen, they:[21]

- don't skim-read
- read one word at a time
- need to decipher words: can't just recognise them
- lose concentration if they have to scroll
- have trouble with searching.

Around 30% of web users are in this category, and all sites that target a broad audience (such as government sites) should use text that the average 11-year-old could read. Plain language is the natural way to simplify text, and fast readers benefit as well as those with reading problems.

The deliberate, standardised use of plain language is also necessary for another reason. Authorities display a persistent tendency to protect their power with obscure, difficult, fancy, mysterious language—to make documents a test of IQ and education rather than a message from writer to reader.

Only in the 1940s did advocates in academia, government, and the armed forces begin using the phrase *plain language* much. By the 1970s, the phrase had graduated into a movement, which is still rolling—and still necessary—today. It's needed to counteract a century or two when teachers mainly focused on grammar, spelling, and punctuation. Time after time, pedantry won over clarity. With plain language, writers start by saying what they mean, and fix grammar and punctuation later. (When you write plain language, you make fewer errors anyway.)

So, hooray for plain language, now a legal obligation for government agencies in many countries, as well as an achievable ideal.

The rules of plain language go online

Some are tempted to be blasé about plain language, purely because it has been with us for so long. However, the principles deserve a closer look now that so much communication is conducted online. In fact, the use of plain language increases the accessibility, usability and credibility of any web page.

The main rules of plain language follow. You will immediately notice that they go far beyond considerations of vocabulary and syntax.

1. Write for the reader, not the writer

Chapter 3 examined some important implications of this very rule: writing for readers who are stressed by circumstances. It is the fundamental rule of plain language. It underpins every other rule and is the essence of usability. Everything you do, you do for the reader. Every improvement of the text makes the reader's job easier.

Writing for your readers means trying to give them a satisfying experience. Remember that they want to feel competent and in control. Too many web sites and intranets leave readers frustrated. If you enable readers to make progress, they feel good.

So how do you do that?

- Write clearly: this empowers readers, instead of making them feel patronised or stupid.
- Use *you* and a conversational tone of voice whenever possible: this improves understanding and retention.
- Write always from the reader's point of view: don't tell them how great you are, but show them how *their* problem can be solved.

2. Use familiar, simple vocabulary

This is probably the best known rule of plain language. In fact, many people imagine it to be the only rule. It has special power online, improving the usability of web and intranet content.

Remember how resistant most online readers are to actually reading every word? Even on paper you can see at a glance—without reading—that the following sentence has too many long words:

> The underlying messaging facilities of an XML-based Enterprise Application Integration/Business Process Management architecture provides a viable solution for any process-centric requirement.

Blink! You didn't even try to read that sentence, did you? Good decision. Your eyes registered an unusual dearth of mini-words. You didn't reason logically, 'Too many long words and too few short words probably indicates a series of noun phrases, clogging up the syntax. The reward for deciphering such a sentence is unlikely to justify the effort. It's only an example anyway. So I won't bother reading it.' No: the sentence didn't look right so you just skipped it. Your own readers will do likewise.

By the way, Rule 1 takes precedence: *familiar* means familiar to your intended reader, not to yourself. Therefore, a plain language page intended for aeronautical engineers would legitimately use technical expressions such as *vortilon*, *bipass mid-stem reverser*, and *yaw damper*. Even so, wherever possible, everyday words are preferable, such as *exterior pre-flight walk-around inspection*.

To follow this plain language rule, imagine a voice in your ear saying, 'I'm your audience! Use the words I use, not some grandiose or woolly paraphrase!'

The by-product of obeying this rule is a biggie: improved search results. When you use the same vocabulary as your intended audience, you automatically introduce keywords that will influence the page's position in search results. By contrast, when the language on a web page is obscure or vague, its position in search results will suffer.

3. Use simple grammatical structures

This is an inclusive rule covering classic advice about using short, simple, positive, active, logically constructed sentences. Frankly, if you write short sentences, you are much less likely to write rubbish. A quick and simple enforcement tip: never write a sentence longer than 21 words.[22] Result: a more user-friendly web or intranet page.

The rule of short, simple sentences is even more important online than on paper. F-readers see text initially as a blur of grey, subliminally registering full stops as white space—and white space brings relief to eyes and brain. Without conscious thought, you somehow know that the following quote is a single sentence, and you back away.

> A managed workflow, application integration interface, or trading partner interaction can all be described, composed, and implemented with an orchestrated flow of structured XML documents and messages—documents and messages that are processed according to message content, formatting requirements, and business logic contingencies.

Again, online readers are ruthless, trusting their first impressions. *Looks hard? Out of here.* Life's too short to struggle with 43-word sentences, particularly when you perceive them as dots of light on a screen.

4. Be concise

This is a mighty important rule. Conciseness is famously tied to the usability of online content. Conciseness is a hallmark of plain language, and everything about plain language conspires to make writing more concise. Visitors to your site are in a hurry, as we have seen. So:

- first, write as you would speak
- next, cut the words back by half or even more.

On web pages, irrelevant chatter, needless explanations, and rampant verbiage prevent people from finding the information they really need.

> Studies of content usability typically find that removing half of a website's words will double the amount of information that users actually get.[23]

Isn't that amazing? To put it another way, the more you write, the less people will remember. A razor is too gentle a tool for today's business writing. Rather, writers need to attack their first draft with a vacuum cleaner or mulching machine. Plain language online requires the relentless removal of redundant words, sentences, paragraphs, sections and pages.

All attempts to be extra nice on the web are counter-productive when they are wordy. Here is an example of time-wasting burble.

> Whatever your age, even if you are nearer 50 than 60 and retirement is still some way off for you, you may want to find out what you will be entitled to when you reach State Pension age (remember, you don't actually have to retire to get your State Pension).

Online writers should resist the urge to introduce, elaborate or explain. Don't tell me what to do: show me!

A concise page is not necessarily a short page. Concise prose says a lot in a few words. A 300-word page that makes 5 points is more concise than a 200-word page that makes one point.

5. Structure content in a logical way

As we shall see in the next chapters, documents online require a rigorous structure. The top of the page matters most and F-language is the key. If a page begins with an irrelevant or vague headline and summary, it is doomed.

6. Write documents that are easily read and understood by the intended readers

The intended readers ought to be able to understand a document at first reading, even on paper. Imagine that: never having to read a business document twice. Think how much time that would save! This rule becomes even more important when business documents go online, given the pressures on online readers.

Rule 6 also means web content must be accessible. Target readers must be able to access the information on a web or intranet page regardless of their computer, browser, preferences, or tools. Readers with disabilities must get hold of the same information as everyone else. Accessibility is largely a technical concern, but obviously, the writer also has some responsibility here: difficult writing is inaccessible.

7. Use easy-to-read design

A plain language document looks easy to read. You glance at a nicely balanced flyer from your bank, for instance, and you feel confident that the information will be understandable, well organised and maybe even trustworthy. As for web content, the plain language writer plays an important role in creating a page that looks good, for example by providing plenty of headlines, and never writing a paragraph of intimidating length.

8. Use correct, consistent grammar, spelling and punctuation

Have you ever noticed a solitary error of grammar, spelling or punctuation on a web page, and left in disgust? You are not alone. According to B.J. Fogg of the Stanford Web Credibility Project:

> Typographical errors and broken links hurt a site's credibility more than most people imagine.[24]

The plain language writer will also notice and correct other slips and faux pas. The next screenshot reminds us of the danger of clichés, especially ones involving body parts.[25]

Product & Service Guide
Find the right solution for your needs.

Thank you for your interest in LexisNexis®. We'd like to show you how we put research solutions and strategies with innovative technologies to benefit you, your business, and your bottom line at your fingertips.

More about style

When you've been using the web for a while, you realise that online writing style must be carefully calibrated. The writer must walk a tightrope between being stuffy and being sloppy. You're aiming for credibility... but you must also convey a somewhat personal, human touch. How do you convey the right tone? How formal should you be? How personal?

First let's state the obvious: your choice of style will be influenced by the site's strategy and audience. But within those constraints, plain language is extremely versatile. For example, scientists and academics are notorious for obscure, longwinded writing—yet many distinguished professors manage to make themselves perfectly clear. And skilled journalists can obey every rule of plain language while using a strongly individual tone.

Look what happens when the rules of plain language are broken.

> In a January 25, 2005 Case Management Order in the pre-license application proceeding for the U.S. Department of Energy's anticipated application to construct a spent nuclear fuel and high-level radioactive waste repository at Yucca Mountain, Nevada, the NRC pre-license application presiding officer board ordered DOE, the State of Nevada and the NRC Staff to confer regarding procedures for privilege logs and challenges to privilege claims in that proceeding.

You probably gave up on this sentence before the half-way mark. If you did read it, you are probably none the wiser.

The quoted sentence is 68 (yes, 68!) words long, and the main point doesn't come until the end. That fact alone suggests the writer is dangerously unaware of the rules of clear communication. Cynics might suspect the obscurity is deliberate. A long, complex sentence such as this has a lecturing tone. I feel as if the writer is trying to bully me into blind acceptance, because I am too stupid to figure out what the meaning is. On the web, such a tone alienates readers.

Get a bit personal

A personal tone is an important ingredient of powerful online content. Relax. Don't be a clone. Don't try so hard to sound important because that sounds pompous on the web, which is a strangely intimate medium. People may expect a brisk tone on the intranet, but the rewards of using a conversational style are great: better understanding and retention.[26]

The people at 37signals put it like this:[27]

> **Would you read it if you didn't write it?**
>
> Nearly all corporate sites commit the sin of dullness in their writing. It's as if the clients and their consultants believe that if the design is good, all is good. Not so.
>
> Writing is not the place to skimp on your budget. Seduce me, entice me, entertain me with words. Don't be cryptic, don't be stupid, and please don't be dull.

You know it's true! The impact of corporate-speak on most readers is decidedly negative. Boring! Even pages on corporate sites can and should have some individuality.

Call me *you*!

Here's a solid gold tip: use the magic word *you* in web content whenever possible. That little pronoun:

- helps the writer focus on the reader's needs
- makes sentences shorter
- makes writing easier to understand
- suggests a human voice
- engages readers at a subconscious, emotional level.

Another useful word is *we*. Using *we* allows you to write more clearly, using more active verbs, and saying who does what. It helps to humanise web content, so that it is obviously written by a human being, not a machine. But beware: overusing *we-we-we* is a well-known way to alienate readers. As a rule of thumb, *you* should outnumber *we* every time.

Be objective to be persuasive

You are in the business of persuasion, implying read my page, use my page, take action, don't phone for more information, fill out the form, and above all—trust me!

But here's an anomaly: hype is counterproductive on the web.

Here's another: writing objectively does not mean being impersonal. Enthusiasm is a treasure—but attempts to manipulate or coerce are strangely transparent online.[28]

Yes, but...

I know, I know: the world would be a poorer place if all documents were written in plain language. I should know—I'm a poet. I love Proust with his 200-word sentences. And even as I lay down the law about avoiding obscure words, I'm relishing prose like this:

> The berg is a record of Antarctic ice shapes no less than of ice substances. Its structural cryology chronicles ice deformation, much as its stratigraphy chronicles ice deposition.[29]

However, poets, Marcel Proust and Stephen Pyne were not writing business documents. If you give business writers an inch, they'll take a mile. Firm guidelines are a blessing in disguise to business writers and their readers.

5.

F-headlines: flying the flag

This chapter deals with the first powerful F-rule: writing headlines that make an instant impact on skim-readers. If the F-pattern is like a flag-pole, headlines are the flags. They're waving at you! They demand attention. People may read nothing else but the headlines on a page, so headline writers must be cunning.

Upgrade the headlines and you upgrade the entire intranet or web site. If you could do only one thing to improve the usability of a web site, my advice would be to do just that.

```
[Logo] [a banner, not a flag]

menu      Headline     is like a flag
menu
menu      Flagpole     other content other content other content other content other
menu      Flagpole     content other content other content other content other
menu      Flagpole     content other content other content other content other
menu      Flagpole     content other content other content other content
```

By the way, here's how I define these terms:
- *page headline*: the first, biggest headline on the visible content of a web or intranet page
- *sub-headline*: other headlines lower down the page content
- *heading*: a short generic label such as *Our Products* or *Methodology*; not a headline.

```
[Logo]

menu      **This is the page headline**
menu      The page headline describes or summarises an entire web
menu      page.
menu
menu      **This is a sub-headline**
menu      A web page may have any number of sub-headlines. They
          describe or summarise the following chunk of information.
```

Other people use terms like *header* or *heading* or *teaser*. Not me. I'm pretty fussy, because each term has its own connotations. For example, you will notice I use the word *sub-headline* instead of the more familiar *sub-heading* in this context. Headings, as defined above, never work as headlines. They are too short.

Headlines have a mighty impact. Bad headlines frustrate and confuse readers, wasting time and money. Yes, money! Jakob Nielsen has estimated that for a company with 10,000 staff, a single badly written headline on an intranet home page wastes almost $5,000.[30] Good headlines speed up reading, comprehension and navigation. And marketers have known for decades that they can get a spectacular increase in sales merely by changing the headline of an advertisement or web page.

When people F-read, the headline at the top of the page is one piece of text that naturally attracts attention. Obviously, therefore, every page needs an excellent headline—not a label, not a header, not a hint, certainly not a teaser—but a headline. Sub-headlines must also be cunningly crafted.

Great headlines don't happen by accident, luckily. What's lucky about that? Well, to write a great page headline, you have to know exactly what you are trying to say. You are forced to create pages with a strong focus. And when you write sub-headlines, you are forced to structure the text into self-contained chunks. That's all good.

Have only one page headline

First things first: the page headline should be obvious. If a page appears to have two or three headlines at the top, it seems the writer cannot decide what the page is about. That's a worry.

A page with four headlines follows. Which is the page headline? What is the page about? It is not at all clear.

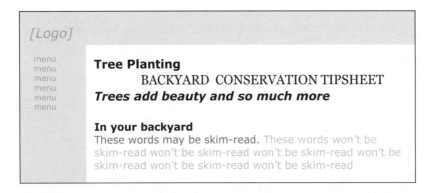

One headline would have been quite sufficient and much more decisive, like so:

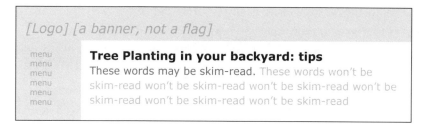

Perfect headlines are left-aligned, not centred. A surprising proportion of readers literally cannot see a short headline that is centred, because the headline isn't part of the F-shape. They look in the top left hand corner of the F: nothing there! They do not look to the right and see the headline.

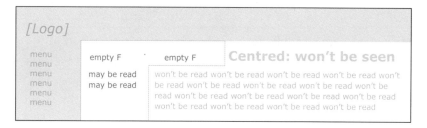

The essentials of an excellent page headline

The perfect page headline for a web or intranet page is:
- a clear guide to the content that follows
- positive, explicit and serious
- unique and specific: the only page with that headline
- front-loaded with keywords.

The perfect page headline even makes perfect sense in other contexts. Just as well, because it is likely to be used in various places, for example as link-text on the home page or the site map.

Don't mess with a good headline. When people click on a headline that is a link, they expect to jump to a page with exactly the same headline. Otherwise they waste time trying to figure whether they are on the right page.

A perfect headline tells the story. John Morkes strongly recommends using an active verb every time; this converts a label to a headline.[31]

Lessons from newspaper headlines

Let's learn about headlines from the masters: newspaper sub-editors.

Anyone who reads a newspaper knows what traditional headlines do: they summarise a news article. They tell the reader enough about the story to make an informed decision about whether to read the news item or not. Online newspapers

write headlines to exactly the same criteria. Examples from the BBC:
- Two sought over tourist's murder
- Delhi swelters amid power crisis.

Editors of news web sites are pretty wary of using headlines that are smart-aleck, silly or just too witty for their shirts. They have two important reasons for writing headlines that are literally true—no joke.

First, they know how impatient online readers are.

Second, they know the same headline has to work out of context—on the home page, in emails, in RSS feeds, as links and so forth. Paper publications do not have the same problem. The headline *Toffee on the nose* becomes meaningful only when placed directly above an article about the departure of an ear, nose and throat specialist from a town called Toffee. But when free-standing, that headline is meaningless and annoying.

Research confirms the traditional sub-editor's wisdom. The Poynter Institute and Stanford University found that on news sites, people prefer straightforward headlines to funny or cute ones.[32]

A *heading* is not a *headline*

Printed newspapers also demonstrate the difference between headlines and headings. Headings are generic labels for recurring sections of a newspaper and are recycled day after day: *World News, Business, Arts, Classified Advertisements* and *Sports* are typical headings. One sits at the top of every newspaper page.

By contrast, headlines are unique and specific to the article. A sub-editor attempts never to use the same headline twice. Ever. In a lifetime.

So that's one of the first things you can do to upgrade headlines on a web site: test them by imagining them in a newspaper. For example, you would never see, *Who are we?* as a headline in a newspaper, and it doesn't work well on a web site either.

Short generic headings are perfectly fine in a navigation bar but should be banned as page headlines. Yet millions of web and intranets have these identical page headlines:
- About Us
- Services
- Applications
- Staff Calendar.

These are all fine as menu items and hopeless as headlines. A few more words would turn those headings into a headline, unique and specific, whether for a web site or intranet:
- About the Family Fry-up Company
- TV aerial repairs, maintenance, and sales
- Apply for travel vouchers, taxi chits, company cars.

Longer than you thought

A good page headline is nearly always longer than your first attempt. Again, check your newspaper, either in print or on the web. How many words in a headline? Here's a rapid survey of the top headlines of a few online newspapers on 21 March 2007.

- NY Times: 6, 10, and 9 words (nytimes.com)
- LA Times: 5, 5, and 5 words (edition.cnn.com)
- BBC: 5, 5 and 4 words (news.BBC.co.uk)
- CNET: 7, 6, and 5 words (news.com.com)
- Times: 6, 8, and 7 words (www.timesonline.co.uk)
- Telegraph: 6, 5, and 7 words (www.telegraph.co.uk).

On these newspapers I couldn't see a single headline shorter than four words. So we can conclude that for headlines on major international news sites, one word is never enough, two words are never enough, three words are never enough and four words are rarely enough.

It is no different on your web site or intranet. Aim to write headlines of 4-10 words. In the list below, only the last two examples are adequate as a page headline—and I prefer the last one:

- Courses
- Undergraduate courses
- Undergraduate courses 2006
- Undergraduate courses 2006, Linguistics and Literature
- Undergraduate courses 2006, Linguistics and Literature, Seddon Polytechnic.

Teasers: forget the very word

Now you're clear about why the word *header* can mislead content writers. How about *teasers*? Unfortunately, that's the word used by certain content management systems instead of *headlines*. A teaser is a tantalising flirt, promising one thing but delivering another. Bad, bad, bad. That's the last thing people want as they go hunting and gathering information on the web. A wasted click is annoying, not fun.

F is for front-loading

Remember, in first and second gear people are mainly F-reading. Obviously, the page headline and sub-headlines form bars of the F (or flags on the flagpole), where most people's eyes come to rest briefly. These sweet F-spots must contain essential information. But can you also see how the very first words of the headlines matter more than the later words?

```
[Logo]

menu     First words     will be read...    last words may be read
menu     may be read     won't be read won't be read won't be read won't be read won't
menu     may be read     be read won't be read won't be read won't be read won't be
menu     may be read     read won't be read won't be read won't be read won't be read
menu     may be read     won't be read won't be read won't be read won't be read
menu

         First words     will be read...    last words may be read
         may be read     won't be read won't be read won't be read won't
         may be read     be read won't be read won't be read won't be
         may be read     read won't be read won't be read won't be read
         may be read     won't be read won't be read won't be read won't be read
```

To satisfy F-readers, so they can get the gist of a page in the blink of an eye, writers must front-load headlines with keywords. I'd better define those terms.

Front-loading means starting a piece of text with a few words that carry some weight. Front-loading is important for headlines, links, paragraphs, list starters, list items, and paragraphs, because their initial words are located on the flagpole of the F. The initial words remain on the F, regardless of a reader's font or browser window size.

Keywords are:
- words that mean something specific
- keys to the subject matter of a web page
- words people might type when searching for a page on a certain topic.

Here are two headlines, which correctly begin with keywords:
- Childhood obesity: answers for parents
- Kids' cell phones: answers for parents.

The specific topic of the pages comes first: *childhood obesity* and *kids' cellphones*. Those important words will appear on the F. The second phrase (*answers for parents*) may be overlooked by skim-readers. It is less important, because it is more general and does not contain keywords. But the specific topic, the subject matter, is rightly placed first.

The writer could have considered reversing the phrases in the headline, like this:
- Answers for parents: childhood obesity
- Answers for parents: kids' cell phones.

Bad idea! Then the words in the F-bar would be *Answers for parents*. That doesn't tell us what the page is about. Readers could miss the point of the page entirely.

Still having trouble recognising keywords? Here's another clue. Ask yourself which words would people type when looking for a page like this one: *childhood obesity* or *answers for parents*? *Kids' cell phones* or *answers for parents*? Simple, isn't it?

I've got another way of identifying keywords. It's very crude— linguists, avert your eyes—but it helps some writers with the all-important skill of front-loading. There are three types of English words:

1. Keyword candidates: these are usually phrases or groups of several words, mainly nouns, verbs, or adjectives. They mean something and are often slightly unusual. Keywords should dominate headlines. These are keywords: *childhood, obesity, kids, cell phones.*
2. Common words: these are so common they are not worth typing into Google. Some of them, such as *the, of, not,* and *so,* don't even have a meaning, just a grammatical function. These are common words: *answers for parents.*
3. Cake-words: these include PR words, vague words, and opinion words whether positive or negative. They provide padding, not substance or meaning. Examples: *good, worst, lovely, super.*

To consolidate the message, here are a couple more examples of good front-loaded headlines, which start with keywords:

- Espresso coffee—online ordering the easy way
- Home phone plan help-line.

Bad back-loaded headlines, which start with non-keywords:

- The easy way to order espresso coffee online.
- We're here to help you choose a home phone plan.

Write plenty of sub-headlines

As people scroll down a page, the page headline disappears from sight. The words lose all context. Without sub-headlines, people get a bored or anxious feeling—and may depart without attempting to read that great grey wall of words.

Therefore, subdivide long pages into smaller chunks of information, each with its own topic and its own sub-headline. A chunk might be just one paragraph or several paragraphs.

On a long page that is mainly text, frequent sub-headlines are desirable. Make sure at least one headline is visible on the screen, regardless of scrolling. That's approximately one headline for every 100–200 words.

An academic article may have longer stretches of prose without sub-headlines than other online content, as it develops a complex line of reasoning. In such cases, the writer can bring relief to the viewer's eyes by other methods—for example, front-loading paragraphs with keywords, and including the occasional very short paragraph.

Headlines and sub-headlines can collectively summarise the entire content of the page. For example, if people read nothing else on the following page, they would still get a good grasp of the content.

> [Logo]
>
> menu
> menu
> menu
> menu
> menu
> menu
>
> **Plan Fakaofo vacation with care**
> If F-readers skip this sentence, it's not too drastic.
>
> **Pacific atoll: population 500**
> If F-readers skip this bit, it doesn't matter. If F-readers skip this bit, it doesn't matter.
>
> **MV Tokelau: take sleeping mat for 30 hours on deck**
> If F-readers skip this bit, it doesn't matter. If F-readers skip this bit, it doesn't matter.
>
> **Transport schedule liable to change without notice**
> If F-readers skip this bit, it doesn't matter. If F-readers skip this bit, it doesn't matter. If F-readers skip this bit, it doesn't matter.
>
> **Snorkeling, fishing, sleeping, reading**
> F-readers won't read this, but it doesn't matter. F-readers won't read this but it doesn't matter.
>
> **Obtain permission from elders in advance**
> F-readers won't read this, but it doesn't matter.

Focused content: one page, one topic

You cannot write a good headline for a confused page. You cannot write a good headline for a page with two or more topics. There's no escaping this basic rule: every page should have only one, clearly defined topic.

It is a bad mistake to put two or more topics on a single page. This often occurs on an ageing intranet: staff blithely add new material to existing pages, fuzzying the original focus.

If you cannot write a headline that summarises the whole page, take another look at the page. Perhaps it has two topics, a vague topic, or a jumble of topics. First focus the page. Then write the headline.

Suit headline style to content type

In length and style, newspaper headlines are an excellent model for web and intranet headlines. But most online content is not news, and often needs a slightly different style of headlines. In fact, the type of headline can give a useful clue about the type of content.

The company style guide ought to include guidelines for writing page headlines. Some suggestions follow. The distinctions may seem finickity, but if you just provide examples of the style you want, most staff writers will imitate them without difficulty.

Basic style for headlines

Write headlines for most content types as a 4-10 word summary of the subject matter on the page, for example:
- Induction seminar for new staff, Washington office
- Latest news from regional officers.

Headlines for news stories

For news pages on a web site or intranet, write a short sentence, or compress a sentence by omitting the verb.
- New CEO welcomes restructuring challenge
- $120,000 saved by plain language contracts.

Headlines for procedure pages

Front-load headlines and include the word *procedure*, for example:
- Respond to government requests for tender—procedure
- Procedure: sabbatical leave applications.

Headlines for policy pages

Front-load headlines and include the word *policy*, for example:
- Establishing pay rates for temporary and part-time employees—policy
- Email policy for public sector employees.

Headlines for interactive pages

Start headlines with a command verb, for example:
- Search our database of articles on geophysics
- Book Sydney conference room online.

Headlines for tips and help pages

Start headlines with *How to* or an *-ing* verb, for example:
- How to convert a text document into a PDF
- Preparing for a job interview—tips.

Headlines for chapters in long documents

The name of the chapter should be the page headline. Every page should show both the name of the chapter and the name of the long document.

Plain language reminder: write for the reader

Writing for the reader is the primary rule of plain language, so headlines should be written for the benefit of the reader, not yourself. Think first: what does your target audience want to get out of this page? What are they trying to do?

Write for readers, not mind-readers! You know who you are, but we don't. You know what your page is about, but we need to be told—in the headline.

For example, in a large organisation there could be 20 different training units, and hundreds of intranet pages about training. Writers within each training unit assume that *training* refers to their own training. So they write useless headers like this:
- Training information
- Information about training.

What training? What information? Who is the page for? If you write for your reader, a longer, clearer page headline would result, for example:
- IT training resources for regional offices
- Online training for intranet content authors
- Seminar: Complying with Privacy Act. Sydney, 4 May 2007.

Some finer points about headlines

Positive language is recommended for all business writing, but is downright crucial in headlines. If people misunderstand your headline, they will misunderstand your page. Negative language tends to be both confusing and depressing. Worst of all are headlines with two or more negative words, and negative questions.

By *negative* I naturally include literal negatives such as *not*, *never*, and *nobody*. I also include words with more subtle negative connotations, such as *deny*, *miserable*, *unless* and *reject*. Readers are unlikely to bother with negative headlines like the ones below—it's too much effort to decode their meaning. They are even more unlikely to say, 'Gee, wonder what they mean, must read more.'
- If you hate health, don't click here
- Visa refusals may not result in entry ban.

Another point: it is usually better not to ask questions in headlines—keep the questions where they belong, on an FAQ page. You see, questions tell only half the story, and readers are looking for answers. Instead of writing the question: *Who are we?* write the answer: *Your business travel arranged by HR-Travel*.

A good page headline is multi-functional

If you now realise that page headlines are crucially important, that's good. But wait—there's more.

Unlike headlines printed on paper, the headlines of web and intranet pages are often used in several different places. Therefore they must make sense out of context.

For example, a well-written headline will make sense when another web site lists it as a link, as in the following:[33]

> **Consumers and Families**
> ○ <u>Verify Licenses Board of Behavioral Sciences</u>
> ○ <u>Online Mobilehome Title Search for Requestor Account Customers</u>
> ○ <u>State Lottery</u>
> ○ <u>Tax Refund Status</u>
> ○ <u>Pay Your Income Taxes Online</u>
> ○ <u>Electronic Services</u>
> ○ <u>File Your Income Tax Return Online</u>

In 1999, Jakob Nielsen listed his top 10 mistakes of web design. They included headlines that make no sense out of context. Years later, this remains a problem. But the good news is that if you follow the guidelines in this chapter, your headlines will automatically make sense as a link in other places, such as:

- on a site map
- on your site's home page
- on other web pages on your site
- on other web sites
- in an e-mail
- on a list of resources or articles.

Finally, a well written page headline can even double as the hugely influential page title, with the site name tacked on to the end.[34]

Headlines are like pebbles tossed into a lake: they ripple outwards into ever widening circles.

Headlines for blogs and newsletters are recycled in Facebook and Twitter. They are forwarded by email and smart phones to wider groups. When they are stored in a company content management system, they are retrievable and they may have a very long life.

Fortunately, if you can write a great headline for web content, you can write a great headline for any channel: the same principles apply. An excellent headline works in any medium.

6.

F-summaries: do or die

Every web page and intranet page must have a summary straight after the page headline. Make this a rule. Just do it!

You may think this is a particularly bossy remark, and it is true that certain intranet pages might make sense without a summary if their headlines were totally, guaranteed, 100%, infallibly clear and complete. However, it's a bad idea to treat the summary as optional. If you do, content is likely to quickly backslide into a non-structured mess.

Writing F-headlines and F-summaries are essential 21st century writing skills, because they can be applied to nearly every document written for work—certainly not just to web content. Every email, report, memo, proposal, and news item should have a clear, comprehensive headline (or subject line or title) followed by a summary or key message. Naturally there are exceptions, for example, blogs, bad news letters and sensitive PR communications. But when documents are consistently structured this way by default, all business writing benefits.

Structure matters heaps online

The *structure* of a document doesn't refer to the meaning or message, but to the way it is built: the scope, relative and absolute size, relationships, functions, and sequence of its parts. Structure is important for all writing, and excessively important for online content.

Awareness of structure in writing is not intuitive: it has to be learned. Many on-the-job writers never consider the structure of their writing: they concentrate exclusively on meaning.

To understand structure you need to shift to long-distance focus and see the page as a whole. It can be difficult to steer your attention away from what you are writing—'Hello!'—to its place in the document's structure.

There's a parallel in group discussions. Most people, most of the time, think only about what they're going to say—OK, maybe some people also think about what others are saying! Only skilled communicators can simultaneously track meaning, structure and process. They do more than follow the argument. They also notice how long is spent on each topic, who speaks most, and how much of the agenda has been covered. They notice whether a comment develops the topic further, strays from the topic, summarises, paraphrases, or closes the discussion. They notice who feels squashed, who feels bored, and what goals are apparently held by individuals in the group.

Luckily, there's plenty of help available for writers who need to get to grips with structure. In fact, much technology is pushing us towards categorisation of content.

- XML is a coding system that breaks text down into elements such as *<recipe>*, *<step>*, *<ingredient>*, *<instruction>*. This forces writers to name the function of each piece of content they are writing. XML treats even tiny pieces of text like data.
- To some extent, most publishing tools help writers to become aware of structure: templates identify parts of a document according to function, not meaning. So you enter text in fields with labels such as *page headline, page summary, body, links*, or *sub-headline*.
- Even Microsoft Word helps writers to think about structure, provided they use the Styles facility. At its most basic, Styles requires you to decide whether a headline will be first, second, or third level.

But right now, all writers need to know is that the first sentence or two of any document should be a summary, which for online content is doubly important.

Why every page must have a summary

After the page headline, the summary is your second big chance to show exactly what any web page is about. A good summary saves your readers time and gives them control. After reading the summary, they should know for sure whether this is the page they want.

On some sites, the page summary may be recycled in search results by an internal search engine. This has huge implications, as you can imagine. If this is the case on your site, the writer has a pretty big responsibility.

In short, if a web or intranet has no summary:

- the content can become a muddle
- readers get confused about the main point of the page
- on some sites, search results will be unsatisfactory.

Why the summary must be the first content

As we've seen, the summary is crucial. So (obviously) it must be placed in the top bar of the F—straight after the page headline. That's a top spot in every sense: a place where nearly everyone will glance, because people read the top of the page if nothing else. Knowing what you know about F-reading, you would be crazy to waste the first paragraph on anything but a summary.

If you put the summary anywhere else, it is likely to be missed. If people don't see a summary at the top, they won't know where else to look. And then, guess what? After a split second, they've gone.

The top of the page is the conventional place for the summary, and that alone is a strong reason for always putting it there. On the web, conventions are comparatively new—otherwise I wouldn't have to make this point.

By contrast, paper books have been around for a long time, and the conventions don't need explaining to authors. We expect every book to have certain elements in certain positions: a title on a title page, chapter names or numbers at the beginning of every chapter, and page numbers top or bottom. Conventions save time: if chapter names were in the middle of a chapter, it would be very annoying. Putting a summary in the middle or bottom of a page is equally annoying for online readers. They want the essential information first: so give it to them.

Make the summary short. Ideally, it will be around 10-25 words.

Another nasty thing tends to happen if pages do not consistently begin with a summary. Long after a page is published, other staff writers insert irrelevant information at the top of the page, making matters even worse. They feel free to commandeer the summary space because the page has no obvious structure.

If you use a publishing tool or content management system, you will probably see a field named *summary*, *description*, or *abstract*. That's where you enter the page summary (doh!). It will appear as the first paragraph.

Example of a template with a summary field

Page headline	
Summary	
Body	

Five ways to write a page summary

OK, so what do we mean by a summary? The terminology associated with web content can be pretty confusing, for the simple reason that it is not standardised. *Summary* is the word I use, but your organisation may talk about *descriptions* or *abstracts* or even (the horror!) *introductions*. To confuse us further, companies selling content management systems seem to take pride in using their own perversely idiosyncratic terminology.

Relax. We are all talking about the same thing. The jargon jumble reflects the fact that we do have options. *Summary* happens to be the word I personally use to cover all possibilities. You just have to decide whether you will summarise:

- the meaning of the page's content
- the topic, purpose, or scope of the content
- the key message of the content
- the purpose, function, or audience of the content

As for style, write simple sentences in plain language. Not dot points, because they turn to mush if summaries are recycled in search results.

1. Write a classic executive summary

You can write a page summary exactly the same way you would write the executive summary of a report: by summarising the meaning of the content.

Not everyone knows what an executive summary is, so here is a reminder. It covers all the main points of a document, using natural language (not dot points or lists). Executive summaries are usually the first section of every report or proposal, but are equally useful in web or intranet content.

The concept of the executive summary arose this way. Imagine meeting your CEO on the ground floor of the office, getting into the elevator together, and being asked to summarise a report before you get to the 14th floor. There's an obvious time constraint: you have less than a minute to give the summary, which they need immediately for a board meeting. You must tell the CEO all the essential facts, so that he or she is well prepared, able to ask the right questions and participate intelligently in discussion. (The rest of the document can be discreetly skim-read during the meeting.)

Think of the executive summary as a very short version of the entire web page. It is appropriate for most types of web or intranet pages, especially those with lots of information. (On short pages, an executive summary can be redundant.) In a scientific article, it might be called an informative abstract—but you don't need to know that.

For a web page, your executive summary will be just one short paragraph. Don't repeat sentences from the bulk of the page: rephrase in plain English.

Q: I haven't read this chapter. What's in it?

AN EXECUTIVE SUMMARY OF THIS CHAPTER

A summary should start every web page. It can be written in various ways, for example as a summary of the whole page, a description of what the page is about, or just the key message. Search engines may use these page summaries, so they must be written correctly.

2. Write the key message

In many cases, what you need to state upfront is the key message. A key message summary states the one thing that people need to know, even if they learn nothing else. It is appropriate for pages that include one urgent point, or one on which everything else depends. For example, a web page might give a country profile for travelers, with facts about population, climate, currency, exports, tourist attractions and language. If a major emergency hits that country, a new summary would state the key message:

> We strongly advise you not to travel to East Timor at this time because of the extremely dangerous security situation. Australians in East Timor should consider departing if they can do so safely.

The key message model is ideal for all short pages: you start with essential information, important for every reader. It has the advantage of being fairly easy to write, but contains traps for the unwary. For example, you certainly need to review the page regularly, for the key message may change.

Some web pages consist of a single paragraph. In such cases, the first sentence should state the most significant point of the paragraph, in other words, the key message. You'll find this type of content in an online encyclopedia or on a museum site, for example.

A real-life scenario for the key message summary is easy to imagine. Say a colleague missed a meeting about future parking arrangements for staff, including plans to develop a large new parking area. At the end of the day, you share an elevator, and she asks you what the meeting was about. Instead of giving her a short version of the whole presentation (in other words, an executive summary), you think it is more important to give her the key message:

'From tomorrow you can't park behind the supermarket or you will get a ticket.'

You have delivered the key message, which will stop her getting fined. If you had time, you would say more, for instance, 'Use the JBS parking building until the new facility is built next year.'

Q: What is the main thing I need to know from this chapter?

KEY MESSAGE SUMMARY OF THIS CHAPTER

You must learn how to write summaries for web pages or you will get into deep trouble as a content author.

3. Write a page description

This kind of summary, the page description, is pretty easy to write. You don't have to give the meaning of the content. You simply summarise the topic and scope of the page content, so the reader knows what will be covered.

Frankly, page descriptions are less useful than executive summaries, which are suitable for practically any web or intranet content. Page descriptions give less than half the story and can be boring. The upside is that they're easy to write. They are ideal for content such as:

- procedures, where an executive summary or the key message alone risks misleading people
- scholarly articles, where readers are interested in detailed analysis, and the conclusion might be complex or unproven
- draft policies open to public discussion, where your tentative conclusions are open for debate: an executive summary might shut the door on discussion
- pages that must be written in two minutes flat.

You can begin with a simple phrase such as:
- This page describes…
- This page outlines…
- Read about…

The page description is the equivalent of what you might say to a colleague who asks you about an article you have just had published. He does not want to be told your findings, just the topic and scope of the article. You say,

'The article reviews four brands of editing software and makes recommendations according to budget, workload, and the type of documents being edited.'

Although the page description type of summary does not convey your actual findings or recommendations, in many cases, it contains enough information for readers to decide whether they want to read the page.

If you read scientific research articles, you will recognise this kind of summary. That's right: it's a descriptive abstract.

Q: What's this chapter about?

A PAGE DESCRIPTION OF THIS CHAPTER

This chapter gives reasons for the use and positioning of page summaries, and describes five ways to write a page summary.

4. Write a use-of-page summary

For some web pages, you can summarise when and how the page is to be used. This is a summary of the page's purpose or function—not its meaning, key message, topic or scope.

The use-of-page summary is especially useful for pages that enable people to take action, rather than just read. Examples:
- computer applications such as Payroll
- dynamic or interactive pages such as online forms
- search pages
- procedure pages.

In real life, you often give or receive a use-of-page summary. For example, you are looking for some letterhead paper. The manager shows you which one to use: 'Policy Department staff use this letterhead when corresponding with Ministers.' That's all the information you need. You don't want to know what is on the letterheads, just what they are for and who should use them.

> Q: What is this chapter for?
>
> A USE-OF-PAGE SUMMARY OF THIS CHAPTER
>
> Content managers use this chapter to introduce essential summary-writing skills to their online content authors.

5. Combine different types of summary

Often, you may decide to write a page summary that combines two or more types of summary. When you know how to write the four basic summaries, this is hardly difficult. For example, you could:
- describe the page and state when to use it, or
- give the key message and summarise the remaining content, or
- describe the page, say who should use it, and summarise the content.

Bad ways to start a web or intranet page

You now know 5 good ways to write a page summary. Unfortunately, there are also at least 5 bad ways to start a page. Anything other than a summary in that first paragraph is bad, bad, bad.

All too commonly, web content starts with no summary at all, with a slow, roundabout approach to the topic, or with some completely irrelevant information. By leading up your main point slowly and circuitously, you force your main point further down the page, so here are a few rules:
- don't start with an introduction or background
- don't start with an explanation
- don't start by writing about the technology of the page
- don't start with a little chat, a red herring or afterthought.

1. Don't start with an introduction or background

If you are a researcher, academic, or policy writer, you may have a habit of starting every document with an introduction or some background information. You lead the reader slowly and carefully to your main point, which is at the bottom of the page.

However, people reading the vast majority of web or intranet pages do not want an introduction. They want to know immediately what the page is about, and then they want the key information.

Actually, the very word *introduction* is incongruous on a web site or intranet, because a web site has no beginning and no end. In a book, an introduction is printed first, before Chapter One—but on the web, people go straight to the page they want.

There is no such thing as the first page on a web site. As your readers trawl for useful information, pages have no hierarchy and no order. Certainly it is good to be able to dig deeper, finding more information about a topic of interest. Certainly most sites need a rigorous architecture, and they do have a home page. But the concept of reading pages in sequence is alien to web technology.

So do not think to construct a page in this sequence:
1. Introduction.
2. Main point.
3. More information.

Instead, construct a page more like this, giving each new section its own clear sub-headline:
1. Summary of information, key message, scope, or use of page.
2. Chunks of information in descending order of importance to the target reader.

2. Don't start with an explanation

Aim to make interactive content self-explanatory, so that an explanation is unnecessary. Readers instinctively ignore explanations like the following:

> Click on the link below to see your account details. When you are on the next page, you can change details such as your profile, address, and credit card type and number.

Online, the more you explain, the more confused your reader becomes. Imagine readers saying, 'Show me, don't tell me!'

When writing online content, write clearly and concisely, and trust your readers. Put help on a separate page: don't clutter up your content with repeated explanations of how to do something like click on a link, for example.

3. Don't start by talking about technology

Once upon a time, my children, long, long ago in a far off land, home pages began with advice about which browser and screen resolution to use. This was the *Best-Viewed* starter, which can still be detected on some primitive sites. There, instead of discovering something about the content and purpose of a web page, viewers receive a little lecture on technology.

Since those half-forgotten days of yore, nearly every aspect of web sites and intranets has improved. Think of browsers, screens, viewers' skills, designers' skills and CSS. What's more, did you ever—even once—even for a minute—consider changing your browser or screen resolution just to see a particular web site more clearly? You did not. You went straight back to Google in search of a web site that looked OK on your own screen with your usual browser.

Sometimes, technical advice is justified, for example if a plug-in such as QuickTime

Player is necessary for video or audio content. Just don't put your *Best-Viewed* announcement in the slot where the summary should be.

4. Don't start with a little chat, red herring or afterthought

If you stray from the 5 types of good summary, you may accidentally create a false start for the page—in other words, you'll begin with a red herring, irrelevant information, a false clue, a random thought, an afterthought. That immediately gives people a false impression of what the page is about. Not only does this irritate some readers, it also destroys the structure of the page, and will be disastrous if recycled in search results.

Some writers think the first paragraph is an opportunity to bond with the reader and set a friendly tone. Bad idea! A little chat will simply annoy. Friendly chat may be OK in a staff newsletter that is archived promptly. But it is certainly not OK on a web or intranet page that remains online for more than a week or two, and it is never OK in search results.

5. Don't start with anything that won't look OK in search results

Read on.

How search results use summaries

No mere writer can determine what summaries a search engine like Google will display in the wild. However, a customised search engine can display the page summaries, the ones in the visible content, in search results. Imagine the repercussions if all web content included a suitable short summary: all search results would be useful, helpful, informative and accurate, at least for customised search engines. Oh, the joy!

Each of the five good types of summary works very well indeed when displayed in search results. No problem. But if writers don't know the rules, or persist in putting rubbish in the summary slot, search results will be utterly useless.

This tip doesn't just apply to web search engines: it is also relevant to all document management systems. Take this as a strong incentive to ensure that everyone in your organisation who writes on the job is trained to write page summaries.[35]

Keywords in the summary

Search engines look for keywords in the summary. Actually, when you write a good summary, it will inevitably include keywords. For example, on a page about a tsunami in Sri Lanka, your summary will surely contain the keywords *tsunami* and *Sri Lanka*—true?

Just to be sure, when reviewing content, always check that the summary is loaded with keywords, especially at the start. Front-loading pays off. Obviously that is impossible with a page description, which starts with something like *This page describes*. Just get to the point immediately afterwards.

Search results display a limited number of words, so the first 16 or so words matter most. You soon see the point of front-loading when your summary is cut short. This just one more twist to F-reading and F-writing.

After the summary: chunking

Fantastic progress—you can now structure the top inch or so of any document. Maybe you're thinking sardonic thoughts: 'Whoop de doo. Six chapters to show how to write one inch, big deal.' But hey, the top inch or two is the most important bit by far, and the changes you make here will have a powerful impact. F-headlines and F-summaries will improve all business documents, and make them fit to publish online.

Moving on: how about the remainder of the document? It too needs structure. In relation to web content, you have probably heard this advice many times: break down content into small chunks. Let's figure out what this means.

After the page headline, the summary is the first chunk of content on any page. Together, they provide the most significant clues to what the page is about.

How big is a chunk? (How long is a piece of string?) It could be one paragraph or 5, but it shouldn't cover more than half a screen. I know that's still extremely vague, but it's about as specific as I can be without imposing ridiculous constraints.

After the summary, put chunks in a logical order—logical from the reader's point of view, not the writer's. Online, this usually means moving from the most important points (at the top) to less important information (at the bottom). You may recognise this as the *inverted pyramid* structure, recommended for most business documents and the norm for news stories: big picture at the top, little details at the bottom. Key information first, at the top of the F. General information at the bottom, where F-readers do not venture.

Aim to place chunks in this order on a web or intranet page:
- information essential for all target readers
- important information, useful to all target readers
- next most important information, useful to most target readers
- least important information: useful to a minority of readers, nice-to-know for others.

Furthermore, every chunk should have its own sub-headline. That's very important for readability, usability, and accessibility.

7.

F-links and cufflinks

F-links are the last of the big four: the rock-bottom, fundamental features of good web content.

Let's assume you know how to write plain language (in every sense), F-headlines and F-summaries. When you get the links right, you will have conquered all the basics.

First, let me stress that this chapter is about links in the body of a web page, the links that content writers are responsible for. It's not about links that are part of the site-wide design, such as those in the navigation menu or breadcrumb trail. Those are part of the navigation system—not content, and not the concern of content writers.

Why links are such a buzz

Links are not just an add-on to web content: they are the essential difference between paper and online copy, the footprint of the internet. Links enable people to jump around a page, from one page to another, to another site, or to another kind of document altogether. It's usually a bad sign when a page has no links in the content, suggesting it's a document written for paper, or that the writer is inexperienced. A page without links is like a shirt without buttons (or cufflinks), formless and disconnected.

Moreover, links (including their visible text and invisible titles) have secret powers. The way link-text is written has great impact because:

- links stand out on the page, so F-readers notice them
- some people read only the links as a clue to the content
- people with disabilities commonly study link-text first
- links strongly influence usability
- search engines give extra weight to words in and near links.

A few years ago, Xerox's Palo Alto Research Center (PARC) came up with a famous theory, *the scent of information.* They compared people searching a large web site with animals foraging for prey, the prey being information. Curious, Jared Spool and his colleagues at User Interface Engineering investigated the design features that supported foragers as they followed the scent. They found that the placement and length of links on the page are critical.[36]

In other words, links in the text are extraordinarily powerful, and there is more to them than meets the eye. When links are well chosen, well placed and well worded, readers click with confidence and doggedly follow a 'scent' to the information they need. They get that delicious sense of control and satisfaction. When links are badly judged, placed and worded, readers click the Back button and may abandon the site.

Clearly, links are worth mastering. Think strategically. What links should you insert? Why? What effect will they have? Where will you put them? What words will you write as link-text? These are interesting decisions.

Decide what links your reader needs

First of all, always assume there will be links in your web content. That's how the internet works! Being aware right from the start helps writers to deliver the right amount of essential content. Superfluous or nice-to-know information does not belong on your page: it belongs on another page, and you can link to it.

It's logical to refrain from lifting text from other pages. Whether writers copy-and-paste or copy-and-paraphrase is not the point. The point is, if an authoritative version of certain information already exists elsewhere, then as a rule, new pages should just link to it. A copied version copy is redundant and sure to go out of date.

Think about your target audience. What links would be genuinely useful to them? Don't send them to another page without a very good reason, for example to find:

- more detailed or selective information on the same topic
- the next step to be taken, for example in a procedure or tutorial
- a tool they need right now, such as a form, calculator or plug-in
- background information, such as the policy behind a procedure or the history of a product
- a glossary (but briefly explain tricky terms on the spot)
- a text equivalent of a graph.

Here is one bad reason for adding a link: because you feel like it. Every link should be the result of a deliberate decision, not an impulse. In the following screenshot, the dot-pointed links are logical and necessary. They allow readers to select their next move. Readers do need to know where the nearest shelter is—but generally each reader will need only one link.[37]

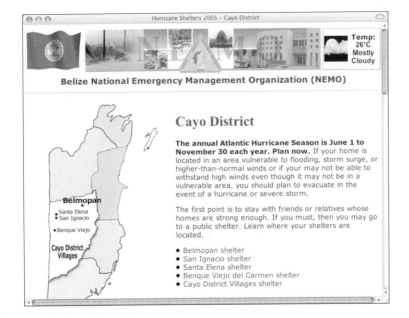

Place links on the F

Systematic placement of links is a sign of professionalism, makes for easy skim-reading, and creates a calm, orderly impression.

The word *F-links* is a broad hint that links should be located on the F. That means placing links hard against the left-hand margin. If links are left-aligned, skim-readers can't help but see them, and are not distracted by links left, right and centre. Some content management systems enforce left-alignment of links by default, for good reasons.

The only way you can make sure links are left-aligned is to place links at the start of a paragraph, in a headline, after a line break, or in a list. The other basic rule is to put links as close as possible to the relevant information.

The links on the following page about moving to Brisbane are consistently placed, easy to read, and orderly.[38]

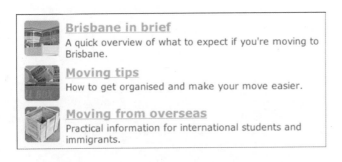

Where you have several links with a similar purpose or topic, place them in a list, as follows.[39]

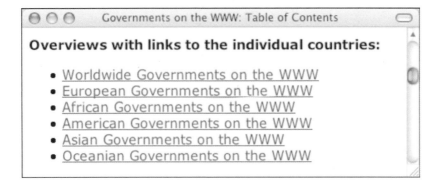

But a list that's too long is a list that's ignored. When there are too many items, people often get bored and simply stop reading. (I do that. Do you?) So when a list threatens to get out of control—say with more than about seven items—it's wise to break it up with sub-headlines, line-breaks or lines of plain text. Sub-headlines guide people towards the list they really need to study. Index pages always need subdividing in this way.[40]

Register Your Company	Register to Pay Taxes
• Registering a Domestic or Foreign Corporation • Registering a Limited Liability Corporation • Registering a Limited Liability Partnership • Registering a Limited Partnership • Reserve a Corporate Name (PDF 145 KB) • Electronic Corporate Name Database	• Tax Registration • New Hire Reporting

Some pages are necessarily long. In these cases it is often good to list the sub-headlines at the top of the page, as direct links (bookmarks) to the respective sections.[41]

If you use bookmarks, or simply if the page is long, you may want to provide a link every few paragraphs to Start of page or Index, so that readers don't feel trapped in a long page. (Not everyone knows a shortcut to the top of the page.) However, this practice presents some problems, particularly for speech-based browsers and for printing out.

Bookmarks, like other links, should be left-aligned. Centred links are harder to skim-read, as you see:

Worldwide Governments on the WWW
European Governments on the WWW
African Governments on the WWW
American Governments on the WWW
Asian Governments on the WWW
Oceanian Governments on the WWW

Same with right alignment: it slows reading and just feels weird, except in a language that's written right-to-left.[42]

Avoid link-spatter

Link-spatter occurs when you choose words within prose at random, and highlight them as links. This is the old-fashioned way to position link-text, and strange to say, many reputable sites still do it. An example follows.[43]

Links placed any old where in the text can alienate your reader. They can be annoying, and they can make the page (and the writer) seem disorderly or confused.

Jan Spyridakis points out that links embedded in a sentence disrupt the natural syntax of a sentence.[44] They attract attention, and often a readers click on a link before reading the full sentence.

Here are some good reasons to avoid link-spatter.
- It is much harder to write dual purpose link-text that makes sense both intrinsically and in mid-sentence.
- When skim-reading, a significant proportion of people literally see nothing but the links. That's just the way they are! With link-spatter, those links may seem a chaotic jumble.
- When links are embedded in paragraphs, you cannot control whether links appear left, right or centre. They often wrap over two lines, making them difficult to read.
- People take longer to read the text. First, they fixate on the link-text because its style attracts the eye. Then they go back to the start of the sentence to get the complete meaning. The eye zigzags between links and complete sentences.

How to write link-text that works

For every link you provide in content, you need to write link-text. Those are the words people click on; traditionally they have been blue and underlined.

Link-text is charged with energy. Link-text shouts at readers *Look at me! Look at me!* Link-text is not passive: it either helps or hinders people in their struggle to finish a task or find information. And search engines treat link-text as clues to the page topic. Yet many writers squander this amazing opportunity by stuffing their link-text with nothing-words.

Link-text should be more than a link. It should be a signpost telling readers what they will find when they click on the link—both its topic and format.

Here's a stroke of luck: you already know how to write good F-links because you know how to write a good F-headline. We have discussed the fact that that headlines should describe exactly what is on the page, be front-loaded, and have 4-10 words.

Follow exactly the same principles when writing link-text for content.

- Describe what content is on the target: that is, the web page (or file) that opens when somebody clicks on the link.
- Frontload your link-text by starting with keywords. Be concise: don't waste precious space on nothing-words like *the* and *about*.
- Use 4–10 words. They should all be all meaningful and help to clarify the content of the target page.

The simplest way to write link-text is to use the page headline of the target web page. Or if you are linking to a PDF, use the title of that document as link-text. That's what people expect, and it's good to meet expectations.

This principle assumes that the document you link to is blessed with an excellent F-headline. If the headline of the target page is inadequate, you may need to start afresh.

Longer links are better links

Links in the content of a page should obviously be much longer than links in a menu bar. Menu links have to fit into a narrow space. When you write link-text for content, you should include much more information.

At this point, let me mention a bad habit that has become entrenched. For some strange reason, writers have often been advised to keep content links as short as possible, and to make sure they match links appearing in the menu. We've been told that if a link in the menu says *About Us*, then links in the text (and headlines, for that matter) should say exactly the same thing: *About Us*. You know that's rubbish. You know that headlines should not match menu links, but should contain more information. Exactly the same principle applies to link-text.

Jared Spool's research showed that the best performing links were long—between 7 and 12 words long. Links that worked contained *trigger words*—the exact keywords that the reader is hunting for.[45] The report explains:

Longer links say more. [...] it's a game of probability. A seven-word link is more likely to contain the right trigger words than a one- or two-word link.[...]

If the optimal length of a link is a game of probability, why don't links that are 13 or more words work well? At some point, the trigger words get lost in the surrounding text. Too many words in the link and the users can't see the individual trigger words they need.

So feel free to write long links: research is on your side. I have only one reservation about UIE's 7-12 word guidelines: when link-text wraps over two lines, it can be confusing.

One more little point, and I mean little. (This is where fine-tuning verges on the neurotic.) When you write a list of links, try to vary their length. This gives a ragged right-hand edge to the list, which is easier to read than a series of links of the same length.

Describe the subject of the target page

Forgive me for stating the obvious, but link-text should clearly describe the subject of the target page. In fact, it should state the obvious.

Your aim as a writer is to provide sufficient information in the link-text for readers to decide whether to click. All readers are on a treasure hunt, hunting for clues that will lead them closer to their goal. They are dying to see certain specific keywords. When those keywords are in a link, they leap off the page: readers spot them in a blink. Then they're confident and they click.

Obviously, the following examples of link-text are far too vague:
- Local Bureau
- GST
- Application forms
- Schedule.

You can usually improve bad link-text by adding a few words to make the topic absolutely clear. For example, these links are far more useful:
- Air Pollution Control Bureau, Hamilton County
- Calculate your GST return
- Building permit application forms
- Induction seminars July-December 2007.

But adding words is not enough. Every word in a link must be a working word, adding key information. There's no point in adding nothing-words. The following links may be longer, but they are just as vague and useless as the original short ones:
- Local Bureau in your community area
- GST – click here for valuable information
- Application forms available online
- Schedule for the current period.

Newspaper web sites always have great headlines: therefore they have great link-text. These examples were taken from www.bbc.co.uk on 29 January 2007:

- Two killed in Kenyan carjacking
- Crowds greet British royals in US
- Boost for Iraq bird populations
- Antarctic hill surprises experts

Excellent link-text is also to be found on many government sites, for example:[46]

- Catalog of Federal Domestic Assistance
- Disaster Assistance for Victims
- Housing Loans for Very Low to Moderate Income Individuals in Rural Areas

Don't be funny, don't be cute

Links are no joke. A frustrated clicker is a grumpy clicker. Don't even think about using fancy language in link-text.

Clickers want to see their own words in links, words they recognise, words they are hunting. Keywords. Every word in a link is a chance to spark recognition and action. Any other word is just a distraction, and that includes the organisation's marketing language and acronyms.

Problems with *Click here*

I never dreamed that in 2007 it would still be necessary to mention this, but unbelievably, some organisations continue to use *Click here* and similar phrases in link-text. Presumably they believe people still don't understand what link-text is for. I had plenty of choice when I selected the following embarrassing example.[47]

AIDS/HIV Outreach Hamilton County Health Department (423) 209-8272	Click Here For Details
Air Pollution Control Bureau Hamilton County APCB website (423) 643-5970	Click Here For Details
Agendas for Commission Meetings Hamilton County Commission (423) 209-7200	Click Here For Details

Look, if somebody online doesn't know how links work, it's not the writer's job to teach them. A word of advice from a child is required—not *Click here*. However, if you know someone who still needs convincing, here are the obvious reasons for avoiding *Click here*. The phrase:

- conveys absolutely nothing about the target page
- is nonsense when people skim-read link-text
- looks ridiculous when a page is printed.

Other sobering reasons are perhaps not so well-known. Firstly, not everybody clicks. For example, some use keyboard shortcuts, or foot or voice commands. Some do this by choice, others because they are disabled.

Secondly, many people (including blind people) listen to online content through voice programmes, instead of reading off the screen. They often tab from link to link for a quick preview of a page's content. It's intolerable if all they hear is *Click here Click here Click here Click here.*

Thirdly, every *Click here* is a wasted opportunity to improve search results. *Read more* and *More information* are no better.

No nasty surprises

Links are associated with nasty surprises. People expect links to take them to another page of the same type (usually HTML), on the same web site or intranet site, in the same window. Anything else can be a nasty surprise—unless advance warning is given.

In fact, links can lead to a wide range of file types. Some can't be accessed without special software. Some take a very long time to download. Some links lead to a completely different web site, perhaps one with less credibility.

Before clicking, people want to be confident about the target file's content, format, and ownership. Otherwise clicking could waste time or crash their computer.

The writer's job is to tell readers exactly what is at the other end of the link, and prevent readers from clicking on a link that would not be useful to them.

Does a link go to another site?

If so, say so. Name the site, and if necessary, add or link to a disclaimer. Otherwise, readers may blame you for the faults of the other site. It is often helpful to provide the URL—but not as link-text, because the URL tells only half the story. It shows the link leads to an outside web site, but not what the page is about. A site-wide policy decision is needed to maintain consistency. For example, some sites bunch all external links in one place with a disclaimer. Others handle external links something like this:

- Slim Kids Campaign (www.kmoh.gov.kz)
- Slim Kids Campaign (www.kmoh.gov.kz)
- Slim Kids Campaign (Kazakhstan Ministry of Health web site)

Does a link open in a new window?

If so, say so. Your site should follow a consistent policy for opening links in new windows, doing it only for a darn good reason. For one thing, when a new window opens, the Back button doesn't work. This can damage the site's usability.

Does a link open a different type of file?

If so, say so. Sometimes you need to link to a non-HTML target. Your target might be a Word, PDF or Excel file, an interactive form, or a window in the reader's e-mail application. Or a Flash movie, audio file or PowerPoint presentation. Then it is particularly important to warn readers:

- the format of the target file (for example, PDF or RealPlayer)
- how large the file is (the number of kilobytes and if possible, pages).

Without these details, readers may have to wait while a large file slowly downloads, only to discover that they do not have the necessary software. This can be infuriating.

Many web sites and intranets automatically create the required data and display them in or near the link-text. That's cool.

Exceptions? What exceptions?

Naturally, blogs have developed their own conventions. Blogs are often written at speed, spontaneously, in a casual style. Promiscuous linking is common. Link-spatter is the norm. Most people don't care.

All the same, it's worth thinking about this.

Jakob Nielsen listed this as one of the top 10 design mistakes on blogs:[48]

4. Links Don't Say Where They Go

Many weblog authors seem to think it's cool to write link anchors like: "some people think" or "there's more here and here." Remember one of the basics of the Web: Life is too short to click on an unknown. Tell people where they're going and what they'll find at the other end of the link.

It turns out that even blogs can left-align links. On Plastic Bag, Tom Coates just writes super-long F-links.[49] He gets it both ways: quick and casual writing that is nevertheless skim-readable.

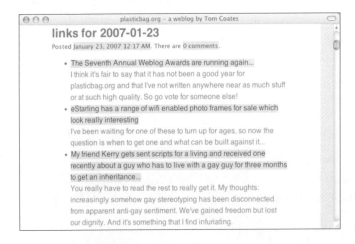

Links and paper documents

There's a fly in the ointment. I've said that documents written for the web work well on paper, and that's true for virtually every issue discussed in this book. But how do you write link-text for a printed document? Links can be clickable in PDFs and Word documents but they are not clickable on paper, and they often don't make sense on paper.

Yet links in single-source documents are certainly not a lost cause. Every organisation needs a policy to cover links for printed documents. A universal rule is unlikely, when on-the-job writing includes so many genres. Procedures, news stories, academic articles, calendars, annual reports—one solution will not fit all cases. But possibilities abound. For example, links in printed documents can:

- be converted to footnotes giving URLs
- be converted to references in an index
- be reproduced as is when the wording is appropriate.

I'll be watching developments on this front with interest. Long term, the non-clickable nature of paper may be its downfall in the workplace.

8.

The feng shui of online content

The look and feel of a web page is the first thing that strikes the reader. Everyone has an opinion about the design. In fact, more than any other factor, the design influences credibility. If the page looks dodgy, people assume the content is dodgy. Design is so powerful that it is tempting to blame the designer for all a web site's problems.

Certainly, the design must be appropriate: a designer's site must look gorgeous, a government site honest and worthy, a charity site fairly frugal, a children's site appealing to children.

But that is no concern of most content writers. Unless you double as a designer, put the site's look and feel right out of your head. On the other hand, your content also needs designing, and it is largely your responsibility to make the content look good.

The Serenity Test of good content is: 'Does the page look spacious, calm, and orderly?' Regardless of site design, the writer can usually achieve this with the text.

Before they start reading, people perceive a page of text as an image. Your publishing tool or style guide should determine most formatting features such as fonts, page width and alignment. But within these constraints, you, the writer, organise your text into a certain shape.

Feelings, feelings

Picture your readers flicking from search engine results page (SERP) to a web page, back to the SERP, and on to another page. Web pages flick past their eyes like frames of an old silent movie. And the mere appearance of each page arouses feelings: no page leaves readers feeling neutral.

Without reading a word, people look at the content on a page and feel... something! Maybe anxious, because they can't see any obvious headlines. Maybe confused or annoyed by content that seems disorganised. Sometimes the appearance of a page makes people feel downright angry—for example, if they encounter the dreaded grey wall of words. Often they feel insecure, sometimes even humiliated, because the text seems too difficult: they imagine they must be stupid or ignorant, because the text is daunting.

You can shape and format your text in such a way that the reader feels calm and confident. Calm, because the page looks well organised. Confident, because they automatically assume the text is correspondingly clear and easy to follow.

Words are scary

Words en masse online are scary. Even highly literate people complain about words on the web. In usability tests and training courses, I find many professional people flatly refuse to read certain chunks of text. These are not stupid people: they read difficult text every day on paper.

'It's too wordy,' they say. 'There are too many words.' Academics say it. Lawyers say it. Journalists say it. How can they tell, at a glance, without even reading a word? Most of your intended audience will instantly reject any text that appears to be—not is, but appears to be—difficult, boring, muddled or ugly. Uncannily, they can spot in a split second:

- the keywords, if any
- the likely location of important information
- irrelevant text
- unreadable, boring, obscure, or useless text.

The F-reading phenomenon strikes some observers as a sign that people are stupid. They sneer about dumbing down documents for web users. But the opposite is true: today's readers are smarter than any before. They judge a web page by appearances, and their judgement is usually correct. For the writer, it's a case of smartening up, not dumbing down. People will F-read online regardless of the writer's wishes.

Is a picture worth 1000 words? Words on a screen form a kind of picture. To make a text-picture attractive to the F-reader, extreme formatting is often required. Shape your text accordingly, providing rewards on the horizontal bars and the flagpole of the F. Your readers' eyes dance down the left-hand margin, absorbing one or two words at the beginning of paragraphs. Don't waste this opportunity.

Considering all the messy, chaotic, and boring pages people have to deal with, two things bring visual relief at first sight:

- order
- white space.

So keep in mind the imaginary, orderly F, and find ways to add white space, which brings relief to tired eyes.

Polish the horizontal bars of the F

You already know how to write the all-important first headline and summary. In that quick first glance, readers will appreciate the summary being pretty darn short.

Ideally, readers will also see at least one more headline—the second bar of the F—on the first screen. That will be immensely reassuring. 'Phew,' they think, or rather feel. 'This is not going to be a wall of words.' To switch metaphors, the iceberg syndrome applies: people assume that what they see on the first screen is typical of the whole page.[50] They'll scroll only if the top of the page looks orderly, informative and relevant to their needs.

Keep headline levels simple or you'll smash the F

In general, two levels of headline are quite sufficient for online content: one for the page headline, and one for all other headlines on the page.

Numerous levels can be confusing and counterproductive, because your readers can only see one screen's worth of content at any time. As they scroll down, they have no idea whether the sub-headlines that appear are Level 1, 2, 3 or 4. They can't see enough of the document to differentiate, so the whole point of multi-level headlines disappears.

Keep paragraphs short

This is a strange formatting issue for online content, unlike anything encountered in printed text. A paragraph that looks quite palatable on paper can change its shape alarmingly when viewed on your neighbour's computer.

Online, your readers don't see the text as you do. They view your page in many different ways. Screen resolution varies widely, as do the size of screens, fonts and windows. Consequently you have no idea whether a certain paragraph will occupy one centimetre or 5 centimetres on your readers' screens. If your paragraphs appear to be long, F-readers may feel disturbed. They assume reading will be hard work. All you can do is restrict paragraphs to about 60 words, particularly at the top of a page.

The only words in a paragraph that you can guarantee will be placed hard left, and therefore likely to be noticed, are the first few words.

Vary the size of paragraphs

I contradict myself? Very well, I contradict myself. I told you this is about extreme formatting! This is a simple trick you can apply after the document is written.

I have observed that many people are reluctant to read a page with equal sized paragraphs. They automatically think the text will be boring, because the page looks boring.

So before publishing a page, check that paragraphs vary in size. A mere tweak will make the page much more appealing: soothe your readers by including the occasional ultra-short, single-sentence paragraph.

Pre-digest all lists

Lists are excellent in online content: quick to skim-read, orderly, and usually meaningful.

But lists can turn to custard if you're not careful. Firstly, make sure they are not too long. The human brain says *Boring!* when it sees a long, unbroken list. This is usually correctible by subdividing the list or combining some items. Say you had a list of 18 scholarships. They will generally fall into smaller groups such as post-graduate scholarships, research scholarships, and travel scholarships. By putting them into logical subdivisions below headings, you make the visual impression of your content much more friendly. The serenity score of the page rises.

Nested lists (lists within lists) are frequently used in government and academic documents. Your organisation may require you to structure text this way. If so, now is a good time to consider changing the house style guide, because nested lists are problematic in web content.[51] Why? Because nested lists:

- destroy the F
- lose meaning as soon as the reader scrolls down the page.

> **A seriously non-F-patterned page**
> Burble burble rhubarb rhubarb I am slowly getting to my point.
> 1.1 Before the nest begins
>   1.1.1 Nested list
>   1.1.2 Nested list
> 1.2 Where am I?
>   1.2.1a Not another indentation!
>   1.2.1b Oh no
>   1.2.1c Stop now, I've had to scroll!
> - Here comes a dot point
> - And another one
> - Stop now, I can't see the top
> - I can't remember how this list began.

Avoid fancy formatting

Any fancy formatting of text interferes with the reassuring appearance of your F-writing, so keep formatting simple. You can probably guess that solid capital letters and italics in the text create visual noise and confusion. And use bold with discretion, as in headlines. A summary in bold attracts many readers but disturbs some.

One of the worst formatting sins for online content is to underline text for emphasis. People expect underlining in link-text and only link-text. Have you ever clicked and clicked on a piece of underlined text, expecting it to behave like a link—but nothing happens? Enough said.

I sincerely hope your site forcibly left-aligns all text, including headlines, lists, and links. Obviously, any text that is centred, right-aligned or justified will slide off the F and demolish the serenity of the page.

The terrors of tables

Here are the rules.
- Use tables for data.
- Don't use tables for text layout.

Using tables for text layout is a crime beloved by certain groups of on-the-job writers. For this type of information, many use tables for text by default. They use tables because they haven't learned any other way to arrange text. They use tables because they are used to tables. And as knowledgeable professionals, they are not likely to cease using tables until they are given a very good reason.

Lists of competencies are sometimes laid out in tables, as follows.

A. Demonstrates understanding of formal structures in own work group	B. Demonstrates understanding of the informal structure within own work group	C. Demonstrates understanding of the organization beyond own work group	D. Demonstrates understanding of organizational realities	Dem(undei of un࿊ orgar i:
Knows what is needed to do the job. Knows who to ask for what (i.e. "chain of command", rules and regulations, structure, values,	Recognizes the accepted and unspoken way of doing things and uses this knowledge to get things done. Uses knowledge of what is and is	Develops and uses informal and formal relationships beyond own work group. Uses knowledge of what's going on around one's own	Demonstrates use of ongoing power relationships within the organization (e.g. alliances) with a clear sense of organizational impact.	Unders reason; ongoin within organiz takes tl accoun decidir course

Perhaps this once seemed a logical layout to use on paper, making for easy comparison. But it never was pretty, and the screenshot above shows why tables are an unwise choice for layout of text online.
- Tables confuse the F-reader: you can't read across a horizontal line at the top, and your eye just doesn't know where to go to make sense of the information.
- On certain platforms, the right-hand columns may not be visible.
- While tables on paper do force text to stay in a certain position, that doesn't work on web sites.

On paper or online, there's no reason why this type of detailed information needs to be in a table. Competencies are often displayed as plain text, as below.

> **Information Literacy**
> Demonstrates the ability to determine the extent of information needed, access information effectively and efficiently from a variety of sources, evaluate information and sources critically, use information effectively to accomplish a specific purpose, and use information responsibly and ethically.

Tables certainly have their place online—but for displaying data, not prose. The line between data and prose is a wiggly one. Sticking with competencies, the next table displays them as data, not prose; and the table is not too wide for display in a browser window. This time, thumbs up!

Procedure	Didactic Only	Lab Competency	Clinic Observe	Clinical Competency
Administration of Local Anesthesia	X			
Air Polishing				X
Alginate Impressions				X

But how about the next table? Personally I consider the contents too wordy to display in a table on a web or intranet page. Is *Innovation Taking risks, adapting quickly to change, leading the change process* prose, or is it data? Doesn't look like data to me.

Competency (See links below for more info):	Behaviours:			
	Administrative Support	Professional	Managers	Executive Managers
Innovation Taking risks, adapting quickly to change, leading the change process	Enhances processes or products.	Develops new approaches.	Fosters innovation in others.	Creates a culture of innovation.
Leadership Positively influencing people and events	Acts as a role model.	Does long term coaching.	Anticipates and plans for change.	Communicates a compelling vision.

Never look at tables as an easy option. Whatever your opinion of the table above, you can see that tables require a professional touch. The inconsistent alignment, the clumsy entry *(See links below for more info):* and the overuse of bold are clues that the table was created by an amateur. In an attempt to make information tidier and more accessible, the writer often makes it messier and less accessible.

Speaking of accessibility, W3C has three standards that apply to tables. They boil down to this:

> don't use tables for text, and if you do [!], you must provide both a summary and a text equivalent.

So why would you bother in the first place?

The W3C standards aim to make all web content accessible. Accessibility will be discussed in more detail in later chapters. Suffice to say that many people do not read web content: they listen to it being 'read aloud' by screen-reading software. Initially, the software was unable to read tables cell by cell: it could only read left to right, line by line. This makes sense when reading data, but not when reading prose within a table.

Look again at the last table. Screen-reading software is expensive, so many people continue using early versions. Their software might 'read' the table above as:

> Competency. Behaviours:
>
> See links Administrative Professional Managers Executive
>
> below for more Support Managers
>
> Info

Take these tips to heart, and you'll be safe:
- use tables for data only
- make all tables short and narrow enough to fit on most screens
- if you need a table, ask a designer to help.

Smart tables

And now for tables that really earn their keep. Used skilfully and for a good reason, tables online are invaluable. The Asian Development Bank (ADB) site uses a table to present its catalogue of publications.[52] Viewers can choose how to view the publications in a database—sorted by Year, Category, Title, Country, Subject or Author.

Dynamic tables are invaluable, reshuffling data as the reader requires. EnergyStar presents search results in a dynamic table.[53] Just by clicking on column headers, you can sort the results according to model, screen type or screen size, without leaving the page.

Easy as 1, 2, 3 (not)

On a screen, digits are easier to read than words. They stand out on paper too.

There is a reason why digits grab our attention, and I suppose it is neurological. Digits use a different visual language, so they stick out like ships in a sea of ABC words.

The legal convention is to put both, as in *within three (3) days*. That would be pedantic overkill in non-legal documents. We need a style that will work on paper and on web sites—and online, digits win.

Most everyday writers know one or two simple rules for writing numbers on paper, such as *Use words for numbers up to ten, and digits for higher numbers* and *Spell out numbers at the start of a sentence or headline.* However, it never was that easy: the Australian *Style Manual* devotes 15 pages to the issue![54]

Editorial style guides will need to be revised, so that one style fits both paper and web writing. It's no use having two sets of guidelines, because mountains of documents are published both online and on paper. It's absurd to think we should have two versions of every document, or to switch between two editorial style guides. Sooner or later, digital rules must rule, and that means digits. Here's a start.

- Use digits not words, even for numbers under 10 and numbers at the start of a sentence.
- Exception: use words for numbers *one* and *zero*, because 1 looks like l and 0 looks like o.
- Exception: use words for short numbers that are not data.

New guidelines will keep writers on their toes. As always, we will need to make some fiddly judgements, case by case. For example, take the phrase *Easy as 1, 2, 3*. Strictly speaking, that should be *Easy as one, two, three*, because those numbers don't represent data. Well, there's a sort of literary reason, plus I want 1, 2, 3 to stand out even if they are not data.

This book exists as a PDF and also hard copy, so naturally, I am making online style the default style. You will notice apparent inconsistencies. That will be common until we all get used to digit domination.

Jakob Nielsen explained the power of digits on 16 April 2007 (www.useit.com).

Add white space

White space inspires hope and even confidence in the reader. White space is created by:
- black dots, whether full stops or dot points
- left alignment of all text, including paragraphs, headlines, lists, and links
- short paragraphs
- plenty of headlines
- pull quotes.

The fact that full stops are unconsciously perceived as white space is yet another reason for writing short sentences.

> *Pull-quotes attract skim-readers.*

Most fancy formatting is counterproductive. But pull quotes add that precious white space, and attract skim-readers.

Regardless of topic, good writing is essential. But to interest and attract people, to convince them in a twinkling that a page is worth visiting, something more is needed. The text must be tailored and arranged to *appear* calm and orderly, according to principles that we might call virtual feng shui.

9.

Function and dysfunction

Every piece of content has a function—or it jolly well ought to have. Content is not merely decorative. It is used for something. But what?

Every web page should have a purpose. It always has an effect—but is it the effect you intended? Boredom is an effect. Quitting the site is an effect.

By the way, I'm talking about function in the sense of *what something is used for*. I'm not talking about functionality, which means *technically, it works*. Obviously, every web page should function properly. For example, links should work. But that's another story, and not the province of everyday business writers.

Function is a combination of purpose and effect, the intended use plus the actual use... or so I was told in my youth. The formula is a little more complicated than it appears, because writer and reader are using the content for different purposes. Well written content can satisfy both parties.

- The writer should have a purpose when writing any page. Yet strangely, most writers are only vaguely aware of their purpose. That's why so many pages fail. If you don't have a goal, you can't succeed except by accident—in fact you can't even monitor how well the page succeeds.
- Online readers nearly always have a purpose; they are usually hyper-aware of their purpose and whether the page enables them to succeed.

No function means dysfunction

No function is another way of saying *no use*. A page without a function is worse than a waste of space. Every redundant page erodes the credibility and usability of the site.

Online content sounds passive, like documents pegged on a clothesline. Indeed, many web sites were initially used as containers for inert, unchanging information. There is a place for inert content, but it should still have a function. Even when apparently just browsing, people grab what they need, and the writer should make information easy to grab.

But people online usually have a specific goal. As technology has become slicker and people smarter at using the internet, expectations have risen.

Two goals for the writer

A skilful content writer will have two goals: one identifies how the page is useful to the site owner, the other identifies how the page will be useful to readers.

Imagine a dynamic page that can be used to compare the pricing plans of several telephone companies. The content writer wants to:

- increase customer loyalty by empowering readers and providing rich, accurate, transparent information (this goal reflects corporate strategy)
- enable people to compare the company's pricing plans with those of major competitors (this is the reader's goal).

The target readers' goals will overlap only partially with the writer's goals. Readers don't care about increasing customer loyalty, obviously—but they do want to compare prices. So they may aim to:

- get details about pricing plans from various telephone companies
- select the cheapest telephone plan, not necessarily from the company that owns the site they are using.

What to do when your boss says, 'Write!'

Don't write. Stop. Think. Question. Otherwise you are in dire danger of writing something pointless, useless, purposeless. Something dysfunctional, of no use to man, woman or hedgehog.

Your instructions are likely to be clear about the topic and genre, for example:

Write a report/discussion paper/proposal/course outline/policy/ lecture/ procedure/form/ memo about such-and-such.

In the past you might have just said, 'Sure!' and got straight to work. (You've written plenty of reports before, you can do it standing on your head.)

Instead, be canny: ask some crucial questions before you start. And the most important questions are *why*, *why*, and *why*? Because managers rarely tell you why. They rarely give instructions as clear as this:

Write a lecture that will enable Accounting 201 students to perform a business analysis for a small company, and also improve their efficiency in using our online database of articles. The lecture will be published on the university intranet in HTML format.

It is up to the writer to understand the implications of electronic publication and act accordingly. It's possible your manager is a paper publisher at heart... someone who has dealt with words on paper all their working life... someone to whom the intranet or web site is a novelty, an extra, outside their mind-zone... someone who still cannot see the inevitability or benefits of online publication.

If you don't ask the crucial questions:
- nobody else will
- you and your audience will waste a lot of time
- you will have to severely edit the document later on.

3 short questions: *Why, why, and why*?

1. 'Why am I writing this page?'
'To inform people about the Pensions Board' or 'Because my manager told me to.'

2. ' Yes, but why?'
'So that our citizens know what pensions they are entitled to.'

3. "Yes, but why?"
'Because heaps of people leave it too late to register for their pensions, and then they get angry with us. To reduce unnecessary pressure on staff. To avoid problems and legal repercussions. To meet our constitutional obligations. To improve our efficiency. To raise our reputation.'

Precision questions

A good time to question more systematically is before you write a word. OK, you're not going to make a big deal of this—you've got babies to feed, mountains to climb. But the most lethal question is always the one you forgot to ask. That's the one that turns web sites into dank labyrinths of mouldy junk.

To make sure you cover all bases, consider the following types of questions, adapted from *Question Driven Writing* by Dennis Matthies.[55] People tend to habitually focus on certain categories of questions (asking for clarification until the cows come home) and ignore others (forgetting those deadly hidden assumptions). I strongly recommend zooming through Matthies' system of precision questioning before you start writing, and whenever you get into a spot of bother.

1. **Go or No go**: Why are we considering this page? How important is this content? Is it important to management? To staff? To the public? To whom? Important for what? How urgent is this? Is it genuinely urgent? How strongly is it linked to corporate goals? How interesting is this? To whom?
2. **Clarification**: What exactly do we mean when we describe the intended web page? Is there already a similar page? How do we define this page? What are its parts? What are its uses?
3. **Assumptions**: What are we taking for granted without discussion? That this web page doesn't already exist? That it is necessary? That it is possible? That it will be perfect? That I should write it? That we can measure the return on our investment? That the readers will want it, find it, use it, and appreciate it? That it

won't go out of date? That the intranet is the right place for it? Something else?
4. **Evidence**: Who decided this page would be a good idea? On what evidence? Why would we believe them? Why should we do this? What makes it a good idea? Do we have enough evidence? How can we gather more evidence?
5. **Causes**: What caused the problem? What happened, that we are considering writing this page? What is the root cause? Was there a triggering event? Is the cause inside the system or outside it?
6. **Effects**: What will be the effects of this page? What will be the main consequence? Other consequences? Short-term and long-term consequences? Consequences for the organisation? For the reader? For the writer? How will this affect me and my group? What is the worst possible outcome? Best possible outcome? What could prevent the best outcome? Most likely outcome?
7. **Action**: What should be done? Who will do it? Can a single action (writing this particular web page) accomplish the task? Do others need to be involved (web team, staff, audience, editor)? Do other things need to be done also? Who will do them? Where should the page be located? Where should links to the page be placed?

You'll know which questions deserve your serious attention. Some of them follow.

Where will this document be published?

This is a trick question. If your boss replies, 'Your article will be published in a paper brochure posted by snail mail to all our customers', that may be true. However, assume it will also be posted on a web site or intranet, and write accordingly. Of course, in this case, you can't build in interaction, links, or online applications—but you can structure and write as if for the web. This will only make the document stronger.

Then you won't be embarrassed when your employer suddenly decides to post your article in a blog or on the intranet as an afterthought.

This is well worth probing: in how many formats will this document exist? Will it exist both on paper and online? Will it also exist as a Word document or a PDF?

Yours may be an organisation that has single source documents, maybe in XML. XML requires writers to consciously structure every document. For example, summaries will be coded as such, and headlines must be created by using Styles (not by just bolding and enlarging text).

Regardless of the initial destination of your writing, your responsibility, as writer, is to think internet. When you write for online publication, the document will work on paper too. In fact, it will win accolades. Colleagues will stop you in the corridor and cry, 'I loved your last article! Why aren't they all like that?' But if you forget about the internet until the last minute, and write as if for print, the document usually needs radical editing. It's a pain.

What other information on this topic already exists on our intranet or web site?

Regardless of whether your manager perceives the future document as paper or electronic, search your intranet and web site for other versions. Maybe the information already exists online, but:

- is invisible because of a poor navigation system
- confuses readers and drives them away
- exists only in part or in multiple versions or is spread over many pages.

Identify conflicting or redundant content on the site, and delete it. Only one authoritative version should be online. Otherwise people will still be confused, and they will not trust your new document.

Who is this for?

Typically, web sites are open to the whole world, intranets to all staff or all students. Potentially, your audience is every man, woman and hedgehog. But it's misleading to think of your audience as *everyone*, because every page should be intended for a specific reader, or a reader on a specific quest. Some examples:

- an older person looking to rent an accessible holiday apartment in central Melbourne
- a newly employed lecturer about to request parental leave
- an 18-year-old Toronto resident interested in musical performance
- a small business owner registered for GST.

When you try to write for everyone, your audience becomes a blur. Best think hard about a typical target reader, and address that person specifically. This is true for any sort of writing: you are more likely to strike the right tone when you write as if to a particular person. Some examples:

- your Aunt Jane
- your last teacher
- your nephew.

Remembering all the stresses of reading online, don't set your sights too high when visualising your imaginary reader. Imagine you are addressing:

- your Aunt Jane on a bad brain day
- your last teacher on her way into the classroom
- your 12-year-old nephew.

Even readers with PhDs will vastly prefer to read plain language F-content online. Moreover, almost 40% of the United States population has low literacy skills: why should other western countries be much different?[56]

What do you want people to do?

Read? OK, so your brilliant writing enables people to read your page quickly and easily. That is good. But that is not quite sufficient. Be clear about what you want people to do next—have a nice cup of tea? I don't think so.

Get into the mind of your readers, find out what they really really want to do, and make it very, very easy. Right there on the page, you can enable them to do all sorts of things, for example:
- register or subscribe
- send an email
- purchase something
- comment on a blog posting
- visit a different page
- listen to a podcast or watch a video
- make calculations
- search a database
- get more detailed information on the same topic
- interact a dozen other ways.

A word about online forms

Taking action often includes completing an online form. When completing a form, your readers are at their most sensitive: at the slightest whiff of intrusiveness, you'll lose them. People are much more willing to undertake online transactions than previously, but are still wary of giving personal information to crooks and con artists. They need to be able to cruise the site, checking out the wares, before registering. So:
- don't ask for any more details than you actually need to complete the transaction
- don't ask for any details before you actually need them
- mark the mandatory fields clearly
- show people how far they have progressed in the task
- on the web site, give details of the completed transaction
- automatically email people with details of the transaction.

Completing an online form can be nerve-wracking, and most people probably feel at least some anxiety. Forms should be self-explanatory as far as possible.
- Use conventional words, and very few of them.
- Don't try to save vertical space by spreading fields across two columns: people intent on completing a form are in no mood to notice anything in the corner of their eyes.

And always test, test, test! It's so simple: ask someone to complete the form, thinking aloud while they do it. Don't put words into their mouths or explain anything:

just observe and listen. They will show you whether the form works. If only Vodafone had tested the following form.[57]

Address Type *: Choose one of the following options:	○ Street Address ○ Rural
Address *:	
Town or Suburb *:	
Street Number *:	
Street Type *:	[⇅]

The above form appeared after I had emailed Vodafone using a form on another page. In other words, Vodafone forced me to complete a superfluous form merely to email them. Within a few lines they had thoroughly alienated me.

They want my street address? Excuse me? I had already provided my email address and cell phone number. I was startled, annoyed, and suspicious. I felt like a foreign tourist in rural China, where it's common (I'm told) for local police to request a copy of your passport so they can keep track of you. Westerners tend to find this offensive, even scary.

Take a look at the form. Every line is weird. Figure how you would complete it.
- Should you read across or down?
- Why the choice between *Street Address* and *Rural*?
- What goes in the *Address* field?
- Why a separate field for *Street Number*?

And why on earth a drop-down menu for *Street Type*? A person who is capable of writing *Main* is surely also capable of writing *Street*.

It's not exactly hard to request an address in a form: just copy a good example. Happily, there are plenty out there.

This bad, bizarre form from a major company reminds us:
- never ask for unnecessary personal information online
- don't mess with conventions (such as the order of elements in an address)
- test every form for usability.

The very existence of the following page is sign of dysfunction, because Levi's product page should be self-explanatory.[58] If people cannot order online intuitively, an explanatory web page is unlikely to help. A mere glance shows the page is wordy and confusing. Close reading confirms the hunch with redundant instructions such as *To browse more products within the product category, click "Next" or "Previous", located in the upper right corner of the page.*

> **HOW TO USE THE PRODUCT PAGE**
>
> Each product page features a photograph of the item along with a detailed description.
>
> To view products in different colors and washes, select the color swatches under the header "Washes/Colors". For additional product views, select "See it Bigger" to see a larger product image. For an up-close look at fabric detailing, click "Zoom". 'Select "Rotate" to see the back view image. Click on "Size Chart" for sizing availability and measurement information.
>
> If you would like to purchase an item that is available for sale online, select a retailer of your choice under the "Buy online at" header on the product page. This will link directly to that product page on the retailer's web site. To purchase the product at a store near you, enter your ZIP code under "Find it in a store" to locate the nearest store location.
>
> To browse more products within the product category, click "Next" or "Previous", located in the upper right corner of the page.

An online form from New Zealand's Inland Revenue Department follows.[59] It is simple, easy to skim-read and with all necessary information in the appropriate place. Warnings and help messages are placed exactly where they are needed. The page enables both the reader and the site owner to achieve their purpose. It's a functional page.

Student loan interest write-off 1 April 2006 to 31 March 2007

If you were studying and a New Zealand tax resident during 1 April 2006 to 31 March 2007, you may be eligible for an interest write-off on your student loan. All you need to do is fill in this form and submit it. **Remember, if you have given your IRD number to your tertiary provider, you don't need to submit this form.**

Fields marked with ● are required

Your details

First name(s) ●

Surname ●

IRD number ●

If you don't know your IRD number, call us on 0800 377 778 and tell us your details. If you are calling from overseas, please ring 64 3 467 7020.

If your postal address has changed please enter it here

Street address or box number

Suburb

Town or city

Post code

Contact phone number

Where were you studying during this income year?

Student ID ●

If you don't have this you'll need to contact your tertiary education provider to obtain it.

Type of tertiary education provider ● [Choose a provider type ▼]

Name of tertiary education provider ● [Choose a provider ▼]

The information you have provided here will be sent to the Ministry of Education who will confirm for us whether you were studying full-time or part-time. If you qualify for an interest write-off, we will confirm the amount written off on your next loan statement.

Disclaimer
Please note that due to the nature of the internet, the security of information you supply here cannot be guaranteed. Only click 'Send details' if you accept this risk.

Send details

10.

Focused, free-standing content

F-content is both focused and free-standing. In other words, each page focuses on a single topic, and makes sense in isolation. Strange to say, there's a logical connection between these two features. Let me explain.

Demands of a modular structure

Whereas the structure and size of a book or magazine are visible, the structure and size of a web site are largely invisible. Of course, you can get some idea by looking at the site map. But people don't much care how a web site is structured or how large it is. They typically approach a web page with a task in view. The only information they want is the information that helps them complete that task.

At the development stage, information architects plan a site's structure and navigation system meticulously. They create hierarchies of content (home page, index page, utility pages, secondary pages and so forth) and logical pathways to all the pages within the site.

A majority of visitors ignore the designer's pathways and seek a route straight to the exact page they want. They don't start by visiting the home page: they use a search engine or a link from another site, and with luck will bypass all other pages on their way to the golden content they need.

In other words, visitors treat web pages as a bunch of modules of equal importance. Therefore the writer must do likewise. Any page you write may be the very first one on a site that a visitor sees. So it has to make sense as if it were all alone, free-standing. You can never assume your reader knows who you are or what you do or even what country your site is in. (This even applies to intranets: just substitute *business unit* or *department* for *country*.)

This seems seriously weird to many on-the-job writers and is a hard thing to grasp. Most hard-copy documents can be seen and held in the hand. It's the publisher's responsibility to declare their identity: a letter from your bank comes on a letterhead with name, address and phone numbers; a book has a copyright page with details of the publisher. Strangely, with online content, the writer often has to provide this information.

Imagine publishing a book: writing, designing, printing, binding and publicising it. Then, in an empty shop, imagine ripping the pages out of your precious book, tossing them into a heap, and turning on a fan. Pages fly all over the room. Now walk through the room kicking pages like autumn leaves. Chaos. You cannot see the whole book. There is no book—just heaps of pages. That's how people stumble across your web site. It's almost scary.

The public never sees your 'book' as a whole. They don't care about it. They are somewhere else, asking a search engine for the ten best pages about the Tokelau education system or contracting opportunities in Indonesia. They may look at only one page from your entire site.

Like it or lump it, that's more or less how people perceive your content. As the whole is invisible, every page must be perfect and complete.

Think of content as data

Think of a web site as a virtual database, and the content on a page as data. Some sites are literally databases: they shuffle and reassemble data to create new PHP or ASP pages—Google, blogs, and Amazon do this. Content management systems even treat the parts of a page as data: writers must complete fields labelled *Headline*, *Summary*, *Content Block* or *Link*. Each part is essentially a data entry.

On web sites that generate pages on the fly from a database, it's comparatively simple to update content. A single source of information is much less likely to become outdated or redundant than a site where every page is written by a human.

Asian Development Bank uses blog technology to provide information about business opportunities, jobs, news, publications and what's new.[60] RSS feeds mean people can keep right up to date with jobs, for example, without ever visiting the jobs page again. The page keeps changing, as old jobs are deleted and new ones added to the database.

The writer must ensure that when contractors click on one of these links, they find a page that:

- is about one particular job and nothing else (focused)
- makes sense when printed out (free-standing)
- gives all the necessary details (free-standing).

ADB's content writers use a template that ensures every web page describing a job meets all the above requirements. The top part of one such document follows.

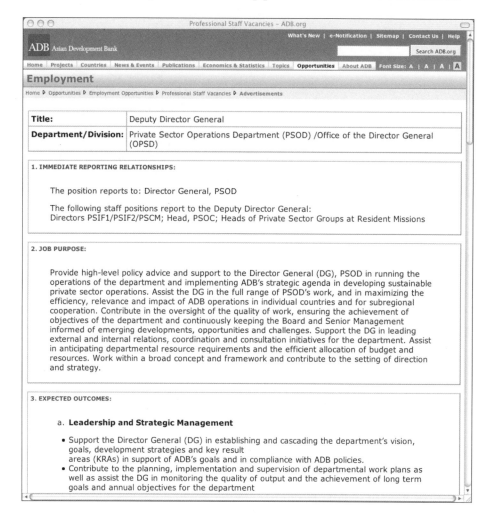

Here's one of ADB's pages giving details of a contract. A single contract. Even printed and out of context, this page would make sense.

> | Indonesia | LOAN: (N) INO 40003-01 | • Objectives and Scope |
> |---|---|---|
>
> **Project Name**
> Poverty Reduction and Millenium
> Development Goals Acceleration Program
>
> • Procurement
> • Environmental Category
>
> **Executing Agency**
> National Development Planning Agency
> Contact :Dr. Dedi M. Masykur Riyadi, Deputy Minister
> Fax. No.:62 21 3145374
> Address :Ministry of Human Resources and Cultural
>   JL. Taman Suropati No. 2
>   Jakarta, Indonesia
>
> • Project Processing Stage
> • Project Officer
>
> **Loan Amount (US$ million)**
> 200.00
>
> **Sector/Subsector**
> Law, Economic Management & Public
> Policy /Economic Management
>
> **Date of First Listing**
> 15 December 2006
>
> ---
>
> **Objectives and Scope**
> > The Project impacts will be to accelerate progress towards achieving the Millenium Development Goals (MDG) in education, and health and contribute to the Government's poverty reduction agenda, and gender equality. The program's outcome is the improvement of access, equity, and quality of service delivery in the education and health sectors within an enhanced national framework for MDG acceleration. It will be implemented in accordance with national priorities as reflected in the current medium term development plan (RPJM). The program will assist the Government in the re-orientation of fiscal expenditures to the social sectors and the reduction of regional disparities.
>
> **Procurement**
> > *Goods*
> > The loan proceeds will be used to finance the full foreign exchange costs (excluding local duties and taxes) of items produced and procured in ADB member countries, excluding

The requirements for free-standing, focused content seem obvious when a site clearly uses a database, as ADB does. However, exactly the same principles apply to every web page. People choose their own paths to find the information they want. Generally, they are seeking a page (like a piece of data), not a site (like a book).

How to write focused content

What is focused content? Simple: it's content that focuses on one topic or task.

How do you know if your content is focused? (Let's consider web pages, although everything from long documents to single paragraphs should also be focused.) Ask yourself what this page is about or for. If you can answer easily in 3–5 words, with no doubt in your mind, that's good.

- 'It's about breeding British Blue cats.' (Good: the page is focused).
- 'It's about British Blue cats and the swimming pool in Khandallah.' (Bad: a page about two things is about nothing. The exception is a personal blog, where anything goes.)
- 'It's about... um...I don't know really.' (Very, very bad sign: the answer should be obvious.)

It will not surprise you that 'What is this page about or for?' is answered by a handful of keywords. That's almost the definition of keywords: words that answer the question, 'What is this page about or for?'

Focused pages tend to be short pages, but not always. After all, an entire book can be about a single topic.

A tragic but typical example of a page with two topics follows.[61] Only the top half of the page is shown. This describes the role of the Irish Pensions Board, the legislation behind its establishment, and its legal obligations.

DSFA » Retired or Older People » Protecting Your Occupational Pension Rights

Protecting Your Occupational Pension Rights

The Pensions Board (An Bord Pinsean) was established by the Minister for Social Welfare under the Pensions Act, 1990. Its main functions as set out in that Act and amending legislation, most recently the Pensions (Amendment) Act, 2002, are:

- to monitor and supervise the operation of the Pensions Act and pension developments generally, including the activities of PRSA (Personal Retirement Savings Account) providers, the provision of PRSA products and the operation of PRSAs;
- to issue guidelines or Guidance Notes on the duties and responsibilities of trustees of schemes and Codes of Practice on specific aspects of their responsibilities;
- to issue guidelines or Guidance Notes on the duties and responsibilities of PRSA providers in relation to PRSA products;
- to encourage the provision of appropriate training for trustees of schemes, and to advise the Minister on standards for trustees;
- to advise the Minister on all matters in relation to the Pensions Act and on pension matters generally.

Occupational pension schemes must register with the Board, and most schemes must pay an annual fee to meet the Board's administrative costs. The Board can act on behalf of pension scheme members who are concerned about their scheme; it can investigate the operation of pension schemes; it has the power to prosecute for breaches of the Pensions Act and to take court action against trustees for the protection of members and their rights. The Pensions Board includes representatives of trade unions, employers, Government, pension scheme trustees, the pensions industry, consumer interests, pensioner interests and various professional groups involved with occupational pension schemes and PRSAs.

All very interesting, no doubt. The Pensions Board has gone through the motions of informing the public about itself, and even provided contact details. But this top half of the page is essentially navel gazing: it's an official document to keep the Board on track.

But wait! Scroll down and we find an urgent warning for older Irish citizens, heavily bolded: 'Don't lose out on your Social Welfare Pension Entitlement'. This message is addressed to all older Irish people.

This page should be split into two, each focusing on a different audience. Or even three: one official document (for the record), one addressed to pension scheme providers, one addressed to older Irish citizens over the age of 65. The reasons are pretty obvious.

- An accurate headline that describes the existing page would be extremely long and confusing—maybe this:
  Irish Pension Board Protects Members of Private Pension Scheme, & Irish citizens: don't Lose Out on Your Social Welfare Pension Entitlement
- It would be hard to write an accurate summary of the page.
- Most people won't scroll to see the urgent message to older people.
- To compound the problem, the Google Search Engine Results Page displays the page title, which uses inhouse jargon and is just a truncated breadcrumb trail: <u>DFSA >> Retired or Older People >> Protecting Your Occupational...</u> But that's another story, discussed in Chapter 13.

How to write free-standing content

Free-standing content makes sense even when:
- people ignore the logo and banner (and they will)
- the logo and banner are not legible
- the logo and banner don't make sense
- the logo and banner don't give enough information.

Hard to believe such things can happen? Look at the home page of the Department for Education and Skills below.[62] Nowhere on the page is a single clue about the country, not even in the footer. This absurd anonymity results from navel-gazing: 'We are British, so naturally everyone else in the world must know who we are. One glance at our logo is enough.'

The UK government portal DirectGov lists central government departments, executive agencies and non-departmental public bodies. Last time I looked at its A-Z list, only 5 of the first 10 sites mentioned the UK (or England, Scotland, or Wales) anywhere on the home page anywhere, not in the content, links, email address or graphics. The worst offenders don't even have *.uk* in the domain name.

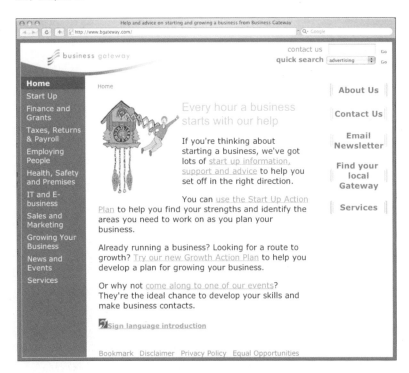

Faced with such arrogant design, a good content writer saves the day by slipping the word *British* into the content, and the nearer the top the better. Best to do this unobtrusively as a matter of routine on every page.

By contrast, Australia's policy is for every government site to sport a standardised logo that includes the words *Australian Government*. And notice the word *Australians* in the tag line below.

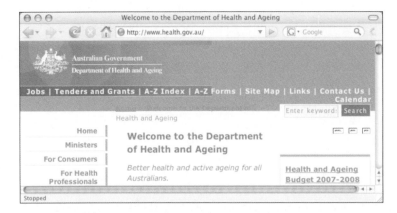

Who would guess that the following logos are for UK government bodies?

A good designer can ensure logo and banner provide sufficient legible, accurate, relevant information. But even a great designer cannot stop people reading the content without reading the banner.

Regardless of design, with a few simple tricks the writer can ensure web pages pass both the identity test and the free-standing test:

- location and site owner mentioned high in the content of every page
- F-headlines
- F-summaries
- absolute dates used, not relative dates like *today* or *in the last year*
- absolute locations used, not *here, in the neighbouring counties*, etc.

Why long documents go pear-shaped online

So far we have been thinking about one page at a time, and there is no exception to the rule that every page must make sense alone. Content managers and editors have some important decisions to make when it comes to long documents that exist on paper and must be published on a web site or intranet. (By *long*, I mean longer than about 5 x A4 paper pages in print.)

You need to make a sharp distinction between two kinds of documents. For that, you need to crawl out of your own cocoon. Most writers sincerely believe that their document, precious, important and unique as it is, must be read from start to finish. But that is rarely true.

Type 1: Pick'n'mix long documents

Most long documents can and should be converted into a bunch of web pages, related but of equal importance. These are focused, free-standing pages that do not need to be read in sequence. The writer might prefer people to read every word, but actually, most people will only want to read a minority of pages. No harm is done by selective reading.

In such cases, there is little point in drawing attention to the linear structure of the original document. The original sequence of pages is irrelevant. Pages from the document can often be scattered in different parts of a web site: put the useful pages in the most logical and convenient location, and don't even think about publishing pointless pages online.

Here's a funny thing: even now you may be thinking, 'Yes, how true—but of course that doesn't apply to the manual/report/policy I'm writing at present. There's no way that could be chopped up and still preserve its integrity.'

Think again. Get a second opinion. Maybe you need both: a few paper copies of the complete historic document for reference, plus many mini-web pages located where people will find them in their time of need. For example, somewhere in your workplace may lurk a two-inch thick delegations volume that describes, analyses and lists all the rights and obligations of all staff at every level of every type of work in every location to take and delegate responsibilities under all conceivable situations. Whew! Even that one sentence turned out horrible—so imagine the complete volume! Now, the two-inch volume still needs to exist as a reference for lawyers, specialists and the CEO. However, most staff need only the details related to their own current employment situation, translated into plain language. That's what should be online, with one topic per page.

Large portions of the original document do not need to be online.

Here's an example of this subdivision into focused, free-standing pages. Remember the fat old Microsoft Users Guides we used to have for Word and Excel? They're museum pieces now. We consulted such manuals for specific problems—when numbering ran out of control or a spreadsheet crashed, for example. Contrast those 800-page manuals with the nifty Help on our screens today. We don't need a 2-inch manual. We just need to know how to fix our latest disaster. And now we can find that information in two clicks.

Type 2: Genuinely indivisible documents

By contrast, a minority of long documents must be published as a whole, because people need to read them from go to whoa. You can't force people to read that way, but at least you can make the size and scope of the whole document really obvious, and enable people to download it complete. Such documents are not over until the fat lady sings.

Documents that need to be published as a whole either have a linear structure, moving inevitably from start to finish, or genuine integrity of meaning. Some examples are:
- anything that tells a story: for example, short stories, history of a company
- chronologies, historical information
- instructions or procedures that must be followed in sequence in order to complete a defined task
- documents where people could make errors or be misled if they believe they have read the entire document (for example, a legal opinion, requirements for tendering, or medical advice)
- papers that depend on analytical reasoning that is not completed until the end.

At the very least, every page of a long, indivisible document should show the larger structure extremely clearly, for example, with:
- a list of chapters at the top
- links to *next* and *previous* pages
- a link to the complete table of contents
- the actual table of contents (short version).

Canada's document on a Common Look and Feel for the Internet 2.0 demonstrates the above points nicely.[63]

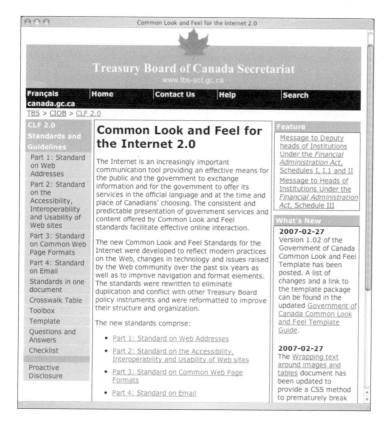

With this type of document, long pages are often a necessity. To split a topic merely to shorten a web page is counterproductive. Readers need to be confident that each page covers a topic completely.

Most genuinely indivisible online documents need a complete table of contents. The conventional version is not a pretty sight. The antique 1.1.1 numbering system is ugly, and often used in official documents. Don't ask me why so many writers feel the urge to add three different levels of dot points to three levels of numbering. The following example strays far from the skim-reader's F-pattern, and notice how cluttered it looks?[64]

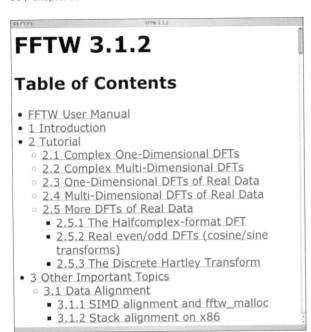

Microsoft Office Online gives advice on creating tables of contents.

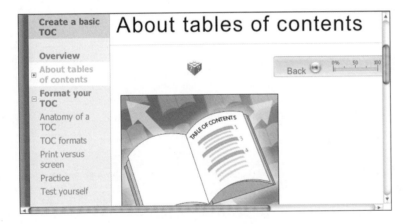

Here's the start of an unpretentious table of contents that is easy to skim-read, from the North Carolina Department of Environment and Natural Resources.[65]

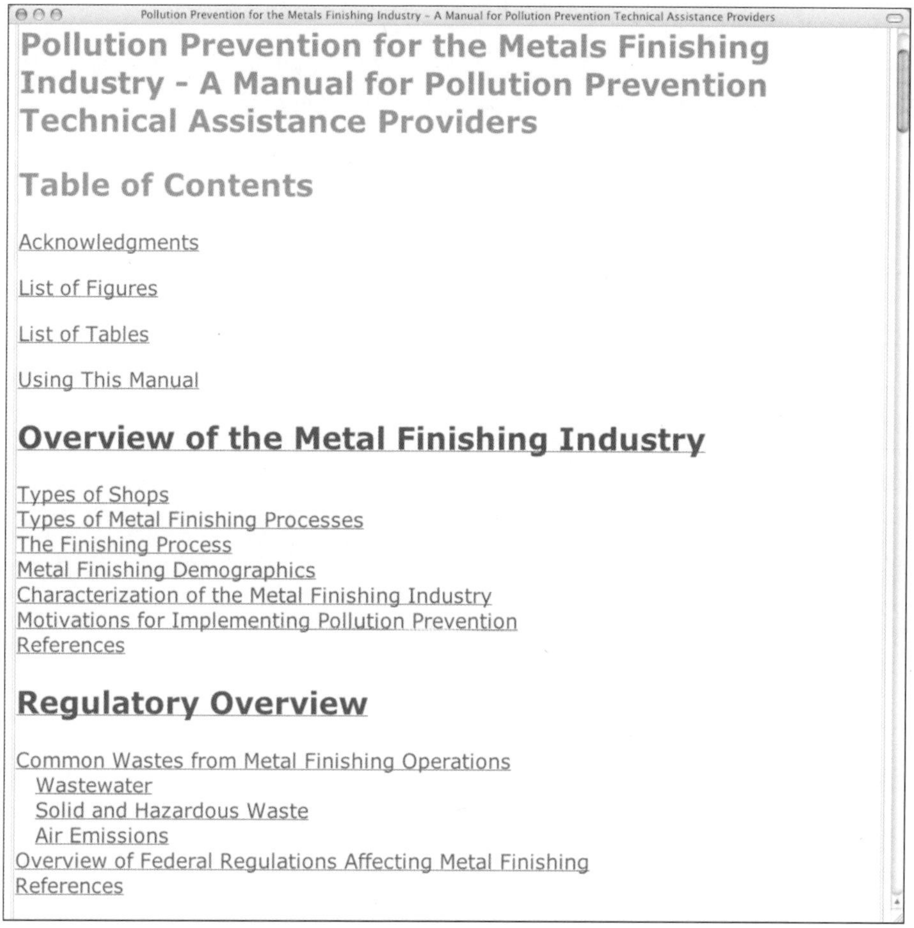

> # Pollution Prevention for the Metals Finishing Industry - A Manual for Pollution Prevention Technical Assistance Providers
>
> ## Table of Contents
>
> Acknowledgments
>
> List of Figures
>
> List of Tables
>
> Using This Manual
>
> ## Overview of the Metal Finishing Industry
>
> Types of Shops
> Types of Metal Finishing Processes
> The Finishing Process
> Metal Finishing Demographics
> Characterization of the Metal Finishing Industry
> Motivations for Implementing Pollution Prevention
> References
>
> ## Regulatory Overview
>
> Common Wastes from Metal Finishing Operations
>   Wastewater
>   Solid and Hazardous Waste
>   Air Emissions
> Overview of Federal Regulations Affecting Metal Finishing
> References

In the next screenshot, the FAO makes a web-friendly decision, simply listing chapters in the table of contents of *Multilateral Trade Negotiations in Agriculture: A Resource Manual*.[66] They left align everything. This is F-writing, beautifully skim-readable. Readers can picture the scale and structure of this substantial document without being overwhelmed, and that is the whole point. Notice how complete and clear the chapter headlines are… that is crucial, and no coincidence.

> Foreword
> Acknowledgements
> Introduction
>
> **Part I. Introduction and General Topics**
>
> 1 Trends in world and agricultural trade
> 2 International trade: some basic theories and concepts
> 3. Instruments of protection and their economic impact
> 4. Agriculture in the GATT: a historical account
> 5. Dispute settlement
> 6. Trade and the environment
>
> **Part II. Agreement on Agriculture**
>
> 1. Domestic support measures
> 2. Preparing for negotiating further reductions of the bound tariffs
> 3. Export subsidies
> 4. Market access I: tariffs and other access terms
> 5. Market access II: tariff rate quotas
> 6. Safeguard measures
> 7. Special and differential treatment
> 8. Continuing the reform process in agriculture: Article 20 issues
> 9. Decision on measures concerning the possible negative effects on LDCs and NFIDCs
> 10. Trade and food security: options for developing countries
> 11. International trade in fishery products and the new global trading environment
>
> **Part III. Agreement on the Application of Sanitary and Phytosanitary Measures (SPS) and Agreement on Technical Barriers to Trade (TBT)**
>
> 1. History of the development of the SPS agreement
> 2. SPS agreement: provisions, basic rights and obligations
> 3. Agreement on TBT: an overview
> 4. Introduction to Codex Alimentarius Commission (CAC)
> 5. Introduction to the International Plant Protection Convention (IPPC)

The case for PDFs

You can already see that publishing long documents online presents a few challenges, and we haven't even got started on the topic. Long ago, Portable Document Files (PDFs) were considered a quick and easy way to avoid decisions. Just PDF it—end of problem. The long document is snapped into one read-only file, with the original formatting intact.

No? No. PDFs are still inaccessible to some people, although the technology has greatly improved. If you work for a government agency or any organisation that is concerned with accessibility issues, check your government guidelines. You'll probably find something like this:

> The primary format for all content available on government websites *must* be HTML.

That's another way of saying:

> Use HTML for all important documents intended for the public, and don't use PDFs unless you have a very good reason.

Very good reasons might be that the document contains many maps or mathematical symbols, or is of interest only to a small number of specialists. The site owner's convenience, on the other hand, is not a very good reason for publishing by PDF. As a general rule, offer PDF as an additional format, not as the only format. Let the reader choose.

Governments attempting to enforce this rule have met with some resistance, understandably. Meanwhile, take care creating the PDF:

- Start with an accessible document: use Styles meticulously. (Consult *PDF techniques for WCAG 2.0* on www.w3.org.)
- include date and version number in the footer
- provide metadata for the PDF file
- bookmark chapter headings.

If you are offering a long document online as a PDF:

- summarise or describe the document before forcing people to click
- always include [*PDF, #KB*] in or near the link-text
- if possible mention the number of pages: that matters more than kilobytes when it comes to printing a PDF
- include a link to download Adobe Reader on each page with PDFs; you might want to explain the benefits of using the latest version
- remember that HTML is the default technology for government documents online.

Australia Government Information Management Office (AGIMO) handles PDFs well on this page of checklists—as we'd hope![67] The icons indicate PDF format.

AGIMO | Better Practice Checklists

Better Practice Checklists

1. Providing Forms Online   (238kb)
2. Website Navigation   (276kb)
3. Testing Websites with Users   (296kb)
4. Use of Cookies in Online Services   (275kb)
5. Providing an Online Sales Facility (286kb)
6. Use of Metadata for Web Resources   (285kb)
7. Archiving Web Resources   (288kb)
8. Managing Online Content   (288kb)
9. Selecting a Content Management System (298kb)

Starting from scratch with long documents

At times you may be forced to publish a long document online that is worse than hostile—it's a danger to shipping. You know the scene. It's copyright—it was written by a committee—it's due yesterday—the lawyers have signed off on it and gone home for the summer. It sort of worked on paper, perhaps, but it sure doesn't work online. You rack your brains (pull-quotes? a summary in a box? photo of sunset in Tahiti?) but nothing can save it.

Ultimately there's only one solution: prevention. Every document, including major tomes like policy manuals and national reports, should be planned with online publishing in mind. Don't write a word without visualising the document on a web site or intranet.

It's long documents that cause the most trouble when online publication is an afterthought. A manager asks you to rewrite a staff manual, assuring you it will be printed. But you know better. You know that as soon as the manual is finished, the CEO will say, 'This is excellent. We must put it on the intranet.' Save the tears by structuring and wording every long document as if it were destined for publication online—in HTML, not as a PDF.

Looking ahead, here's a checklist for the next time you are involved in writing a long document.

1. Write 4–10-word F-headlines for every chapter and section. Never be satisfied with labels such as *Background* and *Conclusion*: provide a complete and crystal clear headline.
2. Don't number chapters or sub-sections of chapters unless you can honestly see this as one of those rare indivisible documents.
3. Restrict sub-headlines within chapters to two levels.
4. Start every chapter with an F-summary—yes, every chapter.
5. Subdivide content rigorously, not only according to its topic, but also to its function.
6. Use plain language or die.
7. Spell out acronyms the first time they appear in every chapter—yes, every chapter!
8. Think links.
9. Left-align the table of contents.
10. Don't duplicate information that exists elsewhere: link to the original page.

New looks for long documents

Publication on the web is not a punishment: it is an opportunity. Your web team may be able to suggest exciting new ways to display the information in your document and make it more usable. Consult them: they're dying to try out some great ideas that you haven't even dreamed of.

Test, test, test

A pick'n'mix long document can be tested in the usual way, because it's just a bunch of web pages.

But how do you know whether your long, indivisible document will work online?

Check it yourself first, then ask a few other people to test it. Watch them read it, and ask them to think aloud as they do.

- Do they look confident?
- Do they understand it?
- Can they always tell what document they're reading, what chapter they're in, how big the document is, what it's about, and which sections they've read?
- Can they print out a page of the document and still have this crucial information: name, version and date?
- Can they read the table of contents easily?

11.

Fresh and factual content

Readability, credibility and findability all benefit when content is fresh and factual. Fresh means the opposite of old, stale, unoriginal and out of date. Factual content has something to say: it isn't just waffle. Factual content has more keywords than cake-words. (*Factual* content can include opinion, if it is supported by facts; but we're concerned with business writing, not games, poetry or fiction.)

People trust sites that update content frequently. If there is no recent sign of life on the home page, we tend to doubt the value of the entire site. Untended web sites are gradually overtaken by redundant, outdated and trivial content (ROT). Would you trust information on a site whose most recent news item is months or even years old? Thought not. ROT can erupt on any page—not just news pages.

Google, the search engine that thinks like a human, favours pages that are frequently updated, and boosts page ranking accordingly. (That's one reason why certain blogs score highly with Google.) The longer a site languishes without change, the further it slips down the ranks of search engine results.

Factual content is what people are looking for when searching. We type into the search box *accommodation Bondi* not *best place*. Objective prose is read faster and retained better than emotive prose. We trust sites that provide accurate information and refrain from vacuous superlatives like *best, finest, amazing*.

Spot the ROT

First and second generation web sites and intranets are full of ROT. It's almost inevitable unless you have a system for reviewing content regularly.

R is for redundant content, which comes in two main forms: content that exists on more than one page, and content that is pointless and useless. Duplicated pages are redundant and can have serious repercussions. If you have 2 (or 10) pages on the same topic, they are bound to differ as one gets updated and the others are left to rot. Then nobody knows which information to trust.

The larger the web site, the more redundant pages: it's simple maths. If your intranet has 200,000 pages, and nobody can find a page on a particular topic, somebody creates another one. Ad infinitum.

O is for outdated. Pages that use the word *new* for something long established. Pages that mention people who have left the organisation or the job. Pages that announce events that have already happened. Obsolete versions of policies and rules.

T is for trivial content: pages that are essentially about nothing at all.

Stop the ROT

First of all, write no unnecessary page. Never write another version of content that already exists on your site: link to it. In fact, consider very carefully before you write another version of content that already exists on somebody else's site. It's better to identify the authoritative version and link to it. This will entail more research and less writing.

Keep links alive: use software to check for dead links frequently, and fix them or delete them. Dead links don't impress people or Google.

Humans sometimes spontaneously tell you about dead content, including links. Then all you need to do is react. You can go further, making it easy for readers to contact you with feedback or questions.

But getting rid of ROT doesn't just happen. I don't see many people twiddling their thumbs at work, and deciding that this would be a nice day to review the intranet for ROT. It needs to be a requirement, and it must be systematic. Build garbage disposal into the job description of certain staff members. Then send automatic reminders to review web content and delete, archive or rewrite ROT. At set periods after content is published, writers get an email advising them to check the page and update if necessary. And if they don't, the relevant manager is advised. And if the manager doesn't update the page, the CEO is advised... just kidding, but you get the drift.

When I searched Google using the keyword *next club meeting*, 9 of the first 10 results were announcing meetings that had already occurred. One had happened 7 months earlier.

> FRIDAY, APRIL 13, 2007
>
> **Next Club Meeting Thursday, April 29**
>
> Our next general meeting will be Thursday, April 19, 2007. Featured speaker to be Ed Cox, John McCain's point man in New York, for his Presidential campaign. Like we mentioned last

Lack of money is one reason for ROT, but so is lack of organisation. *Coastal Awareness Day 2004* is not a good look.[68]

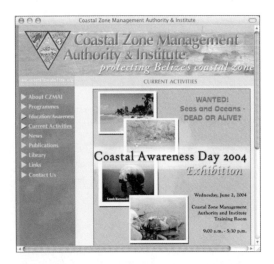

Today was tomorrow yesterday

All emails have dates automatically attached, and so do news stories and press releases. But most web pages don't. People hunt for clues in content about when it was written. Write timeless (if not deathless) prose. Some web pages don't need updating regularly, for example scholarly articles or the history of your organisation. But many are worse than useless if they are out of date. Know the difference and show the difference in your writing.

- Use exact dates, for example, 24 February 1940. Avoid all relative expressions of time such as now, today, in the next six months, soon and recently.
- Don't rely on Last Updated footers.
- Put a date in the content of every page that needs it.
- Date all news items, memos etc.

People change jobs

Future-proof content against change of personnel. Strategy here concerns security as well as ROT.

On an intranet, include details about skill sets and responsibilities in the staff directory. Then a link to the office page in the directory will provide all the personal information required by staff. If possible make the directory a single, authoritative source for contact and professional information.

- In content, for the most part, name offices or roles, not individuals.
- Link to the staff directory or contact page instead of duplicating email addresses.
- In content, use generic contact email addresses, such as enrolment@yourschool.edu.

My *here* is your *there*, my *we* is your *you*

Never assume readers know where you are. A web site has many signposts, and some belong right there in the content, the words you write.

- State actual locations such as *Mt Victoria, Sydney, Tokelau*.
- Don't use relative expressions of place such as *here, there, in the next county, 40km north* (of where?).
- Define what you mean by geographic terms such as *Far East, North Asia, Pacific Rim*; explain once briefly or use country names.
- At least once near the top of the page, state your identity; don't rely on the logo alone, as page content may be quoted out of context. (You knew this. Just a reminder!)

What ROT

A quick flick through environmental web sites revealed the following examples of outdated content. And what about the millions of pages that don't even mention a date?

> The project is expected to be completed in May 2005.

> This £1.2 million scheme is planned to start in December 2003.

> 2005 Projects - A list of 2005 projects will be updated shortly.

> The program commenced in May 2000 and is still active. The current review is expected to be complete in late 2005.

> Projects for 2001.

> Take advantage of the early bird registration and get 15% discount on the registration fee, when you register before the 15th of February 2004.

It's fine to use relative expressions of time such as *over the past few months* if you are absolutely certain your text will always have a date attached to it, as below:

> October 2006. Over the past few months, we have heard from many of our alumni.

Search engine technology is constantly changing. Naturally, my first thought on reading the following tutorial was 'When was this written?'[69] In fact it was last updated on 6 July 2006. I think that date should be right at the top, giving an absolute reference point for words such as *still* and *currently*.

The next tutorial should die, don't you think? If you are ever asked to write something similar, don't even think about agreeing. Just provide a link to an authoritative site that is constantly updated, such as www.SearchEngineWatch.com.

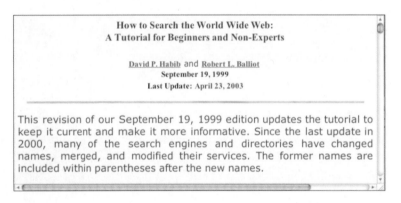

The list of search tools on the next tutorial is our clue that it was *Last modified 07/09/01*.[70] No doubt it was useful and innovative at the time.

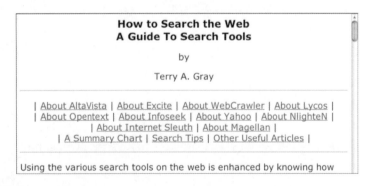

How to write factual content

Straight up, let me assure you I don't advocate that every web page must consist of dry facts. On the contrary, personality and imagination are like water in the desert. No—I'm just reminding you again that a web page must be about something specific, and it must say something or do something. Proof that a page is about something (!) lies in the words. Every cake-word among the keywords risks alienating your reader. They're like speed bumps on the road, slowing readers down, making them question the veracity of the content.

Keywords: *software development, usability, coding.*
Cake-words: *ground-breaking, wonderful, outstanding.*

News stories work well on the web because they always have these features:
- exact date
- keywords
- facts
- concise style
- a headline packed with keywords
- a concentrated summary at the top, packed with keywords
- inverted pyramid structure, moving from most to least important information.

Yet even abstruse, theoretical pages can be factual. And some content can be old yet not outdated.

Maja Milcinski's abstract has wall-to-wall keywords, despite being about emptiness and the void.[71] For Milcinski, *nothing* is a subject in itself. This is an example of content that is fresh in the sense of original, but does not need to be fresh in the sense of constantly changing. On the contrary, it is a copyright article of enduring interest to philosophers.

Philosophy in Asia

Impermanence and Death in Sino-Japanese Philosophical Context

Maja Milcinski
maja.milcinski@uni-lj.si

ABSTRACT: This paper discusses the notions of impermanence and death as treated in the Chinese and Japanese philosophical traditions, particularly in connection with the Buddhist concept of emptiness and void and the original Daoist answers to the problem. Methodological problems are mentioned and two ways of approaching the theme are proposed: the logically discursive and the meditative mystical one, with the two symbols of each, *Uroboros* and the open circle. The switch of consciousness is suggested as an essential condition for liberation of the Ego and its illusions. Rational logic as well as the sophisticated meditative ways of selflessness and detachment are suggested when treating the Chinese and Japanese philosophical notions, and examples of the discussed topics from the texts given. The instructive seventh chapter of the classical Daoist work, *Lie Zi*, is analyzed in detail and put into contrast with the answers given to that problem in the Greco-Judeo-Christian tradition.

Fresh and factual home page

All New Zealand's 21 District Health Boards (DHBs) are strapped for cash. They don't spend much of their scarce resources on web content. In August 2008, 8 sites had settled for stale, unchanging blurb on their home page, with no news or outdated news. The Auckland DHB home page was typical. It's hard to imagine that anyone bothered reading it.

Facts on the South Canterbury DHB home page were badly diluted by cake-words (italicised)—I have no idea why, because a DHB is hardly responsible for scenery.[72]

> South Canterbury District Health Board serves about 54,000 people living in the *beautiful* region bounded by the *grandeur* of the Southern Alps to the west, the *sparkling* Pacific Ocean to the east, and the Rangitata and Waitaki rivers to the north and south. South Canterbury includes the main centre of Timaru, located approximately halfway between Christchurch and Dunedin on the South Island's east coast, and a number of *picturesque* towns and smaller rural settlements.

I'm happy to report that within 3 years the web presence of most DHBs had been revitalised. For example, the South Canterbury DHB home page now shows a contact phone number and obvious links to news. Most DHBs update important content. Nevertheless, in September 2011 the Auckland DHB home page still featured a 250-word letter from the CE about the DHB's aim and vision and focus and goals: this bore a horrible resemblance to the blurb that was squatting there in 2008.

Employment Opportunities (recent additions)

Select any to find out more

| View | Personal Assistant to the Director of Nursing and Midwifery, Greymouth |
| View | Mental Health New Graduate Programme 2008, Greymouth |

>> See all current Employment Opportunities

2008 WEST COAST DHB INNOVATION AND EXCELLENCE AWARDS

"ACHIEVING A SUSTAINABLE FUTURE"

The West Coast DHB is proud to announce the launch of the 2008 Innovation and Excellence Awards, run in conjunction with ACC. The aim of the awards is to recognise and publicly celebrate the commitment and innovation demonstrated by local organisations in serving the health needs of the West Coast population.

Popular Links

These are the pages that interest our visitors most.

- Awareness Calendar 2008
- Board & Committee Papers
- Consultation Documents
- Coping with Depression (NEW)
- Find a Hospital, Practice/Medical Centre, GP, Midwife or Specialist
- Newsletters
- Policies and Procedures
- Projects
- Southern Cancer Network (NEW)
- Sustainability Project Forum (Members only)

>> More popular links

What's New?

- Tuesday, 19th August 2008

  INCUBATOR

12.

Photos, figs, Flash and audio

Content is not just words, of course. On-the-job writers frequently want to use other media. Images play a big part in business content, and Flash, video and audio become more significant by the day. The web team takes care of all images that are part of a site-wide design, for example the logo and any decorative flourishes. But writers are responsible for some important technical aspects of images in their documents.

Do you need images?

First question: do you need images? What for, specifically? Will people even look at them?

The right image, strongly relevant to the written words, can speed comprehension, spark up the content, and contribute valuable information. Unfortunately, the web is saturated with pointless images—generic photos of smiling models. These contribute nothing, and readers are too smart to look at them. Eye-tracking research has shown that most people ignore these pictures.[73] They spot them in their peripheral vision and reject them outright as boring, phony or meaningless.

Here are some examples of generic photos that will be ignored.[74] Just don't bother!

The same research shows that captions are very good value. When people skim-read, captions are among the few items outside of the F-pattern that attract immediate attention. Captions are also vital for those using screen-reading software. Write them just like ALT-text, discussed below.

Making images accessible

When content has images, the issue of accessibility immediately raises its ugly head. This is because many people cannot see the images, and not just because they are blind. They access web content differently by using:

- special software for the partially sighted
- text-only browsers (they are fast!)
- browsers with the graphics turned off
- unusual computers or browsers
- mobile phones or other handheld devices.

At the very least, images in web content need a text alternative. And the logical person to write the text alternative is the person who inserted the image originally. The same principle applies when content uses Flash, video, animation or sound: someone has to write an alternative version in plain text. Text—that antique method of conveying meaning—is still the only one accessible to virtually anyone using virtually any computer.

The W3C standards and most government web standards give top priority to this requirement.

All images need ALT-text

Simple images just need a few words of ALT-text in the code. Usually, writers are automatically prompted to enter ALT-text when they publish an image in content. It must provide in words the information people will miss if they don't see the image.

When content has appropriate ALT-text, all these people know what images are on the page, even if they can't see them.

What happens when a page has no ALT-text

The Snails of Britain web page[75] was constructed entirely of images without ALT-text. On my computer, I see the page as below, complete with all its images.

People using an image-free browser such as Lynx see the same page with file names in place of the images—and these particular file names are pretty well information-free, as shown in the following screenshot.

```
Snails of Britain - Nature ...
image8.gif

        [img10.gif]
        [img11.gif]
        [img12.gif]
        [img13.gif]
        [img14.gif]
        [img15.gif]
        [img22.gif]
        [img24.gif]
```

Imagine people listening to the text of the web page read aloud. Because the Snails page has no ALT-text, those people would hear a computer voice reciting, '*Image. Image. Image. Image. Image. Image...*' or possibly, '*Image8. Image9. Image10. Image11...*'

However, if we provide ALT-text for the images, everyone can get some idea of what is on the page, because at least they can see or hear phrases such as '*Snails of Britain*' and '*White-lipped snail*'. The ALT-text is less informative than the pictures, but it sure beats *Image. Image. Image...*

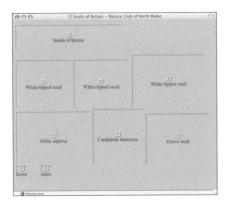
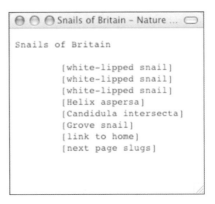

| *Snail* page with ALT-text, as seen with images switched off. | *Snail* page with ALT-text, as seen on an image-free browser. |

How to write ALT-text for images

Writing ALT-text is not a hard job, and any ALT-text is better than no ALT-text! Generally, your ALT-text should describe the picture as briefly as possible. For example, for the image below:

ALT= "Two hippos browse by waterhole."

Describing an image is not always appropriate. Sometimes you need to think what purpose it serves. As a general rule, state what the image represents, or the point it's supposed to make, or the function of the image.
- Usually, identify the subject, for example *Queen Elizabeth greets Paris Hilton* or *Jonah Lomu scores a try* or *Wooden bungalow with cottage garden*.
- If the image is words, write the identical words.
- If the image is a link, give the destination, for example: *Link to Whales*.
- If the image is a graph or chart, give the headline or caption, for example: *Fig 10: Tasmania population 1990-2000*. (I'll talk about graphs later: they need much more than ALT-text.)

ALT-text should be brief and simple. Follow the guidelines for your site, and limit your ALT-text to around 40 characters. (Writing up to 80 characters may be possible, but not necessarily more useful.)

To test your efforts, try reading the text of your web pages aloud, including all ALT-text. Remember, some people see or hear the words alone.

I recommend ending ALT-text with a full stop and space, like a real sentence, so as to help the computer 'voice' to read it aloud with suitable expression. It's a small gesture that may help some people.

All images need a hidden title too

By *title*, I mean a piece of HTML code, not a visible caption. It's all about accessibility: some browsers don't show ALT-text, but they do show image titles. Including an image title makes sure images are accessible to everyone, regardless of their browser.

Now don't panic: the title of an image should be identical to the ALT-text, so no more work is required. At best, the title is entered automatically. At worst, writers just complete another field in a template.

Web-proof all graphs and charts

Always assume your graphs will be published on the web, and web-proof them as explained below. A graph that looks OK on paper is frequently disastrous online—illegible and inaccessible. I reckon creating graphs is a job for an expert, and unfortunately some common software makes it only too easy to create a bad graph. If you have graphic experts on your staff, ask for guidance. There's a lot at stake.

Whether you are choosing, commissioning, or creating a graph from scratch, make sure it fulfils your purpose. Good graphs and bad graphs are worlds apart; a bad graph may convey no information or the wrong information.

First, think why you are going to use a graph—have a reason! The graph should be honest, giving a true impression of the facts. It should also provoke thought. You need to be sure the graph is easy to read, tells the truth, tells a story, and cannot be misinterpreted. Also, be sure the graph is in the best place, close to the relevant text.

The type of graph should be appropriate for the type of data and should not distort the facts. You might choose a bar graph when comparing quantities, but a line graph when showing changes and trends over time. Sometimes a table is more appropriate, especially when readers want precise figures, or want to track data rather than just make comparisons.

Design tips for web-proof graphs

Keep the design clean, simple and unobtrusive. Your readers' screens have limitations of size, resolution, and colour.

- The background should be white or very pale.
- Never use busy patterns (chart-junk) such as cross-hatching or moiré on graphs; chart-junk is bad on paper but unbearable on a screen.
- The graph must not depend on colour alone to distinguish lines, bars or dots. Reasons: some people are colour blind, and some will print, fax or copy the graph in black and white. Therefore use a maximum of three colours: dark, medium and light.
- Try to use no more than four bars or three lines.
- If possible, don't put any text inside the data box.
- Enclose all relevant information inside a border. Include a caption, the data box, source and measurements along each axis.

Incorporate an obvious caption in the file

Like entire web pages, graphs must make sense when free-standing, out of context. So, obviously—surely it's obvious?—all graphs and charts need an obvious, clear, complete caption that makes sense in isolation.

Putting the graph's caption in the surrounding text is not enough: then the caption is lost when the graph is moved. That's why you need a border around the graph and all its accompanying text. The caption must be saved inside that border as part of the image file, not just added to the accompanying text. Why?

- Images are oh-so-easy to lift off a web page and reuse, legitimately or not.
- Writers may want to recycle their own graphs for a different article.
- Researchers and students copy graphs to quote in their own writing.
- An editor may move graphs when editing or restructuring a web page.

Graphs on the UK government statistics site are pretty good, but not consistently so.[76] The graph below is shown the way it appeared online.

The graph appears to have a caption, but this is an illusion. The words *GDP Growth* are actually the page headline. And it's the page, not the graph, which has a summary: *Economy rose by 0.7% in Q3 2006*.

Maybe that's the caption in tiny writing beneath the graph: *Real GDP quarterly growth*. See it? It is so small as to be completely useless. And as we will see, this isn't a caption, but another bit of text on the web page, separate from the graph.

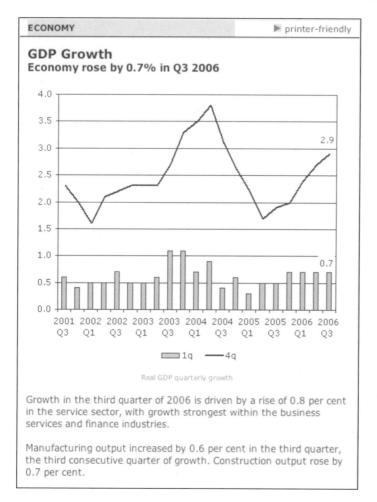

Next we show the JPEG image of the graph. As you see, neither the headline nor the caption is saved as part of the image. That makes the graph in isolation completely meaningless. It can't be reused until a new caption is written and attached. Each time this happens, the image degrades and the risk of error is present.

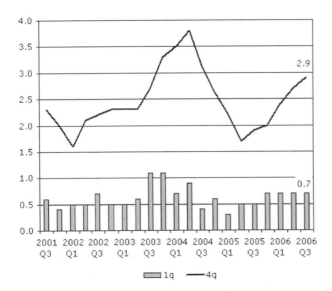

More encouragingly, here are a couple of graphs with adequate captions incorporated into the image file. If only they included one more little word—*UK*—these two graphs would be understandable even here, on a page of a completely unrelated book.

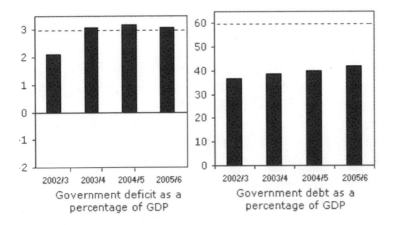

The above graphs show how a good caption can sometimes eliminate the need to state what each axis displays. Figures like *2002/3* don't need explaining, and the phrase *as a percentage of GDP* makes it clear what the vertical axis measures.

By contrast, the graph below has no caption and no indication of what the vertical axis measures. Therefore the graph is meaningless out of context.

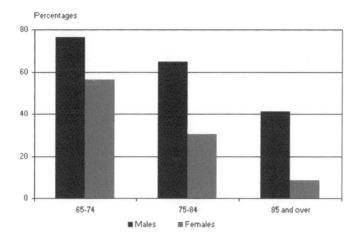

Use a font that's legible online

A legible font in an online graph basically means Verdana, or Trebuchet MS if the words need squashing. Using any other font is just asking for trouble.[77] In the following graph, the letters are blurred even when enlarged for printing.

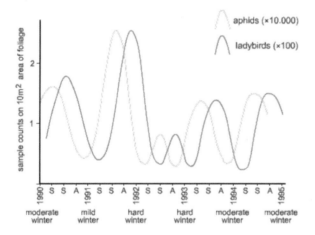

What a difference the correct font makes! Take another look at the two bar graphs about GDP on the previous page. Though small, the text in the graphs is entirely legible on a screen. Naturally, the font is Verdana. And by the way, never use italics in a graph; they are seriously illegible on-screen, especially in small sizes.

After you have found or created the graph for your online content, it should be converted into the format your target audience prefers, for example PDF, JPG, GIF or SVG. (The latter format, Scalable Vector Graphics is not universally accessible yet, alas.)

Complex images: when ALT-text is not enough

All images need ALT-text. But in some cases, ALT-text is not enough. Some images convey a great deal of information and therefore require more explanation.
- Graphs tell a story. They can show trends, patterns, comparisons and changes over time.
- Diagrams and photographs can convey safety features, procedures and fine detail.
- Charts can show direction, hierarchy and sequence.
- Maps can show relative locations, topography and roads.

Having inserted an image that conveys complex information into a web page, the writer must also convey the same information in words. Such images need a text equivalent longer than ALT-text can be. The text equivalent is put on a separate web page. (Its technical name is long description, or longdesc.)

A graph needing a text equivalent

Here's a graph with a decent caption and all necessary information captured within its border. It is simple, but still complex enough to require a text equivalent.

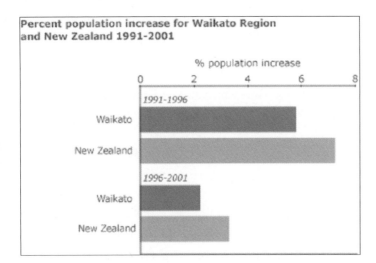

Below the graph on the web page should be a link worded something like this:
- Text equivalent of graph
- Description of graph.

When readers click on the link, they land on a different page dedicated to the text equivalent of the graph, as follows.

Percent population increase for Waikato Region and New Zealand 1991-2001.

The bar graph has four horizontal bars. The vertical axis identifies two regions (New Zealand and Waikato) during two periods (1991-1996 and 1996-2001). The horizontal axis identifies the percent population increase.

From 1991-1996, Waikato's population increased by almost 6%, and New Zealand's by about 7.5%. From 1996-2001, population in both areas continued to grow, but at less than half the pace.

[End description.] Back to graph

How to write text equivalents for graphs

The text equivalent of a complex image such as a graph or chart is a longer, more detailed and complete version of ALT-text. This is necessary to make the information in the graph or chart accessible to people who do not see the image on their screen. Your aim is to give those people the equivalent of the information they would get by viewing the image.

A text equivalent must:
- describe the appearance of the graph
- summarise the main patterns or trends
- sound natural when read aloud
- be understood when read aloud to someone who cannot see the graph.

Your audience for the text equivalent of a complex image is slightly different from your general web audience. Remember, many people will not read the text equivalent; they will listen to it. If listening, they cannot exactly skim-read or re-read. And the text equivalent is their only chance to learn what your graph or chart is about.

Talk on paper as if on the phone. Use natural prose. Use real sentences. Don't be tempted to use dot points or lists! A text equivalent describes and explains, and dot points can never do that. (And anyway, we don't converse in dot points.) For the same reason, you must not substitute raw data. Looking at a graph is very different from looking at a table: it is not equivalent.

In a text equivalent, analysis is required. The word *equivalent* is stronger than *alternative*. The technical term uses two words: *long* (long enough to get the message across) and *description* (not data).

Picture the following situation. You have a graph in front of you. On the phone, you describe the graph to another person. Write as you would speak, in short, simple sentences. Use plain language.

Part 1: Describe the appearance of the graph

This is the easiest part of writing a text equivalent, but the most often neglected. Your purpose is to help readers see the image in their mind's eye—what kind of graph, how many lines or bars, what's on each axis. Always start a text equivalent the same way—this is not the place to be literary! Begin with words that identify the type of graphic, for example:

'The line graph...'

'The flow chart...'

'The bar graph...'

Finish the sentence by outlining the topic of the graph, and stating the variables that the graph measures, compares, or plots.

Here are a couple of examples of Part 1 of a text equivalent. They are not related to any of the graphs in this book: they are just examples to imitate.

- The graph shows five lines. They plot year-ended credit growth for Hong Kong, Malaysia, the Philippines, Singapore and Thailand from 1994 to mid-2004.
- The column graph plots annual net lending flows to Asia, excluding China, Japan and Hong Kong, from 1990 to 2003.

Part 2: Summarise key information in the graph

In the second part of your text equivalent, simply summarise the most important 1–3 points conveyed by the graph or chart. Part 2 is not just facts and figures: it should summarise the information that stands out visually.

That's all! You write a text equivalent in just two steps. In Part 1, you describe. In Part 2, you summarise 1–3 main points.

Don't write any more. Too much information will only confuse the audience, and disrupt the narrative flow of the original page. A good text equivalent is often about 50-70 words. We want an impression only—the same impression you would get from reading the graph itself.

Test graphs and charts online

Never assume that a graph that looks fine on paper will look fine on a web or intranet page. A surprising proportion of graphs online are impossible to read.

Therefore, all graphs should be created and tested explicitly for viewing on-screen. In other words, first load the graph on to an actual web or intranet page. Then study it. If a graph is not legible on the screen, it is not accessible. Start again.

If you're the content writer, you may not have the skill or authority to do this testing personally. But you should ensure it happens; otherwise you may be deeply disappointed when you see your images on the web.

- Test whether colours can be easily distinguished from each other.
- Test for legibility: can you still read all the text and numbers?
- Test for size. (See below.)
- Test online and also by printing the graph in black and white.

The right size for graphs online

If a viewer has to scroll vertically or horizontally to see the whole image on a web page, the image is too big. If a graph is hard to see clearly on-screen, it rarely improves when the size is changed. In fact, it often becomes less legible. The Scalable Vector Graphics (SVG) format solves this problem, incidentally.

Small graphs should be used for simple messages, larger graphs for more complex messages. If you provide graphs in two sizes, both must be legible.

Organisation charts and flow-charts are often too large. They should be big enough to provide the overview you want, but small enough to fit easily on a web page when viewed on an average-sized screen. Consider reducing the amount of information, or subdividing the chart into several pages. If that is not possible, provide a PDF version. (PDF is appropriate for specialised documents that need to be printed.)

When you find a successful formula for online graphs, don't change it without a good reason! Your formula (or brand) will combine format, size, fonts and colours that are easy to read onscreen, regardless of readers' browser, preferences, or screen resolution.

All complex images need text equivalents

Graphs are not the only complex images on the web. Text equivalents are also needed for any image in the content that provides important information. Again, be selective about what you convey in words: why did you choose to use this image—what's your point? Make your point and move on.

A few examples of such images follow: digital camera resolution chart,[78] typical Defense Meteorological Satellite Program Gallery,[79] simple tie knot,[80] red-necked Falarope wings,[81] double helix structure of a DNA molecule,[82] dynobryn plankton.[83]

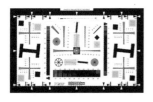 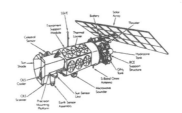 

 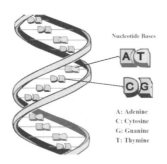 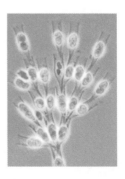

How about maps? A small, how-to-find-us map is easy to handle. But large maps and certain other images are overwhelmingly difficult to describe. Some agencies provide a phone number, and explain the map over the phone.

Using Flash and video

When Flash is used, someone needs to decide whether a full text alternative is required. Today, Flash can be accessible and is very commonly used for tutorials and training. It can be valuable for instructions, demonstrations, 3-D views of a product, content for children, scientific content—and much more.

Flash offers seductive opportunities for sheer creativity. The glamour potential of Flash can be embarrassing in the hands of beginners, but shines in the hands of experts.

For example, the home page of Better Living Through Design features an atmospheric forest scene, changing from time to time.[84] Move your mouse over the little birds and they fly. Subtle. Beautiful. Swift. Purely for branding. ALT-text will suffice.

But if Flash is being used to teach, some people may feel they are losing control, trapped in a movie. This is a very bad prognosis for learning. Your job is to make people feel confident, clever and masterful. The solution is to break the tutorial into small sections, and to provide several obvious alternatives to Flash, including text and audio versions.

As for the text equivalent, forget about covering a tutorial in two paragraphs! Only a full HTML version can be a genuine replacement. And test, test, test with real live people.

Writers may script videos that will be downloaded. This is a specialised area, so I won't say much. Firstly, keep the videos short! It's rumoured that the attention span for video online is 3–5 minutes. Secondly, always warn people exactly what they are about to download: describe the content briefly and state the type and size of the file. This gives your readers choice and control over the content.

Bouncing, floating, climbing data

Graphs illustrate changes and trends, right? So why have we been viewing static graphs online for so long? Hans Rosling is described as a global health expert and data visionary. His Gapminder Foundation has developed free software that can show changes happening in front of our very eyes. Brilliant animated statistics jolt fixed ideas about global trends by presenting the whole picture, decade by decade.[85]

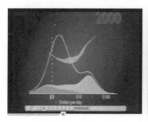 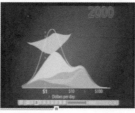 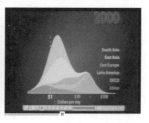

Google makes Gapminder's Trendalyzer software available to all. This exciting tool dramatises the presentation of data on the web.

Audio and podcasts

Scripting and delivering podcasts is now a common task for journalists and business consultants, but how about everyday on-the-job writers?

(Oops, some haven't encountered podcasts yet. These are audio files that people can download from a web site and listen to through an iPod, MP3 player, or phone. It's do-it-yourself radio. People choose what they want to listen to, and when and where they listen.)

The possible uses of podcasts are limited only by time and imagination. For a start, you might find yourself scripting or delivering podcasts over the intranet:
- in-house news for your business unit
- supplementary training for new managers
- weekly updates on a joint project or new initiative
- regular interviews with the CEO
- a quick guide to organisational structure
- induction talks for new employees.

Subject experts may also be responsible for all manner of podcasts placed on public web sites. Think of weekly tips on almost any topic relevant to your business, news, advice for small businesses, introducing the latest properties for sale, and untold training sessions.

In many cases, audio is not just a nice little extra, but the primary way people get information. Supposedly about one third of internet users have some trouble with literacy, and others simply prefer listening to reading. Therefore it's a very good idea to publish certain information as audio files.

You can figure from this that it is well worthwhile getting to grips with the essentials of podcasting.

Six tips for podcasters

1. Prepare, but don't script

Audio is an intimate medium, so you mustn't sound stiff and formal. As a rule, it's best to prepare by jotting notes, doing a mindmap if that's your style, and rehearsing a couple of times. Then you have a good chance of knowing your material and sounding relaxed. If you have to read from a complete script, try to at least sound as if you are ad libbing. Feel free to make a few mistakes.

2. Develop a consistent format

Just like written content, audio content must be structured carefully. Absorbing information by ear can be a strain, so it helps if listeners can anticipate your format. If you start with a musical theme, stick to that forever—well, at least for the first series. Try to keep the length of the podcasts about the same, whether a 2-minute news update or a 40-minute lecture. Start each podcast the same way, for example,

> Hello, my name is _____. Welcome to _____, the podcast about _____. Today is _____, and I'm going to talk about _____.

3. Repeat key information

Because your talk is entering brains via ears, you must be solicitous. Think about the audience: they might be walking, cycling, skating or commuting. Their hands may not be free to stop and rewind the podcast. Distractions surround them. So in the time-honoured way, tell them what you're going to tell them, then tell them, then tell them what you told them. And whenever you mention something that needs to be written down (such as a URL) be sure to repeat it—and possibly again at the end of the podcast.

4. Speak intimately to one friendly interested listener

That's your audience: you are talking to one person at a time, not shouting at a crowd. How personal should you be? Follow your organisation's guidelines. As a general rule, don't expose personal details about your life, but show your enthusiasm about the topic.

5. Don't rush

Many people gabble into a microphone because they are embarrassed or bored with the sound of their own voice. Slow down. Listen to yourself. Change the pace sometimes.

6. Ask for feedback

And listen to it! Broadcasters are made, not born.

Test and test again

Usability testing is especially important with content such as images, video and audio. Testing by even a small sample of 3–5 people always brings up interesting issues, ones you didn't anticipate.

13.

Findable content

What use is content if nobody can find it? You don't need persuading that all documents should be easy to find, regardless of whether they are on a web site or intranet, or in a document management system. That's a given.

I'd like to clarify the role that everyday, on-the-job writers play in the amazing race for great search results. (And remember, whatever you do to make web content findable, you can also do to an electronic document, for example in Word or PDF.)

Not just top search results. Top is fabulous, of course: everyone wants their pages to appear at the top of a SERP[86] (search engine results page: an acronym that will be used often in this chapter). But we also want the words on a SERP to describe our pages fully and accurately.

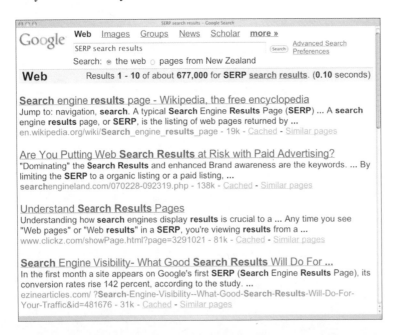

Search Engine Optimisation (SEO) is the art of designing or modifying web pages to rank well in search results. It's simple: search engines, just like humans, are on the hunt for substantial, original, popular, relevant content. (Supply it!) SEO is also complex and technical, one of four jobs on the cutting edge.[87] Many organisations find it worthwhile to pay SEO experts US$400+ an hour to do the job—so I'm certainly not about to explain it in one paragraph. Even if I could, my information would be out of date before this book went to press. Suffice to say a SEO expert might work on strategy, information design, navigation, accessibility, pay-per-click advertisements, inbound links, keyword research, metatags, page ranking, search engines—and much more!

Kalena Jordan's Search Engine College offers an industry-recognised certificate in search engine optimization.[88] The courses offered indicate the range of knowledge needed by SEO practitioners.

- Search engine optimisation (starter and advanced courses).
- Pay-per-click search engine advertising (starter and advanced courses).
- Web site copywriting.
- Web site usability.
- Keyword research.
- Link building strategies.

Another site's advanced training course lists more than 100 topics and 60 search engines and directories.[89] A few of them follow, showing the level of detail required by a professional SEO expert.

Possible SE Ranking Factors	Frames	JoeAnt
Analyzing Real Life Examples of	Gateway Information Pages	Kanoodle
Top Ranking Sites	Gateway Pages: 25 Ideas for Building Quality	Kanoodle's Special Offer
Domains & URLs: SE Ranking	Gateway Pages	Looksmart
404 Error Messages	The Golden Triangle	Lycos
Software and Tools	Google Supplemental Index	Mamma
MSN	Guide to Using FrontPage	MSN Search
MSN Quiz	Hallway Pages	NBCi
	Hosting Companies	Netscape Search
Lesson #4	HTML Issues for SEOs	Northern Light
Link Popularity	Important Steps to Creating Top Ranking Pages	Onsite Search Engines
Link Reputation		Open Directory Project (ODP)
Theme Search Engines	Industry-Specific SEO	Other Engines
PageRank™	Image Maps	Overture (Now Yahoo!)
Site Maps	Java Redirect	Pay Engines
On Site Search Engines	JavaScript	Russian Search Engines
Link Popularity Quiz	Keyword Bid Optimizer	Search Engine
	Keyword Choice	Relationship Chart
Lesson #5	Keyword Prominence	Snap/NBCi
Top Tips & Top Mistakes Made	Keyword Tips	Spanish Search Engines
by SEOs	Keyword Weight	Swedish Search Engines
Site Architecture	Legal Issues	Teoma
Subdomains & Domains	Link Popularity	Topclick
Cascading Stylesheets (CSS)	Link Reputation	UK Search Engines
The Benefits of Using Server Side Includes (SSI)	Local Search	ValleyAlley.com
	Log Analysis	WebCrawler
	Log Files and Robot Manager Pro	whatUseek
Ask Jeeves and Teoma	META & Other Tags	Wherewithal
		Wisenut
		Xoron
		Yahoo!
		Yahoo! Search Marketing

Government sites and intranets are more likely to rely on their own experts for SEO. Government sites can rarely justify the expense of hiring an expert; after all, they have no competition. Intranets are not competing with other sites, either. Nevertheless, in both cases, the aim is to get pages identified accurately on a SERP and listed in order of relevance.

Public vs. internal search engines

Public search engines and directories have their own ever-evolving formulae for ranking pages and displaying search results. Internal search engines, by contrast, can be customised. Internal search engines can search either a particular intranet or web site or the whole public World Wide Web. Smart content writers and a customised search engine can combine to powerful effect.

To remind you how to spot an internal search engine, here are images from Direct.gov.uk and Australia.gov.au.

SERPs look much the same, whether on Google's site or anyone else's. The difference is, your own search engine can be customised. The following screenshot shows a SERP on a Canadian government site.[90]

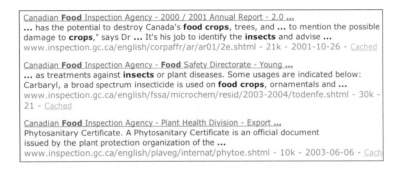

SERP summaries on Google and other search engines may be cobbled together automatically from any content that contains the search term. Like the example below, they don't necessarily make sense.[91]

> **2. Title:** Possible Domestic Policies to Manage Greenhouse Gas Emissions
> **Summary:** Danielle JacquesA/Director------
> ------------------CAL HomeAbout UsCollectionLibrary CatalogueDocument Delivery Services Possible policies to manage g... **Size:** 14 Kb **File Format:** text/html **URL :**
> http://www.agr.gc.ca/cal/epub/2034e/2034-0012_e.html

Search engines make up their own summaries partly because so few web pages begin with a genuine summary, and because it's only human to try and outwit search engines with dirty tricks (such as summaries full of lies). Directories such as Yahoo! have a different system. They use their own humans to write SERP summaries, which are often very different from the ones submitted by web site owners. Either way, writers are not directly responsible for summaries on a public SERP.

The one thing we can control on a Google SERP is the first line they display, the blue underlined link. This is always the HTML page title.

Getting the HTML page title right

The web development team naturally want their internal search engine to present search results that:
- are clear, sensible and accurate
- can be generated automatically.

The most vital element of any search result is the first line, which is a link to the site. With most search engines and directories, that's the HTML page title, virtually unseen and unsung until it appears in search results.

By the way, the HTML page title is not the page headline. See the difference?

Plenty of people choose to view nothing except the first line on a SERP, so it had better do the job right.

The vital decision of how to generate HTML page titles must be made at the site's development stage. The following are common solutions, not all of equal merit.

1. Page headline + site name, in that order = HTML page title. (Perfect, if all pages have F-headlines. Many countries make this standard for government sites.)
2. Reverse breadcrumbs, going from the particular to the general. (Good.)
3. An expert web editor writes HTML page titles one by one. (Waste of time, but at least the titles will work.)
4. Page headline is recycled as HTML page title. (Not too bad, if all pages have F-headlines.)
5. Site name + page headline, in that order = HTML page title. (Foolish backloading: all search results from the site begin with the same words.)
6. Content writer writes a unique HTML page title for each page. (Risky. Expect some *Untitled Documents* in search results.)
7. One generic HTML page title is used for all pages on the site. (Stupid: all search results from your site will show the same title.)

On an intranet, the page headline followed by the name of the business unit or department will make an excellent page title for SERPs—but only if all content writers know how to write a great F-headline.

Examples of HTML page titles in action

In the screenshot below, the HTML page title is the cryptic word *HR Policies*, with no mention of the site.[92] See it in the top bar, the place you never look?

A 1-word or 2-word page HTML page title is rarely any use. A good title would be: *HR Policies, Commonwealth of Virginia* (headline followed by site name). That would be heaps better. The page's search result relies entirely on its summary to make sense:

Findable content / 133

HR Policies
These Guides provide more detailed information about the intent and appropriate application of **human resource policies**, and explain how **policies** can overlap ...
www.d**hr**m.state.va.us/**hrpolicy**/**policy**.html
- 67k - Cached - Similar pages

Here's an example of reverse breadcrumbs working well as an HTML page title.

Policy Manual | **Human Resources** | **University** of Missouri
University of Missouri. Columbia | Kansas City | Rolla | St. Louis. Skip to content.
University of Missouri ... **Human Resources Policy** Manual ...
www.umsystem.edu/ums/departments/**hr**/manual/ - 19k - Cached - Similar pages

The Australian Universities Teaching Committee (AUTC) structures HTML page titles the wrong way round, putting site name first, headline second.[93]

Putting the site name first in an HTML page title is not good practice for two reasons. Firstly, it foils F-readers. Secondly, all search results from that site start with the same words. This can work with a 1-word site name, but not with a 5-word site name.

Australian Universities **Teaching** Committee (AUTC) - **Australian** ...
This page details the **Australian Awards** for **University Teaching**(AAUT) ... The winners of the 2004 **AAUT** were announced at a ceremony at Parliament House, ...
www.autc.gov.au/aaut.htm - 15k - Cached - Similar pages
    Australian Universities **Teaching** Committee (AUTC) - Home Page
    The 2005 **Australian Awards** for **University Teaching**; Current projects (including Stage 2 of AUTC projects); National **Teaching** Forum and Visiting Scholar ...
    www.autc.gov.au/ - 14k - Cached - Similar pages
    [More results from www.autc.gov.au]

The next screenshots show a good HTML page title. It begins with the page headline (*Careers Information*) followed by the name of the site (*Royal Australian Navy*).[94]

Customising the summary for internal SERPs

The second item in a search result is the SERP summary, also known as a description or abstract.

Content writers can in fact influence the automatically compiled SERP summaries (such as those in Google), but this should never be their primary goal. If they write F-headlines, F-summaries, F-links, and plain language, this will pay off with Google as well as with humans. Let's leave the fiddly stuff to SEO experts.

For internal, customised search engines, things are different. There, the web developers make some crucial choices about what should appear as a summary on the SERP. They can show:

- the first 16-25 words of the summary (first paragraph) on the actual page (perfect when every page has an F-summary)
- a summary written from scratch by an editor or metadata specialist (a waste of precious time)
- a sentence or two automatically generated by the search engine from content on the page (almost inevitably this is garbage).

Option #1 is way the best choice—provided all documents have an F-summary. You know how to do this. Let's see summaries in action.

Even summaries of the very simple *this page describes…* variety work very well on a SERP, provided they get straight to the point.

> Biology Weblinks - Chapter 25 - What Is an Animal? - Glencoe Online
> **This page describes different** creatures you will find in the sea. Use the images and information on this page to design your own Web page for animals found ...
> www.glencoe.com/sec/science/biology/bio2000/ chapter/weblinks.php?
> iRef=25&iChapter=25&iUnit=8&... - 57k - Cached - Similar pages
>
> Patient Education and Learning Resources at California Pacific ...
> **This page describes different** tests that your doctor may order during your pregnancy to ensure the safety of you and the baby. Antepartum Testing Center ...
> www.cpmc.org/learning/layh.cfm?EventPage=layh_
> result.cfm&gt_id=50&ht_id=328 - 83k - Cached - Similar pages
>
> Intute: Science, Engineering and Technology - browse Mechanics ...
> **This page describes different** types of motion, and focuses on the simple harmonic motion (SHM) of oscillating objects. The author includes graphs and ...

Automatically generated summaries are usually flawed, and those on a SERP from Study in Australia are no exception.[95] They all start with the same sentence.

> **Search the Study in Australia website**
>
> Documents 1 to 10 (of 202) matching the query '*help*'
>
> 1. **Study in Australia**
>   **Abstract:** the easiest way to get all the information you need to study and live in Australia Go Study in Australia Welcome to the official Australian Government website for advice on study in Australia. In Australia you will experience a unique kind of education – a learning style that encourages
> 2. **Search for a course**
>   **Abstract:** the easiest way to get all the information you need to study and live in Australia Go Search for a course Australian education institutions must be registered with the Australian Government and meet high standards of quality and ethical practice to enrol international students. These
> 3. **Explore the possibilities**
>   **Abstract:** the easiest way to get all the information you need to study and live in Australia Go Explore the possibilities Australia has education and training sectors offering qualifications from Senior Secondary Certificate of Education to university PhD: , , and . These sectors are linked so

W3C uses Google on its site.[96] Even Google can't manufacture a perfect summary from scratch, so clarity depends heavily on HTML page titles being well written.

> Examples: WAI Web Content Accessibility Curriculum - slide "5.5 ...
> <TABLE border="1" **summary**="This table charts the number of cups of coffee consumed by each senator, the type of coffee (decaf or regular), ...
> www.w3.org/WAI/wcag-curric/sam50-0.htm - 5k - Cached - Similar pages
>
> POWDER Working Group Blog - Meeting **summaries**
> News and opinions from the participants of the POWDER Working Group.
> www.w3.org/blog/powder?cat=56 - 23k - Cached - Similar pages

Other ways writers can influence search engines

Besides writing appropriate F-headlines and F-summaries, trained content writers boost a page's success with search engines in other important ways.

- F-links: Search engines give extra weight to the words in link-text. Skilfully written F-links maximise the benefits of this feature in natural, legitimate ways.
- ALT-text: Search engines can't read images, but they do index ALT-text, which often includes keywords.
- Keywords: These are the fundamental building blocks from which F-headlines, F-summaries and F-links are constructed. The writer who understands and uses keywords is streets ahead of others when it comes to getting good search results.
- Blogs: Frequently updated blogs are strongly favoured by Google.
- Favourite pages: When other sites link to a page, that page is ranked more highly by Google and its imitators.

Favourite pages are the golden apples of search: pages so good, so original that they attract links from other sites. And links not just from any old site—but from hugely popular sites. If my page of potato recipes inspires a link from Aunty Maud's home page, Google will leave my page languishing at the bottom of SERP #999. If Yahoo!, Amazon, Global Gourmet, Rick Stein and Nigella Lawson link to my recipe page, suddenly it jumps to #1.

Software cannot write those pages, so honour the writer.

Benefits of F-writing

Plainly, organisations with large web sites and intranets benefit when staff are trained in 21st century business writing. More importantly, if staff are not trained, search results are almost bound to be inconsistent at best, a disaster at worst. Junk in, junk out.

Every bit of advice in this book has a bright side for search results. So let's look at the ideal scenario.

1. All staff writers can write good F-headlines, F-summaries and F-links.
2. So all web and intranet pages have F-headlines, F-summaries and F-links.
3. Page titles consist of page headline first, then site name.
4. Metadata titles and summaries (more about this later) are accurate and make sense.
5. Bingo! Google gives the page a good ranking.
6. Bingo! The page is findable.
7. Bingo! Search results make sense.
8. Some writers write favourite pages that attract many links.
9. Bingo! Many other sites link to your best pages, boosting their ranking with search engines.

Tips from the horses' mouths

Want your site to do well with Google? (Who doesn't?) Many of Google's tips for webmasters concern the writers.[97] There's nothing new here. What people want, Google wants. Write high quality content and you cannot help but win brownie points with Google. Here's what they say, word for word.

- Give visitors the information they're looking for. Provide high-quality content on your pages, especially your homepage. This is the single most important thing to do. If your pages contain useful information, their content will attract many visitors and entice webmasters to link to your site.
- Think about the words users would type to find your pages, and make sure that your site actually includes those words within it.
- Try to use text instead of images to display important names, content, or links. The Google crawler doesn't recognize text contained in images.
- Make sure that your TITLE and ALT tags are descriptive and accurate.

Yahoo! also kindly describes the kind of pages it wants to index.[98] (Yahoo! is selective.) Skilled writers can fulfil 3 of their 5 recommendations:

- Original and unique content of genuine value.
- Hyperlinks intended to help people find interesting, related content, when applicable.
- Metadata (including title and description) that accurately describes the contents of a web page.

Keywords on the page

Why does Google stress that the actual search terms people use should be on the page? It's obvious when you look at a SERP: the summaries are usually pulled from the page content, with the exact search words in bold. If the exact search words are not on the page, the page won't be listed on the resulting SERP. In the immortal word of Homer Simpson, *Doh*!

- The words people type in Search are keywords.
- Keywords are the words people type in Search.

So there's yet another endorsement of the prime plain language rule: writing expressly for your target reader. And yet another reason for stacking the content with keywords, especially headlines, summaries and link-text.

Oh no, not more about keywords! But hey, even though the principle of keywords is utterly non-mysterious, still many people find it hard to grasp. Why? Because it can be amazingly difficult to get into the head of your reader. You need help—ask a neighbour, an auntie—ask anyone outside the loop of your own jargon.

When writing copy for a page, imagine yourself as an outsider, searching for this very page, or one like it. What words would you type in the search bar? Probably you'll type in 2-5 words, if you use English.[99]

That means as a writer, you need to be aware of at least 6 words or 3 phrases that people might use when searching. Say they are looking for a company like Insurance Technology Solutions (ISO-ITS).[100]

The first two paragraphs on the ISO-ITS home page are packed with keywords. They are not a riveting read, but give plenty of important, relevant, objective information. The target readers of ISO-ITS use the same terminology, so jargon is not a problem here. All the words in bold are the kind of words their target readers might use in search:

ISO **Insurance Technology Solutions** (ISO-ITS) encompasses the AscendantOne® **Policy Management** Suite, seamlessly integrated with **ISO Rating Service**™ to deliver a comprehensive rate-quote-issuance, **underwriting** and **policy-administration** system for **property/casualty insurers**.

ISO Rating Service is the **automated rating** and **underwriting** system from ISO. With a **dynamic rating processor, validated ISO information, automatic updates**, and **tools** for maintaining and **customizing** your **rating** structures, **ISO Rating Service** is your fastest, most accurate way of managing and implementing program revisions

I searched Google using these phrases:
- insurance technology policy underwriting
- policy management insurance
- iso rating automatic
- customizing insurance iso.

In every case, the ISO-ITS page was listed on the first page of search results. That's what you get when the writer uses a high percentage of the right keywords on a page.

Contrast the initial text of a page from Linbeck.[101] Again, you'll see the keywords in bold—this time I could find only two. I couldn't see any other words that a target reader might enter in a search box.

Linbeck is committed to bringing optimal **facilities** solutions to our clients. Our corporate logo, the three-sided pyramid, represents our approach to helping our clients realize their visions. It is the joining of three critical elements to create a symbol of substance and strength: Principles, People and Process.

Principles: Above all, the Linbeck organization is based on a culture of Integrity and Trust. The same family values that guided the company at its inception today are the cultural foundation of the firm. At Linbeck, we understand that being a strategic partner is a true honor and one that requires an intense level of trust.

Finally we discover some more keywords in the fourth paragraph, on Process: Linbeck is a *pioneer of the* **collaborative** *approach to defining,* **designing** and **building projects**.

Too late! These keywords only appear after nearly 200 words of burble burble toot toot. It's not just readers who cherry-pick: so do search engines. They make the logical assumption that the first 100 words or so will state what the page is about.

By definition, a page with a high percentage of keywords at the top is:
- actually about something
- interesting to humans because it is actually about something
- rated highly by Google because it is actually about something.

Metadata that writers need to know about

Many governments require public sector web sites to provide metadata for documents including web pages.[102] Required metadata may include up 19 elements, or even more. Organisations that receive public funding or that simply want to make their sites more searchable are also likely to have a metadata policy.

Metadata consists of snippets of highly specific information about the content of a document. Documents include web pages and intranet pages, PDFs, text documents, slide presentations, journals, audio files, spreadsheets—virtually any electronic file or hard copy containing information. One snippet of metadata tells you who wrote the document. Another snippet tells you what sort of file it is (e.g. Word, TXT, HTML, PDF, XLS, MP3). Another snippet tells you what date the document was written. And so forth.

The purpose of metadata is to enable:
- classification and cataloguing of documents
- retrieval and re-use of information
- version tracking.

Metadata is, in part, a system of cataloguing. With certain metadata in place, every document:
- has a unique identity, even apart from its URL
- can be found by many different pathways, e.g. author/creator + date of publication + subject, or audience + publisher + title.
- can be located in context.

The aggregation of many metadata snippets makes it possible to search for documents according to many different criteria. For example, you could search for *HTML documents about GILS created by Molly Malone, U.S. Government Printing Office in January 1996*.

Much metadata is generated automatically, and needn't concern the writer—for example, Creator, Identifier, Date (of creation, completion, publication or modification), Publisher, Type, Format, Source, Language, Coverage, and Rights.

Two important bits of metadata, Title and Description, can be recycled from the page headline and the summary. If the author has written these correctly, no problem, you're home and hosed!

On some sites, the content writer needs to select or check certain metadata from a fixed list. This isn't difficult. For example, the author may need to check Status, choosing from options such as Draft, Ready for Review, Reviewed, Approved, Final, Submitted, Published, and Archived. Other elements of the tick-the-box variety include Audience, Function, Availability and Mandate.

To deal with metadata, web content writers need:

- training to write F-headlines and F-summaries
- training in any metadata they need to select or check for your specific system
- training to write Keyword metadata (more about this shortly).

Just for interest's sake, here's half of the metadata automatically attached to the chapter I am writing.[103]

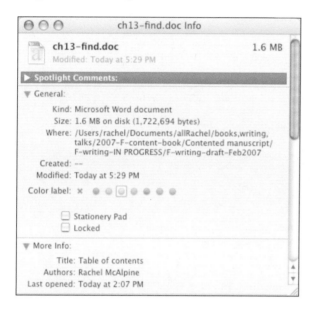

And here's an example of metadata as it appears in the code behind a heavily tagged web page.[104]

```
<title>Government Information Locator Service (GILS)</title>

<meta name="description" content="The Government Information
Locator Service (GILS) is an effort to identify, locate, and describe publicly
available Federal information resources, including electronic information
resources.">

<meta name="keywords" content="government information, federal
information, GILS, government information locator service, pointer records,
electronic information">

<link rel="schema.DC" href="http://purl.org/dc">

<meta name="DC.Contributor" content="U.S. Government Printing Office,
Superintendent of Documents">

<meta name="DC.Coverage" content="January 1996 to present">

<meta name="DC.Creator" content="U.S. Government Printing Office,
Superintendent of Documents">

<meta name="DC.Date" content="Creation Date: January 1996">
```

```
<meta name="DC.Description" content=" The Government Information
Locator Service (GILS) is an effort to identify, locate, and describe publicly
available Federal information resources, including electronic information
resources.">

<meta name="DC.Format" content="Text, HTML">

<meta name="DC.Identifier" content="URL: http://www.access.gpo.gov/
su_docs/gils/index.html">

<meta name="DC.Language" content="Eng.">

<meta name="DC.Publisher" content="U.S. Government Printing Office,
Superintendent of Documents">

<meta name="DC.Relation" content="Individual Agency">

<meta name="DC.Rights" content="Information may be used/reused
unless noted by the publishing agency">

<meta name="DC.Source" content="Individual Agency">

<meta name="DC.Subject" content=" government information, federal
information, GILS, government information locator service, pointer records,
electronic information">

<meta name="DC.Title" content=" Government Information Locator
Service (GILS)>

<meta name="DC.Type" content="Text, HTML">
```

Finally, the Subject and Keywords metadata

Watch out for tricky ambiguous terminology with metadata. (Grrr!) Essentially, at least two metadata categories for *keywords* may exist in your organisation's document management system. One is for Subject, the other is for Keywords with a capital K. Whatever your system calls them, all content writers need to know which is which.

Both Subjects and Keywords metadata answer the question, *What is this document about?* or *What does this page do?* But there the resemblance ends.

The Subject metadata list consists of *correct* terms, drawn from a predetermined set of words, using a controlled vocabulary. The writer must select several appropriate Subjects, for example *Biography* and *Biology*. The writer is not permitted to invent new Subjects, such as *Personal Story*. Subjects are used for classification, putting the document on the right shelf, so to speak. Of course you can't have authors inventing and adding unique Subjects, or classification would be impossible.

By contrast, the purpose of Keywords in metadata is to enable a search engine to find and display the exact page someone is searching for. These Keywords are not necessarily correct terms, but include alternative words that your target audience is likely to use when searching. Writers need to check any automatically generated Keywords metadata carefully, eliminate those that aren't relevant, and add unique Keywords that relate only to that specific page. How?

- Check (again!) that the content includes words people will type in when searching for this page.
- Ask at least two other people what words they would type in when searching for this page.
- Add those words to the content if possible and appropriate.
- Add the words to the Keywords metadata, especially if the words can't be gracefully incorporated into the content.

Yes, really! I promise you will be surprised by some really obvious keywords you never thought of.

For example, the visible content of a page about a government superannuation fund includes the following keywords:

- state sector
- superannuation
- retirement
- income
- contributions
- eligibility.

But the page is intended for the general public, who might search for it using different keywords such as:

- pensioners
- government
- savings
- rights.

The writer should add these words to the content if appropriate. Otherwise, add them to the Keywords metadata.

In one of his newsletters, Gerry McGovern discusses the words people use to search with.[105] These are not always the words you'd want to use in web content, but they can safely be included in the invisible Keywords metadata.

> ... according to Overture, in December 2006, 730,958 people searched for "used car," while only 949 searched for "pre-owned vehicle." Nearly 73,000 people searched for "housewife" (122,000 searched for "desperate housewife"), while only 43 searched for "stay-at-home-mum". Over 30,000 searched for "gay marriage" while 19,000 searched for "same-sex marriage".
>
> What I am wondering is whether when we search, we revert back to older, more basic words. Words that might be cruder, shorter and simpler.

I will search for a cheap hotel but when I arrive at a website, I don't really want to see a big heading saying:

WELCOME TO OUR DIRT CHEAP HOTEL

Findable blog entries: tagging and categories

Blogs have their own systems for making posts findable. You may be invited to supply *tags* for every post you write. You can also nominate *categories*. Tags are a bit like Keywords metadata and categories like Subjects metadata. No need to worry: the software makes it easy and the rewards are obvious.

Search is continually changing

Some significant developments have occurred since 2009. They all affect the kind of search results you can get by optimising web content—but they do not change the guidelines for writing web content.

1. Search engines now impose a personal filter. They analyse the topics of your searches, emails, blogs and social media contributions. Consequently your computer will show a selection of search results distorted to reflect your online activities. When two people search in Google for 'Iran', one sees news headlines, one sees tourist information. Use Google Analytics and user testing to monitor your web site's SEO success. If you test your own sites on your own computer, you'll get a false impression.
2. Google announced a clamp-down on rubbishy, unoriginal, spammy web content. It's now even harder to achieve top search results with poor quality web content. The change was a response to the shameful activities of article marketers (recycling the same article with slight changes on thousands of sites) and SEO content factories (which churn out thousands of keyword-stacked articles daily). An honest, careful, original web writer has nothing to fear from these changes.
3. Facebook is used by millions as a search engine, and Google promotes results pulled from Facebook. LinkedIn and Twitter have also invaded SERPs from the big search engines. Writers: this means that any social media content should be written with care, following the guidelines in this book. If you want your social media writing to be findable, you can't just blurt things out.

14.

Web Me-Too and what else is new

A short history lesson follows. Web 1.0 sites make information globally available and searchable. Web 2.0 sites gather data about web users—our interests, name, age, health, wealth and education—and use it to deliver what the individual apparently wants. (Think Amazon.) Now Web 3.0 is here: social media rule (think Facebook), active participation is the norm, and enormous archives are open to the public (think Data.gov). These changes affect all business writing. Web 4.0? Maybe it's already here.

Theory and practice

The concept of Web 2.0 was heavily publicised when Time magazine named *you* (you, me, everybody, the great unwashed) person of the year for 2006:

> For seizing the reins of the global media, for founding and framing the new digital democracy, for working for nothing and beating the pros at their own game, Time's person of the year for 2006 is you.[106]

What was the big revolution about? Participation! Here's how one journalist perceived the exploding Internet in December 2006:

> I do think the Internet is going from a series of semi-interesting billboards to a 24-7 worldwide dialogue. It's gone from a joke to being a force in retail, advertising, politics—and everywhere else.[107]

What do the classic Web 2.0 sites have in common—for example Amazon, Flickr, YouTube, MySpace, Blogspot, Wikipedia and iTunes? According to Tim O'Reilly, co-coiner of the term Web 2.0, they generally:[108]

- deliver services, not software
- have dynamic, database-backed sites
- are almost infinitely scalable
- trust and cooperate with the user.

So what? Most people are barely aware of what is going on behind the scene of the screen—and that is the whole point. What we notice is the impact of these changes. The best web sites make it easy to do such things as:

- use new software without pain—it's seamless and superbly usable
- create a blog, recommend a book, upload a video, or talk to the world
- get instant summaries of new content on their favourite sites through Really Simple Syndication (RSS)
- get all manner of fresh data (such as stock quotes and weather forecasts) on their cell phones
- comment on other people's postings
- track who is linking to their own blogs.

Social media web sites are being used in fascinating ways. At first sight, SecondLife.com is a world for personal entertainment. But scratch the surface and you'll find Harvard University's virtual campus for extension courses, and NASA running virtual space trips. Facebook was established as a way for people to keep in touch with friends; now businesses use it for marketing, meetings, sales and customer support. Bill Gates and the kid next door both post their thoughts on Twitter.

Wikis take collaboration to extreme lengths: anyone, or anyone in a particular group, can alter existing content. This may or may not be moderated. A famous example is Wikipedia: you can contribute on any subject you like. Wikipedia is flawed, but the wonder is that the majority of entries are so good. On a smaller scale, wikis have long been the default method of co-writing papers in many universities.

> **Welcome to the** Second Life **Wiki,**
> that any Resident can edit.
> 1,720 articles created.

The strange thing is, many of these facilities have been available for at least 15 years. But with earlier technology, everything was a hassle for you and me. The idea of creating your own online diary in 5 minutes was unthinkable: even with templates and publishing tools, the job was fraught with problems. Now it's all very, very easy, and as a result, the Internet is changed forever.

A wake-up call for on-the-job writers

A great deal of legitimate content on intranets and web sites is still just static information. It's still crucial that writers know exactly how to make static content usable, readable, and findable. Nevertheless, internet technology and philosophy has long outgrown the simple model of one-way publishing. Site owners and content writers must understand this, or be left behind.

Your target readers now have higher expectations of your site. In the past, you could get away with *shut-up-and-listen* content. Today, whether your readers are citizens, students, customers or fellow workers, they are intuitively requesting something different:

- involve me!
- use me!
- listen to me!
- treat me like a collaborator, not a passive vessel!

Opportunities abound for genuine consultation, because you can have real conversations within a community of interested parties. In an organisation awake to Web 2.0 possibilities, every employee can spontaneously offer innovative ideas, which the entire organisation can discuss in detail. Projects can be jointly managed online. Genuine co-authorship can happen in wikis before your very eyes. You can call a meeting with any number of participants throughout the world, and allow it to run for 20 minutes, 20 days or 20 months.

Going for it

At IBM, hundreds of employees have public blogs.[109] Their policy for blogging is a model that has proved its worth.[110] (Incidentally, the policy is also a model of content writing: short, succinct, clear, intelligently structured and easy to skim-read.) *Responsible engagement in innovation and design* summarises IBM's purpose in encouraging staff blogs and wikis. The corporate aim, when the pilot expanded in May 2005, was to help improve IBM's competitiveness in key IT markets by encouraging its tech experts to join in public discussions. The policy document on James Snell's blog spells out the philosophy behind the rules:

> To learn: As an innovation-based company, we believe in the importance of open exchange and learning -- between IBM and its clients, and among the many constituents of our emerging business and societal ecosystem. The rapidly growing phenomenon of blogging and online dialogue are emerging important arenas for that kind of engagement and learning.
>
> To contribute: [...] As our business activities increasingly focus on the provision of transformational insight and high-value innovation -- whether to business clients or those in the public, educational or health sectors -- it becomes increasingly important for IBM and IBMers to share with the world the exciting things we're doing learning and doing, and to learn from others.

According to the University of Massachussetts, 23% of Fortune 500 companies had a public blog, 60% were on Twitter and 56% on Facebook in 2010. Starting a corporate blog should be approached cautiously. This is not to be treated as just another one-way CEO newsletter or media centre. As Jason Ryan says, 'producing half-decent content day-in day-out is bloody hard work'.[111]

The usual mix includes corporate news, interesting trends, and personal ideas and experiences. We expect blog writers to be human, available, and real. The corporate world is wary, with some reason.

As Harvard professor Andrew McAffee observed:

> These tools may well reduce management's ability to exert unilateral control and to express some level of negativity. Whether a company's leaders really want this to happen and will be able to resist the temptation to silence dissent is an open question. Leaders will have to play a delicate role if they want Enterprise 2.0 technologies to succeed.[112]

It's hard, very hard to relinquish control over your own corporate communications. And now that the public has a voice, they are merciless when they spot something phony. Wal-Mart came a cropper when it emerged that two 'independent' bloggers were actually journalists on the Walmart payroll.[113]

Yet although about 8% of Americans have created a blog, it is not likely that work-related blogging will get out of control on intranets.[114] According to Jakob Nielsen, fewer than 1% of internet users participate heavily, and 95% just lurk, observing without contributing.[115] The same proportions probably apply on intranets. Commitment is rare. Cream rises to the top.

Eavesdropping on a professional network of intranet developers, we see how trust can grow with experience. Dorje McKinnon describes his initial conversion:[116]

> 25 Nov 2005: NB - I was VERY sceptical of wiki's until about 2 weeks ago. To the point that I point blank refused to enter into discussions regarding their use in our internal production environment.
>
> The blow that toppled me off my perch was seeing how the developer teams were using the ad-hoc wiki's they've set up for themselves and how much MORE information was being captured. Information that would have walked out the door when that staff member moved department or left for a different company.

Will staff misbehave on a wiki? Six months later McKinnon commented again:

> In my situation we assume professionalism by all staff, this carries over to intranet publishing and wiki use. In seven years with hundreds of staff we have never had any inappropriate material published in any medium other than email.

Six degrees of participation

Consider a draft policy document open for public consultation. In numerous cases, government agencies and NGOs are legally obliged to consult the public or at least key stakeholders before finalising this kind of policy. But how seriously do they take this obligation?

1. Take it or leave it

This is the way of Web 1.0: simply publish a document, with no expectation of a response. Perhaps the fact is mentioned, with an unobtrusively placed phone number or physical address. A reader who wants to comment on this draft policy document has to search for contact details and take all the initiative. A *take-it-or-leave-it* page tends to look like this: just text, text, text, not a link or an email address in sight until you've scrolled way down.

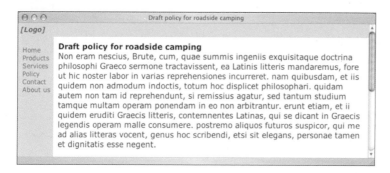

At least the above policy is in HTML format—in other words it is a web page, highly accessible. It's better than the following *take-it-or-leave-it* version, which doesn't publish the policy online—it just provides the policy as a PDF.

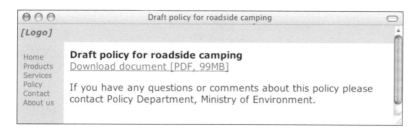

PDFs are fine as a second option, after a basic HTML version has been provided. But to offer only a PDF of a simple text document is at best a half-hearted way of consulting the public. PDFs are less accessible and annoy many readers. Moreover, if people want to quote from a PDF in their response, they can't always cut and paste: they may need to retype the original words one by one.

2. We want email

At the second level, the site owner invites readers to email their opinions. Readers won't know how many people have emailed, or what they've said. (And they need an acknowledgement!)

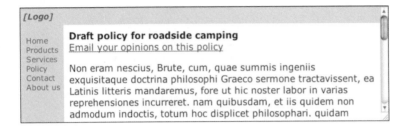

3. We need your help

Readers can respond to specific sections of the document by entering comments in a field. This is two-way communication, but the site owner is still in full control.

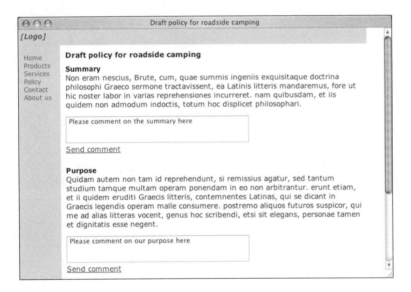

4. Let's talk to each other

This is essentially the blog model, although in the olden days, a discussion board served the same purpose. Now everyone can see comments from different readers; they can respond to one other's remarks as well as to the article.

5. You're the project

At the next level of engagement, the site owner is seriously committed to public consultation. An entire web site is dedicated to soliciting and displaying comments for all to see. Now readers can see they are being taken seriously. The British

Biotechnology and Biological Sciences Research Council (BBSRC) showed how this could be done.[117] Today, other organisations use blogs to achieve a similar level of consultation, and make it all seem oh so easy.

6. You help to write the policy

The ultimate degree of reader participation online is found in a wiki, where readers can add to a document and edit what others write. Wikis are the natural choice for any group writing task. In the screenshot below, the UNDP uses a wiki for full reader involvement.[118]

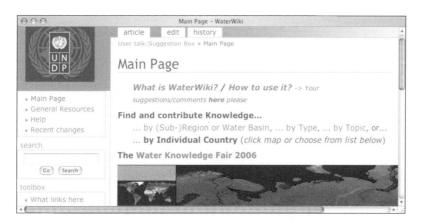

More challenges for writers

Some days I wake up in the morning and pray to the IT deity, 'Please don't make me learn a new software application today.' Writers almost daily encounter new technology, or new twists in the technology we know. The demands can seem overwhelming. But we can't turn our backs on IT: our careers are at stake.

In the immortal words of Marshall McLuhan (printed on paper in a book), *the medium is the message.*[119] He argued that the form of a message determines the way in which that message will be perceived and received. Indeed, the impact of the medium is greater than that of the message, although:

> it is only too typical that the "content" of any medium blinds us to the character of the medium.

We can assume that the medium also determines the way in which the message will be constructed and written or otherwise formed. For instance, we can safely assume that the content of messages chiselled into marble will be very different from those bouncing off a satellite dish.

Tech-fatigue may be why so many on-the-job writers resist learning how to write for the web. It's understandable: if online content is a moving target, why even aim at mastering it?

Many writers get a crash course in new technology when they are forced to use it for the first time. Every contract requires the use of something unfamiliar: a shared hard drive, a content management system, strange templates or databases, a new method of processing photographs or creating flowcharts. OK, so you learn it by lunchtime! This is pragmatic, realistic, on-the-job education, and there's nothing wrong with that. It is human, it is normal, and it is frequently effective. Maybe it is also living dangerously, but you learn well because you really, really need that knowledge. Moreover, we probably learn a new technology best by using it for a real job, not by reading about it. We keep up with technology by the seat of our pants.

One bright spot: the technological demands of Web Me-Too are tiny. It's the strategic implications for management, governance and politics that we need to get our heads around.

Mandatory: an inquiring mind

The writer's best defence is personal experience of the relevant medium, plus an enquiring mind. Rules are meaningless without understanding, and understanding is impossible without prior experience.

Experiment with new media. Sell something on TradeMe. Make podcasts, and listen to them critically. Start your own blog. Use your cell phone or Blackberry to get sports results. Contribute to wikis. What the heck—what have you got to lose?

Learning needs a basis to build on. All learning hooks on to previous knowledge, and people with no previous knowledge of the web won't make head or tail of this book—let alone be able to follow the guidelines. You need to be a regular web user or you won't even begin to write appropriately.

Hang on, you say—you mean there are people in the workforce who don't use the web? Indeed there are. Astonishingly, I am still approached by professional wordsmiths who are reluctant web users yet want a career in writing online content. Some literary people are the worst offenders. Ten years late, they learn that the web is the biggest publishing machine the world has ever known, and they want a piece of the action. That's fine, but Step One involves the very thing they dread: spending time online.

But that's not you, of course, or you wouldn't be reading this book.

Content in the hand

Content is now found on handheld computers such as smart phones. These tiny screens require ultra-concise, unfussy content. iPads, other tablets and even little netbooks also demand that writers understand their technology.

The future of handheld computers is pretty interesting. People read news headlines, weather forecasts, stockmarket results, and sports results on the screens of cell phones and other mini-computers. Intranets can be accessed by people on location or on the move. Extreme portability makes interaction even easier, at least in theory.

Time magazine arrives any way you want: by RSS feed, on your mobile device, by podcast or video.[120]

> **QUICK LINKS:** U.S. | World | Blogs | Business & Tech | Health & Science | Entertainment | Photos | Magazine | Specials | Archive Get TIME RSS Feeds | Get TIME on your Mobile Device | TIME Podcasts | TIME Video

Ponder the implications of MyStory, a ground-breaking soap.[121] Each episode is a mere 2 minutes, and is specially shot for multiple delivery methods. That means TV, computers, and above all, cell phone screens. The tiny telephone screen influences *My Story*'s style in many interesting ways. Long shots would be lost, so head shots and close-ups of detail feature large. Details of the 18-year-old characters' computer screens, blogs, scribbles, texts and cell phone screens are shown—phone screens on phone screens. (Find it on www.nzonscreen.com.)

My Story is commercial TV imitating amateur video imitating commercial TV. It's also Web Me-Too on display.

Professionally made, My Story deliberately imitates the YouTube look and feel, as if shot by drunken teens wielding cell phones. Decor echoes the primary colours of Big

Brother. Clare uses her blog to solve a mystery. The show was on MySpace as well as its own web site, guaranteeing maximum access and interaction with fans.

This is not the future. It's from 2007. Oh yes, and it's cunningly written with extreme conciseness. Multimedia people get the Web Me-Too. Journalists get it. I wonder when on-the-job writers will get it too? They need a helping hand.

As a writer, you may not always be told when your work is destined for a tiny screen. Two tricks for training yourself in micro-writing: use Twitter actively and thoughtfully, and practise reading on your mobile phone. These activities deliver brutal lessons in clarity, conciseness and structure.

Podcasts and Web 2.0

Podcasting is a revolutionary way of delivering news, opinions, entertainment and training. You can record, edit, publish and play podcasts on a web site like BigPod.co.nz. Look Ma, no software! DIY broadcasting is very much in the democratic spirit of Web Me-Too. In August 2006, Pew Internet researchers estimated that 17 million Americans had downloaded a podcast at least once, and numbers were growing.[122] Access to podcasts is easy and ubiquitous. PodcastAlley.com lists at least 30,480 podcasts totalling well over 1 million episodes. iTunes music store makes it ever so easy to download podcasts and listen or watch them any time, any place.

Think iPod—22.5 million were sold in 2006. The iPod is a mass publishing outlet.

The definition of *podcasting* has become rather blurry at the edges. Content is no longer limited to sound but includes video and images. Mainstream media organisations such as the BBC and Comedy Central now distribute their content as podcasts.

There's more about writing content for podcasts in other chapters—because business writing is web writing, and web writing includes podcasting. Many business sites routinely include a video or sound podcast in their content.

People are just as picky about podcasts as web sites. Naturally, to prepare appropriate scripts, writers need to download podcasts to their own iPod or MP3 player, and listen on the bus, out walking, on the plane or train—even in the shower! By exploring the culture from within, you become the consumer, analyse your likes and dislikes—and then you can deliver the goods.

Screen-reading software

This technology was developed for the blind and visually impaired, who cannot see what's on the screen. Screen-reading software delivers content in a computer-generated voice, miraculously making much of the web accessible. It's another way of listening to content.

A screen reader is not Web 2.0 software, although new developments do mean the blind can join the internet community more easily than before.

Maybe you are thinking this technology will never affect you—? It already does affect you, if you write for a government agency. All government documents should be prepared with accessibility in mind. For example, people using screen readers often survey a web page by listening only to the headlines or links. On a badly written page, they hear only useless information, such as *Who are we? Click here.* On an F-written page, they hear real information: *Higher Salaries Commission of New Zealand. We establish salary levels for top civil servants.*

Screen-reading software is not only for the blind. Many people with perfect vision would rather listen to web content than read it. Screen readers can read extremely fast, much faster than humans; they are easier on the eyes; and they suit people with predominately auditory learning modes.

How to write well for this technology? F-headlines and F-links make a huge difference, and Chapter 12 shows how to make images accessible. But when you get a chance, observe an experienced user in action. I promise, you will be amazed. And then you will analyse everything in the content that made reading tough for them, and figure what that implies for the writer. That's inside-out learning.

Reading e-books

Finally, here's some technology that reverses the trend of Web Me-Too by re-introducing passive reading. E-readers are small devices (often the size of a paperback book) designed to present long documents in a highly readable form. About 3.6 million e-readers (including Kindle, Nook, Sony and Kobo) were sold in 2009, and about 6.6 million in 2010. Sales of e-books have risen exponentially in the last few years, and today's e-readers make reading electronic books comfortable and convenient. E-readers are not the only way to read e-books, however: people also use multipurpose devices such as smart phones, iPod Touch and iPads. The classics are at everyone's fingertips now: bring back Proust!

As a writer of e-books, prepare by reading them on these devices—not on the screen of a regular computer. The experience is quite different. Discover the formatting requirements of e-book writing, and follow them to the letter.

And test, test, test

How will you know if new content is working in an unfamiliar medium? Test it. Solicit contributions to your wiki or blog. Ask others to listen to your podcast and give their impressions. Watch someone access your content with a screen-reader. That's all. You are bound to learn something, and it's always fascinating.

15.

Standard pages need a brain

Most web sites and intranets automatically include certain standard pages. It's logical to provide a *Contact* page and a section dedicated to corporate information: they are standard fare for good reasons. However, these pages hold traps for the unwary. Providing them is a no-brainer, but actually writing them requires a brain.

First we'll consider the content on home pages, index pages and site maps, all of which usher readers to the page they really want. Then we'll look at standard pages for *Contact Us*, *Our Organisation*, *News*, and *Press Releases*.

Home page content: fresh and functional

What is a home page? Silly question? Not really. Sure, the home page of a web site or intranet is usually obvious. It is the page people see when they type your domain name in the browser address bar. However, a large site can have many pseudo-home pages within it, one for each section—for example, on an intranet there could be a so-called home page for every separate business unit or academic faculty. Whether these are sub-home-pages or index pages is largely a matter of perception and policy.

By the way, I'm not talking about personal home pages or splash pages. (Mercifully, the fad for splash pages has dwindled.)

The design, navigation and usability of a home page have a powerful influence on readers, generating respect and trust, or their opposites. Home pages should be instantly recognisable as home pages—no scrolling, a slightly different layout, very little text, perhaps more visual interest than other pages.

Home pages matter enormously, because about 40% of visitors see that page before any other.[123] As elsewhere, I'll focus on content alone—the guts of the page: not the banner, logo, design, or navigation, but the words and pictures in the main body of the page. On a large site, a specialist team will usually control the selection and editing of home page content, which concerns staff writers only peripherally. They contribute indirectly to home page content when it links temporarily to a new or revised page. That's when training pays off: then page headlines and summaries can be automatically recycled on the home page and make perfect sense.

Ideally, home page content will include:
- basic information about the site owner
- snippets of news, linking to the full stories
- samples (not descriptions) of the most popular or newest items on the site
- clearly worded links straight to the pages of most interest to target readers.

After fulfilling those basic conventions, a web site or intranet has numerous other options for filling the home page. However, a good rule for home page content (as elsewhere) is *Show me, don't tell me*. With this in mind:
- minimise puffery, maximise facts
- change home page content at least weekly
- use customer language, not marketing lingo or corporate-speak.

Mitsui & Co. (USA) uses its home page for branding alone, blowing its own trumpet instead of reaching out to customers.[124] There's no content apart from what's in the screenshot below.

Fonterra's home page also has its PR angle, but it gives objective facts about the company, and links to key areas of the site.[125] That's more use to visitors!

The University of Sydney's home page content starts with news items, followed by corporate facts and links to key pages.[126] That's a reasonable approach.

> **Sydney researchers share in historic project**
> Sydney University researchers were part of the huge international project to produce the first genome sequence for a marsupial - the South American opossum. More
>
> **Research and innovation**
> The University of Sydney is one of Australia's leading research universities, winning more funding from competitive grants than any other university in the country.
>
> | All about research at Sydney | Centres and institutes |
> |---|---|
> | Research scholarships | Business Liaison Office |
>
> **Learning and teaching**
> With 45,000 local and international students, the University of Sydney offers high quality undergraduate and postgraduate courses in a comprehensive range of disciplines.
>
> | Find a course | Learning and teaching |
> |---|---|
> | eLearning | Scholarships |

6 common mistakes in home page content

1. Identity crisis. It should be instantly obvious whose site this is. Include at least one sentence stating who you are, where you are and what you do. Don't rely on the logo and banner!
2. Mystery location. The humble writer must sometimes compensate for poor branding or design by stating where the site owner is based.
3. Too many words. People do not want to spend long on the home page. They are usually aiming for another page, and excess verbiage just confuses them.
4. Too few words. Back in 2002, the wordless home page was in vogue. Home pages were a playground for designers and an IQ test for visitors. Now most web designers know that a home page without words is a wasted opportunity.
5. Pompous self-promotion and navel gazing.
6. Stale content.

Top pages: index, top content, burble or toot?

Some say the home page is like the foyer of a department store, where visitors get their bearings. Then top pages are elevator pages, which take you to a specific department within the store.

After you click on a link in the navigation bar, for example, *Services*, you usually land on a page sporting the word *Services*. (Sorry to point out the obvious.) This top page, or section-entry page, opens the door to a whole bunch of other pages.

What to do with these top pages? In practice they are often redundant, because clicking on *Services* doesn't just send you to a new page: it also opens a new menu with a list of services. And that's what people are really interested in. They want information about one particular service (or product or course or whatever).

If a site's design requires top pages, those pages should always contain worthwhile content. Essentially, writers have three sensible choices:
- create an obvious index page
- use the top page as a sub-home page, for latest news and links to new content
- present top content: essential facts.

Unfortunately, top pages are notoriously useless. Without guidance, many writers are mystified about how to fill the page, and so they do one or both of the following.
- 'Burble burble! In this section you will find a range of servies. If you want a haircut click on haircut in the left hand menu.'
- 'Toot toot! We are the most wonderful people in the whole world don't you think we are just terrific?'

Top pages in action

Index pages have an obvious function: they provide an index of all the pages within a certain area of a web site. They should *look* like an index page.

Part of the University of Southampton's navigation bar is shown below.[127] Imagine clicking on the *About Us* tab.

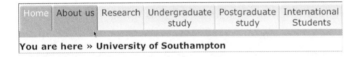

That tab takes you to the top page for the university's *About Us* content, shown below. Notice the new menu on the left showing all pages in the *About Us* section: that's what people really want. What riches are here! Now, the *About Us* page is top of the list, the top page for the section. The text is content of an elevated nature: a letter from the Vice Chancellor. I bet nobody reads it. A typical pointless burble burble toot toot top page, it essentially says, 'We are terrific. Read the menu on the left.'

But wait—there's more and it's better! If we click on *Academic Schools*, the first link below *About us*, we find an index page. Hooray, this really looks like an index page: you can recognise an index without reading a word. It lists 21 academic schools plus the head of school and an email link for each school. Each school name links to a new web site.

The page has a toot-toot message at the top, plus one important factual sentence: *The University has more than 20 Academic Schools which are organised into three Faculties.*

Academic Schools

Teaching takes place across a broad range of disciplines and our students are led by academics who push research boundaries. Students benefit from the latest knowledge and expertise and this, together with the University's strong entrepreneurial culture, makes the Southampton learning experience especially valuable.

The University has more than 20 Academic Schools which are organised into three Faculties.

Faculty of Engineering, Science and Mathematics

- **School of Chemistry**:
  Professor Jeremy Kilburn
  Tel: +44 (0)23 8059 3333
  Email: chem@soton.ac.uk

- **School of Civil Engineering and the Environment**:
  Professor William Powrie
  Tel: +44 (0)23 8059 4652
  Email: civilenv@soton.ac.uk

- **School of Electronics and Computer Science**:
  Professor Wendy Hall
  Tel: +44 (0) 23 8059 6000
  Email: helpdesk@ecs.soton.ac.uk

- **School of Engineering Sciences**:
  Professor Geraint Price
  Tel: +44 (0)23 8059 2840
  E-mail: ses-enquiries@soton.ac.uk

- **School of Geography**:
  Professor Nigel Arnell
  Tel: +44 (0)23 80 592215
  E-mail: Geography@soton.ac.uk

- **School of Mathematics**
  Professor Alistair Fitt
  Tel: +44 (0)23 8059 5141
  E-mail: enquiry@maths.soton.ac.uk

- **School of Ocean and Earth Science**:

Faculty of Law, Arts and Social Sciences
(**www.lass.soton.ac.uk**)

- **School of Art**:
  Professor Bashir Makhoul
  Tel: 02380 596900
  Email: askwsa@soton.ac.uk

- **School of Education**:
  Professor Mary Ratcliffe
  Tel: +44 (0)23 8059 3475
  Email: soeadmin@soton.ac.uk

- **School of Humanities**:
  Professor Michael Kelly
  (Archaeology, English, History, Music, Modern Languages and Philosophy)

- **School of Law**:
  Professor Nick Gaskell
  Tel: 44 (0)23 8059 3632
  E-mail: law@soton.ac.uk

- **School of Management**:
  Professor Richard Lamming
  Tel: +44 (0) 23 8059 3076
  Email: mmtmail1@soton.ac.uk

- **School of Social Sciences**:
  Professor Tony McGrew
  Tel: +44 (0)23 8059 9393
  Email: socsci@soton.ac.uk
  (Counselling, Economics,

Faculty of Medicine, Health and Life Sciences

(**MHLS Faculty Graduate School**)

- **School of Psychology**:
  Professor Nick Donnelly
  Tel: +44(0)23 8059 3995
  Email: kms@soton.ac.uk

- **School of Biological Sciences**:
  Dr David Shepherd
  Tel: +44(0)23 8059 7747
  Email: M.A.Smith@soton.ac.uk

- **School of Medicine**:
  Professor Iain Cameron

- **School of Health Professions and Rehabilitation Sciences**:
  Professor Roger Briggs
  Tel: 02380 592142
  Email: sohprecp@soton.ac.uk

- **School of Nursing and Midwifery**:
  Professor Dame Jill Macleod-Clark
  Tel: +44 (0)23 8059 7979
  Email: uossonam@soton.ac.uk

Next we show another true index page, from IRS.[128] Notice how orderly and straightforward it looks. You can instantly see it's an index of links. We like that.

Burble burble, toot toot

A large intranet or web site may have hundreds of sections, and hundreds of top pages. The vast majority do not contain an index or important content. Consequently, they are almost inevitably confusing or useless or irritating.

A typically pointless burble-burble top page follows.[129] There's hardly a keyword in sight, and the key message is a vapid truism: *Choose from the links below the top banner to find out what's best for you!*

The red flag for burble is the ultimate so-what phrase: *a range of*. They say they have a range of courses. Well, gee whiz, we wouldn't imagine they had only one course. They offer *a variety of* career fields. So? That's what colleges do. *A range of* stands for *we do stuff*. The specifics—which do interest us—require another click.

Another tragic burble-burble top page follows; the content is a complete waste of space.[130] The page:

- duplicates the links on the left
- explains how to use search
- burbles on in chatty truisms
- tells people they can use this section of the site by searching and browsing.

Solve with technology, rules and templates

Writers need help. The problem of top page content is too great for them to solve spontaneously. The web team would do well to find a system-wide solution. Here are a couple of options when developing a site.

Many developers eliminate index pages by forcing readers to select a sub-item in the menu: they make the top level items (e.g. *Public Health* in the example below) non-clickable entry points to a drop-down menu.[131] Hey presto: no top pages are needed.

Standard pages need a brain / 165

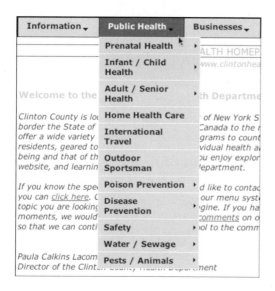

Label pages are another way to eliminate index pages: a top level click just opens up the menu without changing the visible content of the page.

If the site design cannot be changed, I suggest establishing a policy and template for top pages. They should be recognisable as either sub-home pages or index pages.

Contact pages

It seems so obvious, that every web site needs a contact page. But the *Contact Us* page is a hard-won right. In the 1990s, most web sites didn't have such a page—or else they exerted excruciating controls on contact. For example, many sites forced people to complete a detailed form merely to send an email. Multinational companies didn't perceive customer access to be important, and that rascal Boy-in-Garage relished the anonymity of the web.

But today, the web is often the first resort for phone numbers and addresses. People demand contact details on a web site for reasons of credibility, transparency and accessibility, and the contact page is crucially important for business.

Like any web content, the contact page requires thought. It should reflect the needs of users, not the corporate structure. Who do your readers want to contact? Why? How? Give as much detail and choice as you can without creating a monster page: names, postal address, phone numbers, email address. (Of course other people are involved: someone has to answer those emails and phone calls!)

Even if you provide an online form for feedback, give a link to an email address too.

What's wrong with restricting choices to a form alone? Well, an online form can erode people's sense of control. Besides, they need to receive immediate acknowledgement. Otherwise their trust can be shaken. When people complete and send a form online:

- they have no record of what they wrote, unless they print out the page before sending
- they are taken out of their own familiar email environment.

A contact page should look like a contact page. Some look more like *don't-bother-me* or even *piss-off* pages, like this one from Philip Morris International.[132]

> **Contact us**
>
> Before you call or write to us, you might want to look at our frequently asked questions. You may find the answer to your question there.
>
> Consumer enquiries
> Please don't ask us for marketing materials, promotional items or cigarettes. It's our policy not to send out such items in response to consumer requests.
>
> If you're unsatisfied with one of our products please send it, along with details of where and when you bought it, to your nearest Philip Morris International office. You'll find their address on our Where to find us page. Please clearly mark your envelope "Quality assurance".
>
> Media enquiries
> Journalists should call our press office on +41 (0)21 618 4500 or send an email to pmi.pressoffice@pmintl.com.
>
> Please note that our press office cannot respond to general or consumer enquiries.

As for this wordy, gushing, toot-toot page from Toyota.com—what were they thinking?[133] That we would be awed by their generosity in providing more than one way to contact them? That journalists need to be told what a newsroom is? That nobody knows the meaning of FAQ? Puh-lease!

Toyota's marketing team missed a beat. Sure, a contact page works as a marketing device—but once more, *show me, don't tell me.* Show me you respect me as an intelligent busy potential customer. Don't give yourself a medal for communication skills: earn it.

Here's the top part of Princeton University's excellent contact page—concise, comprehensive, clearly laid out, and targeted to different groups of customers.[134]

General Contacts		
University Operator	(609) 258-3000	> Search Princeton People
U-CALL voice directory	(609) 258-2255	
		> Campus Mail & Phone Information
Academic		
Dean of the College	(609) 258-3040	> Change My Contact Information
Dean of the Faculty	(609) 258-3020	
Dean of the Graduate School	(609) 258-3035	> Mailing address:
Registrar	(609) 258-3360	Princeton University
Community Auditing Program	(609) 258-0202	Princeton, NJ 08544
Continuing Education	(609) 258-5226	USA
Administration		
President's Office	(609) 258-6101	
Provost's Office	(609) 258-3026	
Vice President and Secretary	(609) 258-3019	
Executive Vice President	(609) 258-3108	
Recording Secretary	(609)258-3305	
Admission Offices		
Graduate	(609) 258-3034	
Undergraduate	(609) 258-3060	

Wellington City Council's contact page, shown below, is clever and deceptively simple.[135] It gives essential details at the top of the page. And when people click on an item in the A-Z list, they get a popup window with the contact details—nothing else.

Organisation pages establish credibility

Pages about the organisation are a fundamental feature of virtually all web sites and intranets. They usually sport the label *About <Organisation>* or *About Us*. On an intranet, *Our Org.* might be the label. A site could have a single page or scores of pages. This is a convention that's rarely questioned, because it is so useful.

The organisation pages won't be the most popular on the web site. A minority of people will visit them, and very likely visit only once. Nevertheless, the pages are essential, because they establish the site's credibility.

Who will consult the *About Us* pages? Investors, business students, job seekers, potential partners, contractors, distributors and agents, for starters. But frequently people using other parts of the site will flick to *About Us* to check on the owner's credentials. 'Can I trust this site?' they wonder. Most of the answers should be on the *About Us* pages.

These pages often turn into turf war terrain. Someone has to decide what the organisation hopes to gain from the pages, and therefore what content it should provide.

Essentially, the *About Us* section should provide succinct, objective facts. At the very least, visitors must be able to find out the following facts about the organisation:

- name of organisation
- location
- core business
- management team.

About Us pages may include or link to a great many other informative pages, for example:

- corporate history, especially date of establishment
- organisation chart
- strategic plan
- investment information including current stock prices
- list of key customers (with their permission)
- Annual Reports
- Financial Reports
- map of locations (for example, campuses, offices)
- policies that concern the public (for example, environment, equal opportunity).

Government agencies tend to present organisation pages factually. They are not usually trying to sell themselves. For example, the Agency for Healthcare Research and Quality provides a direct, no-nonsense index page.[136]

> **About AHRQ**
>
> Mission & Budget
> Appropriations — reauthorization — profile — annual report
> Strategic Plan
> Vision statements — work plans — performance reports
> Organization & Contacts
> Offices & Centers — key contacts — National Advisory Council
> Map & Directions
> Location — transportation — visitor information
> Events & Announcements
> Conferences — meetings — general announcements
> Job Vacancies
> Full-time positions — expert appointments — fellowships — summer interns

The purpose of organisation web page content is to inform and reassure, not to persuade. The facts will persuade where appropriate. Before investing in a company, I want to know *exactly* what they do.

The 3 most common mistakes made in *About Us* content are:
- using them for marketing hype alone
- basing them on departmental structure
- failing to produce the expected facts.

All content should be objective, concise, and scannable. *About Us* pages are no exception. We go to corporate web sites for facts. Marketing mania has no place there.

Corporate mission statements are nearly always deeply embarrassing in the cold light of public scrutiny. They tend to attract the skeptical response, 'Yeah, right!' Mission statements are valuable for staff and investors. But they should be so placed on the web site as to spare other people the pain of finding them by accident.

I do see signs of improvement this century. For example, in 2002, Microsoft's Corporate Information top page was headlined *What we do* and contained 72 words of self-inflation:

> Microsoft's vision is to empower people through great software - any time, any place and on any device. As the worldwide leader in software for personal and business computing, Microsoft strives to produce innovative products and services that meet our customers' evolving needs. At the same time, we understand that long-term success is about more than just making great products. Find out what we mean when we talk about Living Our Values.

By 2006, this worrying content had morphed into a useful customer-focused index page.[137]

> **Company Information**
>
> Published: June 25, 2003 | Updated: October 14, 2005
>
> Learn about Microsoft's business units and Board of Directors, get contact information, locate a sales office, find out how to participate in the Microsoft Vendor Program, or view our latest advertisements.
>
> **Our Businesses**
> Read about our commitment to customers and find out how Microsoft's seven core business units serve our customers' needs.
>
> **Microsoft Timeline**
> Explore the events and turning points that have shaped our company over the past thirty years.
>
> **Visitor Center**
> Come share in the excitement of our discoveries, explore some of our latest products, and meet some of the people whose ideas and creativity make Microsoft a world leader in computer and software technology.
>
> **Contact Information**
> Learn how to reach us by mail, phone, fax, or e-mail.
>
> **U.S. Office Locations**
> Find a Microsoft office in your district.
>
> **Worldwide Offices**
> Visit Web sites for Microsoft offices around the world.
>
> **Procurement**
> Find out how you can participate in the Microsoft Vendor Program.
>
> **Corporate Governance**
> Take a look at our corporate governance practices.

Fine, that's better! But alas, Microsoft has plenty of counterproductive hype on other corporate information pages.

An absurd top page for *Procurement* follows.[138] It wastes five paragraphs sharing the Microsoft mission—below a generic 5-cm high banner.

Who cares? Vendors need to know about processes and opportunities. Hey, they just want to make a buck! Their decision to tender does not depend on Microsoft's desire to help them *realize their full potential.*

Our commitment to realizing potential extends from our products to our procurement practices—to you.

PROCUREMENT

Our Process
Microsoft Vendor Program
Supplier Diversity
Register Your Interest
Glossary

The Microsoft mission is totally inclusive—not only does it encompass all people; it includes every area of our enterprise:

To enable people and businesses throughout the world to realize their full potential.

We also embrace a core set of values. We look for suppliers of all types of quality goods and services who share those values and can assist us in fulfilling our mission.

We invite you to explore this site and decide if you would like to work with us as we turn our passionate tradition of innovation into opportunities for discovery and growth. Because at Microsoft, it's our belief that the true measure of our success is not in the power of our software, but in the power it unleashes in us all.

Learn More

Our process
Microsoft Vendor Program
Supplier diversity
Register your interest
Glossary

Those marketing maniacs—they just don't get the web, do they? They have written a hymn to me, me, Microsoft. The trumpets are blasting. Nothing is missing except the heavenly choir. Don't fall into the same trap.

But enough bad—here's good. Pages about corporate philanthropy are almost doomed to sound phony. But this one from Mitsubishi USA is specific and factual (despite long sentences and the dread phrase *a range of*).[139]

> **Corporate Contributions**
>
> Mitsubishi International Corporation's (MIC) Corporate Giving Program supports a range of programs addressing civic, human rights and other concerns of relevance to the communities where we do business. The company is committed to spending 2% of its after tax income on these programs.
>
> MIC makes gifts both through a corporate program and through the Mitsubishi International Corporation Foundation.
>
> **Matching Gifts**
>
> MIC also matches employee gifts to non-profits, dollar for dollar, through our Matching Gifts Program, which matches gifts of at least $25 by full-time employees to any 501(c)(3), except to political organizations or for religious purposes. This program, which has an annual maximum of $1,000 per employee, is intended to encourage public service among staff by providing a way for them to respond to community need. And it allows our employees to have a say in where some of MIC's charitable dollars are spent, thus enhancing their involvement in the company's efforts to be a good corporate citizen.
>
> **Corporate Drives**
>
> Mitsubishi International Corporation's New York City headquarters also implements on an on-going basis numerous company-wide collection drives.

Our People pages

What are these pages for? The writer is often attempting to implement a marketing policy, and forgets that readers have their own agenda. The writer's purpose might be one or more of these:
- attract new staff
- boost the organisation's reputation for expertise
- raise the profile of key people
- tell readers who to contact for particular enquiries
- attract new customers, students, distributors or agents.

But why do readers look at these pages? They may have entirely different reasons such as to:
- get a job
- study the organisation's employment policy
- find facts for an article or student report
- evaluate the organisation as a supplier or customer
- decide whether to do business with the organisation.

One constant is that pure hype doesn't work, and is hard to read.

Another constant: talk to me! It would be fair to say that most readers expect an *Our People* page to be pretty darn boring, even if they really want information. A conversational tone can make all the difference.

What a difference a *you* makes!

Marketing writers have a tough job. Someone at Philip Morris USA tried to make the following text objective (good) but forgot to make it personal.[140] It-language prevailed. So the general impression is pompous, bureaucratic, distant and repetitive. Who cares? Who reads?

> PM USA promotes a culture of inclusion for a broad array of stakeholders including its employees, suppliers, customers and host communities. Experience has shown that a wide array of life experiences produces the diverse perspectives required to keep a company moving forward. That diversity combined with effective collaboration ensures PM USA's long-term success.

A different writer conveys similar information on the Philip Morris International site—but what a difference in tone! This is we-language, still potentially dangerous (because it's all about us) but far more personal. The page makes statements of facts: *PM International hires locally*, for instance. And just by starting with one little *you*, it sweeps us into a conversation.

> You might think that because we employ more than 80,000 people around the world diversity wouldn't be a problem. In many senses it's not: we hire locally, so our employees reflect the diversity of the communities where we operate.
>
> But we still have a way to go. For example, we need to address gender equality higher up the ladder. We are working to increase the number of women in senior management. To get there, we are working on our promotion and recruitment practices and redesigning our appraisal procedures.

Be real or be rubbished

Today there's no place for phony content on the web. People used to having their say on blogs and Twitter can spot lies at 100 paces, and are in no mood to tolerate them.

Here's an example of a marketing technique that used to pass without comment, but today is very unwise. The Philip Morris USA *Our People* page[141] has some photos of real employees, each with a short autobiography. Trouble is, they didn't actually write their own autobiographies: a professional writer constructed them all from boilerplate text. For instance, both Darlene (Youth Smoking Prevention) and Darryl (Information Services) end with exactly the same sentence—and pop goes any illusion of authenticity.

> **Darlene**
> Youth Smoking Prevention
>
> I came to PM USA straight from the University of Washington in 1999. My first job was in Sales, working as a territory sales manager in Washington state. This was a great job with lots of autonomy and opportunity. I learned a tremendous amount about the company, particularly its mission and values.
>
> I quickly learned that PM USA is the place for those seeking opportunity and growth. From 1999 to 2002, I received several promotions and moved to Oregon as part of the Sales department. Along the way, I earned an MBA (paid for by the company) at Ohio University.
>
> In 2003, I accepted a position in our External Affairs department, working to develop and manage programs and grants that encourage the positive development of youth and educational initiatives linked to student achievement in our plant communities of Richmond and Cabarrus County, NC.
>
> I enjoy the diversity of the work that my department performs. My entire career at PM USA has been one of continuous growth and development. It is one thing to just have a job. I've had several in my lifetime, but it's another thing to have a career. PM USA provides that and more.

News stories and media releases

Most web sites and intranets have news stories. Some also have media releases. What's the difference?

- News stories have been edited and published for public consumption.
- Media releases are a resource for outside journalists to edit and publish as they please.

It's possible that a brilliant media release might be published in a newspaper just the way you wrote it, but it's far more likely to be changed before publication, or totally ignored. Media releases usually have very long informative headlines, which will be changed by various subeditors to suit their needs.

What on-the-job writers need to know about news stories

At work, you may be called on to write news stories—for example, for the intranet or a newsletter. If your story is picked up for display on the home page, it might need a little polishing by the press officer.

But if your stories follow the guidelines for general online content, they will already have an excellent F-headline—it may even be perfect. This is a great start.

Other tips for writing online news stories:

- use newspaper stories as your model
- include a photo
- stress the angle that will interest your audience
- start with a summary of the entire story
- short is best: write 100-300 words
- use plain language and F-language, of course.

Use experts for media releases

Ideally, media releases are handled by communication specialists who know the rules and know how to please a network of tetchy editors.[142] This kind of writing is not an add-on job for everyday staff writers. They can feed information to the Corp Comms team, but are not necessarily the best judges of what's newsworthy.

The thing is, professional journalists don't need readymade news stories: media releases are just the starting point for their own stories. For this reason, many organisations dedicate a special section of a site to meeting the needs of journalists, or even an entire web site. Indiana University takes press relations that seriously.[143]

Compare media release with news story

Next we show the start of a bare-bones media release made available to all media by Indiana University's Office of Media Relations.[144] Notice the contact details at top right: 2 names, 2 phone numbers, 2 email addresses.

Exercise when young may reduce risk of fractures later in life

FOR IMMEDIATE RELEASE
Nov. 30, 2006

When kids are running and jumping, they aren't just having fun, according to researchers at IUPUI.

◘ Print-Quality Photo

INDIANAPOLIS -- Running and jumping during childhood is more than child's play; it provides lifelong benefits for future bone health and appears to reduce the risk of fractures later in life according to a Journal of Bone and Mineral Research study by Indiana University-Purdue University Indianapolis (IUPUI) researchers. The study is now available in an advance online edition of the journal and will appear in a print edition in 2007.

"Our study demonstrates that exercise when young may reduce the risk of fractures later in life, and the old exercise adage of 'use it or lose it' may not be entirely applicable to the skeleton," said the study's principal investigator, Stuart J. Warden, assistant professor and director of research in physical therapy at the Indiana University School of Health and Rehabilitation Sciences at IUPUI.

Researchers exercised the right forearms of 5-week-old female rats for a few minutes three times a week for seven weeks. The left forearms were not exercised. Bone quantity and structure of the rats' right and left forearms were assessed before and after exercise. Researchers did not exercise the rats for the next 92 weeks -- virtually their entire lifespan. At that point, their forearm bones were assessed again for bone quantity and structure, as well as strength.

All procedures were performed following approval of the Institutional Animal Care and Use Committee of Indiana University.

Now check the start of a news story based on that media release. Megan Rauscher has given the article a new headline, a new slant, shorter sentences and an even more readable style. It is now her story, and she is named as the author.

Early high impact activity key to bone health

E-MAIL A FRIEND

Early high impact activity key to bone health

Last Updated: 2006-12-07 14:22:33 -0400 (Reuters Health)

By Megan Rauscher

NEW YORK (Reuters Health) - Running, jumping and other high impact activities during childhood benefits bone health by increasing the size and strength of the growing skeleton, suggests new research. Moreover, the benefits in bone size and strength induced by exercise during growth persist lifelong -- even if exercise is ceased.

"The lifelong maintenance of exercise benefits gained during growth may help reduce an individual's risk of osteoporotic fracture as they age," said study chief Dr. Stuart J. Warden, director of research in physical therapy at the Indiana University School of Health and Rehabilitation Sciences in Indianapolis.

For their study, Warden's team exercised the right, but not the left, forearms of young growing rats for a few minutes three times per week for seven weeks. They analyzed the amount and structure of bone in the rats' right and left forearms before and after exercise, according to the report, published in the Journal of Bone and Mineral Research.

Error messages and Help

A much neglected type of standard content is those little error messages. They are often rattled off by technical people who are not trained writers, and it shows. The quality of error messages and help text can strongly influence people's perception of the site. Messages like *Challenge token null* can confuse, frustrate and madden us.

> **Have an Account? Login Here.**
> If you already have an account, enter your login information here and click the "Login" button below. If you do not have an account, please click on one of the buttons to the left.
> USERNAME:
> mcxxipo
> PASSWORD:
>
> [Login]
>
> Challenge token null

What's wrong with *Challenge token null*? Let me count the ways:
- It's jargon, not plain language.
- It's abrupt, and sounds negative.
- It doesn't tell me how to fix the problem.
- It's in the wrong place, not obvious, so people waste time staring at the form before they see the message.

From this you can deduce what's needed for a usable, helpful error message on a web site. The guidelines are true even when a technical whiz addresses another technical whiz. Programmers and coders swamp discussion boards with pleas for help over error messages that make no sense.

- Write in plain language—a language used by the human beings who encounter the problem. On most web sites, these are non-technical human beings. They don't even understand phrases like *Helper application not found*, let alone *IEXPLORE caused an invalid page fault in module KERNEL32.DLL at 0257:bff7c743*.
- Be polite and be positive. Cryptic messages like these give us a bad feeling: *Bad file*, *Bad request*, and *Failed to create empty document*. About.com goes to the opposite extreme: so polite that the tip spills out of its window!

- Tell us what to do. It's no use just saying *Failed DNS lookup*. Only technical people know that means they have to check the spelling of the URL, or try again later.
- Put tips, explanations and error messages exactly where they are needed. Then they empower people, giving them confidence to continue. ThinkGeek.com does it right. *Forgot your password?* links to a page with instructions.[145]

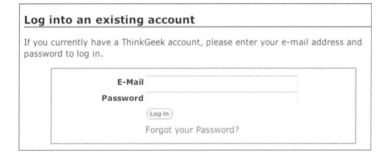

Even the word *Help* has a hidden barb. There's a perception that only losers need *help*, and many people feel inadequate if they ask for help.[146] Solution? Use *Tips* or *Support*. Readers get a sense of satisfaction from finding and using a tip. They're in control, whereas they lose control when they ask for help.

Provide tips and explanations exactly where relevant, e.g. *Why we need your zip code*.

Revising all these messages is a project in itself, requiring an expert writer working alongside IT people.

Test, test, test!

How do you know whether the content on your standard pages is OK? You guessed: you test. As usual, even a few minutes of casual testing can reveal a great deal. There's no mistaking your friend's frown or smile as they look at something you have written. Just do it. All feedback is useful feedback.

16.

The secret life of intranets

Intranets have developed in an interesting way this century, and most of the changes happen behind closed doors. Nothing sinister there: it's just that only insiders get to use the intranet. So what's going on? What has been growing in those secret places—truffles or toadstools?

Intranet consultants and developers get to see a great many intranets close up, so when they comment on trends, it's worth listening. Trends matter to writers—they can't write well if they have an antiquated view of what the intranet is for. And as it happens, the value of intranets is commonly misjudged by top managers. The intranet is no longer a nice-to-have aid to business: increasingly, it is the primary tool for doing business.

Trends in intranets

Jane McConnell of NetStrategyJMC began surveying global intranets in 2006, questioning organisations in Europe, North America and Asia Pacific.[147] In May 2011 at the Intranets2011 conference, McConnell noted that intranets have been through three major stages.
1. Intranets were centrally controlled, chiefly by Communications, IT and HR. Their main purpose was one-way communication from management to staff.
2. Business units took over their own slice of the intranet, and used other tools and platforms such as Sharepoint to meet their business needs. (Governance was sadly lacking.)
3. Social media—networking, micro-blogging, wikis, discussions and collaboration—are now used to some extent in 70% of organisations.

As McConnell sees it, the old, controlled intranet is now just one aspect of a digital workplace. Social media, collaboration and managed content are each part of a whole. The very word 'intranet' has an old-fashioned ring. But I'll use it in this chapter as a convenient code for the digital workplace.

The Nielsen Norman Group has been selecting and reviewing the ten 'best' intranets since 2001. We can reasonably deduce that where the 'best' intranets go, others will probably follow. The 2007 report states:

Looking back, it seems that most intranets were founded in the 1990s, then left to grow haphazardly. In contrast, the current decade is one of consolidation and emphasis on (finally) making the intranet work well as a business tool.[148]

According to McConnell, 2011 shows five megatrends for intranets.

1. Intranets are becoming a front-door into the content, services, tools and applications people need to do their job.
2. Intranets are becoming more team-oriented, as project and collaborative spaces are integrated.
3. Intranets are becoming people-focused, with networking and social media.
4. Intranets are becoming places for real-time communication, with micro-blogging, web conferencing and other tools.
5. Intranets are becoming mobile, through smart phones and other mobile devices.

So, if you thought the intranet was all about communication, think again. That may be what the CEO thinks, but it's not what employees want. Tony Ward says:

> The intranet is not a communications tool; nor a technology. And it's certainly not just a website. The intranet is a business system to support the entire company. It touches and represents all facets of the business, and if executed properly, improves all aspects of the business.[149]

The intranet is the natural home for all business applications. Of course, on-the-job writers are not usually the people who create applications, but smart writers may be required to write key information that makes an application work better.

For example, consider the core tool of every intranet: the staff directory. Unless it's in very poor shape, everyone on the staff uses it to check phone numbers, email addresses and photos, to identify the head of a business unit, or to figure some aspect of organisational structure. A good directory is searchable by name, office, job titles, responsibilities, experience and skills. Microsoft's intranet directory is also searchable by distance from the searcher's desk, on the assumption that sometimes you need help from a person in the same building—or at least the same country. The extra details can be very useful, for example to managers seeking staff with the right skills and experiences for certain projects.

Who writes or edits the job descriptions? This is a skilled task, though you might not think so. Who updates them? A directory with outdated, inadequate or irrelevant information is exasperating. This is just one example of unexciting content that looks more like data than writing, and helps staff to do their job.

Implications for writers: same only more so

If content is not primarily communication, where does that leave content writers—out in the cold? The message for writers is this.

Your readers are at work. Doing their jobs. In a hurry. Like you. They can't stand to be frustrated by wordy, irrelevant, circuitous, repetitive pages. Most intranet content should not just be telling people stuff: it should be helping them to achieve a particular task. Any content that doesn't help them is probably wasting their time.

The principles for writing intranet content are the same as for web pages—and more so. Always be concise—and on the intranet, more so. F-headlines, F-summaries and F-links are always very important—and on the intranet, more so. And as always, be sure who you are writing for, and why, why, why?

In two respects, intranet content differs fundamentally from web content. First, there's no need to sell or promote services or products: intranet content is directed at colleagues, not clients. They want facts unembellished with promotion. Second, there are no competing sites. You have a captive audience.

Unfortunately these two factors can lull writers into a false sense of security. Intranet illusions and delusions are common, and make for sloppy writing.

Many writers have the illusion that an intranet is private. Not so: it is possible that employees will talk about what they see on the intranet—perhaps to a reporter. Intranet areas with obvious security concerns will restrict access, but the majority of content is open to all employees.

Exquisite judgement is required to get the tone and content right for intranet blogs. The spirit of the intranet should be cheerful and friendly, and some writers are too casual. They behave like hosts at a party, failing to introduce themselves, cracking in-jokes, using inhouse jargon, and chattering on at length. Trouble is, the guests don't all speak the same language, don't necessarily know the hosts, aren't even sure if they are in the right house.

- Jokes are dangerous online, and the intranet is no exception.
- In a large organisation, every business unit has its own jargon, including the names of projects. Briefly explain or expand strange terms at the top every page. (Luckily an intranet can have a comprehensive jargon-buster, a glossary that is the first resort for any employee faced with a mysterious acronym.)
- Friendly chatter wastes space (except in social newsletters and so forth). When people are trying to get a job done, extremely brief content is actually much friendlier than chit-chat.

Some staff think that a search engine takes care of search. But no, an intranet search engine depends entirely on the existence of quality content. If the content is junk, search results will be junk.

I've saved the worst for last. Just as web pages often fail to show where they originate, so do intranet pages. Staff writers of a large organisation exist in a cocoon within the mother ship; they write under the illusion that everyone knows who they are. To some extent, good design can make it obvious where content originates. But frequently, staff visit an intranet page and have no idea where it comes from—which business unit, project, initiative, office, or even country. The solution: as with web content, slip these details into the summary or headline, and make sure every page makes sense out of context.

None of the above problems are exclusive to intranets; it's just that some intranet writers relax the rigorous rules of F-writing, believing they are in a safe family environment.

Three problems of intranet content deserve special attention. They concern shovelware, policy and procedures, and conveyor belt content.

Shoveling recycled paper

Shovelware refers to paper-based documents that are put straight on to web sites without revision to suit the different medium. The rude term implies vast quantities: we're not talking about a good old lean-on-the-shovel shovel, but a mighty front-end loader.

In the early days of the web, most commercial sites were full of marketing shovelware—not a good look. But today, it's intranets that are sinking beneath the weight of recycled paper documents.

Writing about HR portals on intranets in January 2006, Mike Theaker said bluntly:

> [...] many are simply "link farms" to HR forms, benefits provider pages, outdated material, and "shovelware" (paper-based HR policies and practices literally "shoveled" onto an intranet site with no regard to content structure, format, presentation, linkage to complementary information, or ease of use).[150]

Theaker picks on HR intranets because he is an HR consultant—but the same problem looms in every section of the intranet.

When intranets were new, the PDF seemed like a godsend, and anyway, who had time to start rewriting all their business documentation? The long-term plan was conversion to HTML... maybe... some day.

Years later, the shovelware scenario is probably no better on most intranets. There is one hopeful new factor, though: by now, pretty well every employee knows and hates horrible intranet content. Chances are, the content they reject is shovelware.

Realistically, the situation cannot change until everyone who writes for work fashions documents with the intranet (or web) in mind. That day is not at hand. This week, thousands of people have been earnestly writing thousands of important documents that are totally unsuitable for the intranet. Next week, those documents will be shoveled on to the intranet. Thousands of other people will waste time and make errors in their work as they attempt to make sense of shovelware. Many of these documents will remain on the intranet for years and years, unchanged.

It's completely barmy to imagine they will be edited for the intranet after sign-off. Think about it... A consultant is contracted. A committee is formed. These people are highly educated and highly paid. Key stakeholders contribute their ideas. Together, the committee writes a policy document. They are thinking about policy, not readers. Then lawyers study the document and make a few amendments. They are thinking about the law, not readers. The CEO approves the document. Then it is published on the intranet—whether as HTML or PDF is not the point: on the intranet it is virtually unreadable, regardless of format.

At this stage, who in their right mind would suggest tweaking the policy to make it useful, readable or even tolerable to intranet readers? The whole laborious process would have to start all over again.

Slowly but surely, organisations are starting to refashion forms, policies and procedures for intranet publication. But they must often feel they are running on the spot, forever fixing content that could have been written properly from the start.

No, organisations will be stuck with shovelware until they take a giant step for usability, and offer training in F-writing to all staff. The solution has been mentioned several times already: all documents need be structured, written, and edited for intranet publication right from the start.

Is it such a big ask? That a bunch of intelligent, experienced, educated people learn to use plain language, F-headlines, F-summaries and F-links? You wouldn't think so. Nevertheless, it will never happen without comprehension, commitment and funding from top management.

Policy, procedures and instructions

Mike Theaker, who has seen a lot of intranet portals, states:

> Many remain at the first level of enablement – online libraries. Unlocking the potential requires innovative thinking about prospective opportunities to transform not just how work gets done and by whom, but what the work is and what can be accomplished.[151]

That's an exciting thought! But let's not go there right now. First let's re-examine the verbose, jargon-riddled, scrambled documents that purport to be policy and procedures. Managers need to understand policy, so they can make informed decisions. Staff need procedures to do their jobs, so that they know who does what and when.

In general, writers need to be clear about what type of content they are writing. The genre influences structure.

Typical content types on an intranet	
Audio	Long documents
Blogs	Media releases
Calendars & schedules	Memos
CEO letters	News
Dynamic/database content	Newsletters
FAQs	Org. charts
Formal reports	Our org. pages
Forms	Policies
Home page content	Procedures
Images and graphs	Process Flowcharts
Index pages	Tips
Instructions	Top pages (with content)
IT help	Video and Flash
Table of Contents	Wikis

Here's the crucial issue with policies and procedures: they are discrete content types that typically get jumbled up together. The result is that staff go looking for procedures—and are confronted with a wordy policy document that has a few instructions buried deep inside.

Who are you writing for? People trying to do their job. If I'm applying for sick leave, I need a form. Occasionally I also need instructions. If I'm granting sick leave, I need a short skim-readable page reminding me who does what, and in what order—a procedure. If I am newly promoted or need to make a decision on a tricky application, I need to read the policy behind the procedure. To get an overview of a series of interlocking procedures, I need a process flowchart. I need links between these pages of different content types: instructions, procedures, policy and process flowcharts.

What I don't need is a web page that's going to take me 20 minutes to read.

The perils of policy on the intranet

A massive proportion of company policy will be published on the intranet. It is reckless to write policy as if it will only appear on paper.

Policy writing needs to follow all the usual guidelines for good web content: it's not special. Policy needs to be web-proofed, like any other business document. However, policy writers need to be unusually alert.

- Policy deals with matters of principle and hypothetical situations, so writers need to take unusual care to use plain language. It's easy to smother readers with long words, long sentences, the mystifying subjunctive and perpetual passive.
- Other problems of style abound. Watch out for an overload of abstract nouns and jargon, and backloaded (periodic) sentences. Some policy writers use a try-hard school essay style, others go chilly and legalistic.
- Policy needs to be policy only: one web page, one topic, one genre.
- Worldwide, archaic policies are regularly tweaked and recycled without regard for their style. They began ugly and unreadable and they remain ugly and unreadable through multiple revisions. Staff writers should use intranet publication as an excuse to rewrite these legacy documents from scratch.
- Eventually, policy is firm and finalised. But along the way, draft policy is often open for discussion. Writers need to make this fact, and the deadline for responses, crystal clear. A note at the end is not enough. See *6 degrees of participation* in Chapter 14 for ways to genuinely and obviously invite a response.

On the web, the audience includes the general public, so priorities are different. But on the intranet, procedures are what most staff are looking for day to day, rather than policy.

Of course I can't show you examples from intranets, which are private. Most of the screenshots in this chapter are from university web sites. These have something in common with intranets, catering for students and staff off campus.

Let's not identify the university that put the next policy on the web, and presumably on its intranet also. This is one of those unbelievably horrible, ugly, unreadable policies I mentioned above. The screenshot is intentionally illegible—its purpose is merely to convey the *piss-off* feng shui of the page, a sub-text conveyed by format. Tragically, this level of ghastliness is not unusual.

Let me save you the trouble of figuring why it breaks all the rules of F-writing.

- Sub-headlines are too few and they don't stand out.
- Sub-headlines are underlined, so they look like links but are not links.
- Link-text for the only link is incomprehensible and inappropriate: <u>Attachment 1</u>.
- Jargon includes *proration* and *noncompensable*.
- 40% of verbs are passive.
- Average sentence length is 29 words.
- Longest sentences are 51, 58, 60, 73 and 86 words.
- Flesch Reading Ease score is 26.8. (Standard score is 60-70; desirable score for policy is at least 45.[152])

SICK LEAVE POLICY FOR ACADEMIC STAFF MEMBERS

SICK LEAVE POLICY FOR ACADEMIC STAFF MEMBERS

This statement explains the appropriate use of sick leave, as well as the number of sick days available, how they accumulate, the order in which they must be used, when they are eligible for payment, and options at retirement.

Sick leave may be used for illness of, injury to, or need to obtain medical or dental consultation for the staff member, the staff member's spouse, children, parent, or members of the household. A staff member may use sick leave for pregnancy. Following the adoption or birth of a child, sick leave may be used for a period of time, not to exceed twelve weeks, to care for that child. No deduction of time from sick leave is made at a time when a staff member is not expected to furnish regular service to the University.

Effective January 1, 1998, academic and administrative staff members who are participants in the State Universities Retirement System or Federal Retirement System (except for medical residents, postdoctoral research associates, and annuitants in SURS or the Federal Retirement System), and who are appointed for at least 50 percent time to a position for which service is expected to be rendered for at least nine consecutive months, will earn sick leave of 12 work days for each appointment year, the unused portion of which shall accumulate without maximum. If these 12 days are fully utilized in any appointment year, up to 13 additional workdays will be available for extended sick leave in that appointment year, no part of which 13 days shall be cumulative or eligible for payment. No additional sick leave is earned for a summer appointment. In the case of an appointment for less than a full appointment year, the 12 days cumulative and the 13 days noncumulative leave shall be prorated.

In the event the 25 days of earned and extended sick leave described above, or any proration thereof, are exhausted in an appointment year, prior year balances may be used in the following order:

1. Noncompensable: sick leave accrued before 1/1/84 and on or after 1/1/98 will be combined into a single balance of noncompensable sick leave.
2. After noncompensable balances have been exhausted, compensable sick leave earned between 1/1/84 and 12/31/97.
3. Subject to the approval of the chancellor, a full-time academic staff member who has completed at least three full years of service may be granted noncumulative sick leave with full pay for a period not to exceed one-half of the staff member's appointment year (including the sick leave already taken). (In the case of academic staff members of university administration offices, the president will act.) (See Section IX/A – 10 of this manual for information on the University's Family and Medical Leave policy.)

An academic staff member who has not accumulated sufficient sick leave and who has not completed three full years of service may, with the approval of the unit, utilize accumulated and unused vacation and/or request leave without pay.

The Family and Medical Leave Act (FMLA) of 1993 entitles eligible employees up to twelve weeks of unpaid (or paid) leave for illness and certain family reasons. In some cases of catastrophic injury or illness, eligible employees may also apply to use shared benefits from the sick leave pool. (See Section IX/C – 39.1 for a description of the Shared Benefits program for academic staff.)

Short-Term and Part-Time Appointments

Staff members on appointment for less than a full appointment year receive a prorated share of the 12 cumulative and 13 noncumulative days. Staff members on part-time appointment receive the 12 and 13 days at the percentage of their appointment. If the percentage of the appointment changes, the previously accumulated sick leave days must be converted to the equivalent number of days at the new percentage.

Postdoctoral Research Associates, Medical Residents, Graduate Assistants, Annuitants in SURS or the Federal Retirement System, and Other Ineligible Appointments

By special action of the University Planning Council, the following academic staff members are eligible for 13 noncumulative/noncompensable sick leave days per appointment year at the percentage of their appointments. (They are not eligible to receive compensation for accumulated sick leave upon termination of employment.)

1. Postdoctoral research associates and medical residents;
2. Graduate assistants and other students appointed for less than 100% time;
3. Annuitants in SURS or the Federal Retirement System; and
4. Other academic staff members appointed for less than 50% time or for less than a continuous 9-month period.
5. F and J visa holders who have not yet met the substantial presence requirement and are ineligible to participate in SURS.

By contrast, the Johns Hopkins sick leave policy has been F-written from scratch.[153]

It's very easy to read online. Sure, the language is formal, the headline is centred, there's one level of indentation, and some of the sentences are long. Nobody's perfect—but this content should satisfy readers. It looks orderly, implying that the policy will be readable and trustworthy. Bookmarks at the top outline the contents, and links take readers straight to the section they need. Sub-headlines guide us safely through the policy.

> *Back to Table of Contents*   *Printer Friendly Version*   *Effective January 1, 2006*
> **Personnel Policy Manual**
> << Section 14: Sick Leave >>
>
> A. **Definition**
> B. **Earning Sick Leave**
> C. **Taking Sick Leave**
> D. **Transfer of Sick Leave**
> E. **Termination**
>
> ---
>
> A. **Definition**
>
> 1. Sick leave is absence with pay for time lost due to a bona fide non-work related illness or injury, pregnancy, or dental or medical appointments of eligible staff members. In the event that the illness or injury of a staff member's child, spouse, same sex domestic partner, or parent requires the absence of the staff member, such absence may be charged to accrued sick leave as provided in Section C.1. below.
>
> 2. The reason for taking sick leave may qualify as a 'serious health condition' under the Family and Medical Leave policy. If the staff member qualifies and the reason for taking the sick leave qualifies, the Family and Medical Leave policy must be followed. (See Section 15).
>
> B. **Earning Sick Leave**
>
> 1. Full-time staff members who work at least 37.5 hours per week accrue sick leave at the rate of 1 day per month to a maximum of 90 days.
>
> 2. Full-time staff members who work less than 37.5 hours and part-time staff members who work on a regularly scheduled basis accrue sick leave on a pro rata basis to a maximum of 90 days.

The Johns Hopkins policy scores noticeably better on objective readability tests.

- Number of words per sentence is 24.2 words.
- Only 34% of verbs are passive.
- Flesch Reading Ease score is 47.5.

When policy includes procedures

Sometimes policy and procedures really must be on the same intranet page. Possible reasons:

- a very short policy
- a make-do solution while policy is being rewritten
- bureaucratic requirements.

In such cases put the procedures first, or bookmark them at the top. Let's consider sick leave, which can get pretty complicated.

The next document combines policy and procedures. Unfortunately the web page is structured upside down, with policy at the top. Let me stress that this is typical of old HR policies everywhere—impossible to skim-read on paper, and even worse online. I hope the screenshot is illegible even to compulsive cereal box readers.

- The top of the page is solid prose: seven paragraphs without sub-headlines or dot points.
- 45% of verbs are passive.
- Flesch Reading Ease score is unacceptably low at 32.1.

- The reader must scroll to discover that procedures are included at the bottom of the page.
- It has no links to the necessary forms, nor any indication of where they can be found. On an intranet, that would be a serious omission.

The following page of sick leave policy is reproduced from a completely unsuitable paper document, complete with elaborate nesting.[154] Without reading a word you can see saggy-baggy content, drooping way down the page without scoring a point; a narrow font; an elaborate tangle of nested lists… Poor F-readers don't have a chance. The horror, the horror!

Happily, good models are also to be found. The University of Otago structures policy so that it works on a web site. The following web page includes policy and procedures, and bookmarks from the top take staff and students straight to the part they need.[155]

> Sick Leave Policy
> - Purpose
> - Scope
> - References
> - Sick Leave Provisions
> - Actions and Responsibilities
>   - Heads of Departments
>   - Staff Members
>   - Human Resources
>   - Accident Reporting & Rehabilitation Policy
>   - Download Sick/Injury/Domestic Leave Record form

Procedures on the intranet

Procedures will be consulted far more often than policy, and they need to be unequivocally clear. A good template helps writers to keep procedures short and snappy. Otherwise, they'll be tempted to create saggy-baggy pages, explaining far more than is necessary. On a procedures page, don't explain— just link to explanations. Explanations belong in policy, not procedures.

Procedures or instructions should be written in the order they occur. They should be numbered, because a numbered list of steps implies that things must be done in that very order. That's true on paper and online. The guideline happens to be backed by research:[156]

> 15.11: Make action sequences clear
>
> Guideline: When describing an action or task that has a natural order or sequence (assembly instructions, troubleshooting, etc.), structure the content so that the sequence is obvious and consistent.

It's also advisable to write every step of a procedure with the same utterly basic sentence construction, always using active verbs: <Somebody> <does> <something>. That's what staff need to know. Not *something is done*. If you omit the who-does-it information, nothing gets done.

How much information to include is often an issue when writing procedures. The intranet makes those decisions easy: write less. Write the minimum, because procedures are everyday work tools, not teaching devices. The procedure page can link to the relevant policy, which will include more detail, and to the office or person who can help train or explain to a new employee. The intranet should also include a generous section for new staff members. Don't write procedures for your Granny on how to suck eggs. Otherwise the intranet overflows with pointless instructions on how to do what you are already doing. An unfortunate example follows.[157]

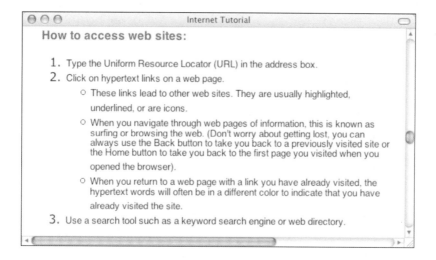

The above page is a tiny fraction of a redundant 3,000-word tutorial on the same level. The subject is *How to access web sites*. But, er, anyone reading the tutorial has already succeeded in accessing a web site! It ends with the words, *Have fun exploring the internet!* It shows no date. Say no more.

Now for some good examples. Notice how they all have a clear, complete headline that not only identifies the topic but also indicates the content type: procedures. On an intranet, it's important to use a consistent format for procedures.

A well constructed template helps both writers and readers. Writers are forced to think clearly, write concisely, and supply the necessary links. Staff soon learn where to look for forms, for instance, saving time and hassle.

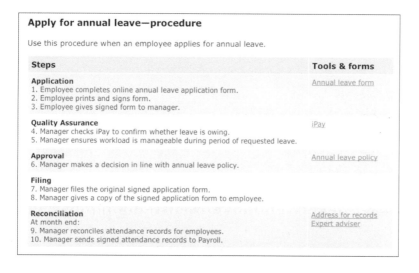

You're wondering... isn't that a table? Yes, and it's OK here. Tables are fine for displaying data. The template helps staff to write procedure steps as if they were data: simple, short, direct, factual.

The next screenshot shows another interesting way to keep policy, procedures and tools separate but readily available.[158] See the mini-menu linking to *Info*, *Steps* and *Tools*? For a single procedure, people can choose to look at only the steps (as displayed), or the background information (such as the policy behind the procedure), or the tools required to carry out the procedure (such as forms). Again, the design forces writers to identify who does what, and keep that information concise and logical.

Notice also the warning in a box at the right: exactly where people need it.

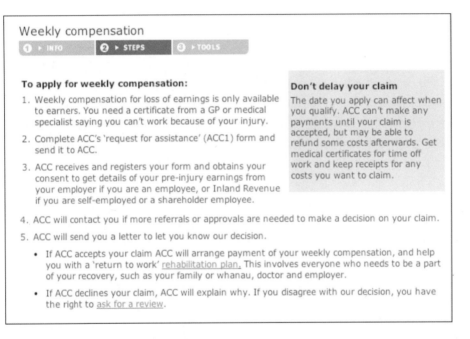

Instructions are simpler than procedures, being addressed to only one person. The distinction is not always clear. For example, in the previous screenshot, the customer is addressed as *you*, but the ACC carries out many of the procedures.

Numbering instructions in their correct sequence is essential. An example from New Zealand Post follows.[159]

Legal dangers of reliance on intranet

A poll run by NETconsent seems to show that:

> nearly 50% of UK organisations could be leaving themselves open to litigation through managing their corporate policies primarily on the intranet.[160]

You might want to take this with a grain of salt, as the statement comes from a commercial vendor, but the poll does highlight the dangers of relying entirely on the intranet to display and manage policy. This is a management issue, and a healthy reminder to policy writers to keep track of all policy pages and delete ROT regularly. The hazards of ROT include legal hazards.

Conveyor-belt content: a web page is not a memo

ROT is an overwhelming problem in most intranets. Sometimes I suspect it is the main reason why intranets are redeveloped.

One reason why intranet ROT becomes such a problem is that staff write web pages as if they were memos. Now, memos hit the desk every day, and one memo often cancels, contradicts or expands on a previous memo. Staff understand this. They read memos in the context of other memos. Memos are not intended to be the last word on any subject: they are part of a running commentary on business and office life.

Memos arrive on a virtual conveyor-belt, and are sent only to the people who need that particular information (or that's the plan). They are usually read on the day they arrive. And they always carry a date.

Many staff writers seem to unconsciously assume that intranet pages are similar to memos. But they are not. Unlike memos, an intranet page should normally be the only, latest, authoritative version of a topic on the entire intranet. Otherwise people get very confused. (Exceptions: news, media releases, newsletters, blog entries, and so forth.)

Memo-writers assume that when information changes, they can fix it by adding a new intranet page, or adding more information to an old intranet page. Suddenly there are five pages on the same topic, all seeming as if they were written that very morning.

From the table below we can deduce some of the unfortunate effects when content writers perceive themselves as memo-writers. The effects can be minimised by supervision, experience, a rigorous workflow system, and smart information architecture.

Memos	**Intranet pages**
Arrive in sequence.	Have no discernible sequence.
Are delivered to those who need them.	Can be viewed by anyone.
Are read on or near the date issued.	Can be read for months or years.
Are read in sequence.	Are read at random if at all.
Are usually read.	May not even be found.
Always carry a date.	Should state when last updated (but often don't).
May be contradicted by later memos.	Should be the only, latest, authoritative version on the intranet.
Are followed by many other memos.	Should have content updated (not extra pages added).
Once issued, are never corrected or reissued.	Should be corrected when information changes or goes out of date.
Can safely use relative expressions of time, e.g. *today*, *next Tuesday*.	Must always use specific dates.
Can safely use names of people.	Must usually state roles or generic contact addresses instead of names, because employees move and change jobs.
Can safely use relative expressions of place, e.g. *in our office*.	Must name the place, e.g. *in ABC's Edinburgh office*.

Writing for the social intranet

Now that so many organisations have social media on their intranet,[161] more staff are writing more content than ever before—blogging, micro-blogging, discussing, commenting and collaborating on writing tasks. It seems staff feel comparatively comfortable writing in this environment, which seems rather casual and spontaneous.

Inevitably, the quality of intranet writing is of concern to management. Intranet managers are looking to clarify governance, impose standards, and provide training for the many staff who now generate internal communications.

All the advice in this book is as relevant to social intranet content as it is to one-way, top-down web content. Staff may at first be surprised at a call for standards, but as the social intranet matures, they tend to see the need and to embrace training.

17.

E-government: because you must

Good web content for government sites has its own flavour, and that flavour needs to be in sync with e-government guidelines and public service values. Special dangers for government content writers are cold bureaucratic language, a lack of engagement with the public, ghastly gobbledegook, space-wasting layout conventions, labels instead of headlines, the inhouse-outhouse syndrome, and (you guessed) documents written without the web in mind.

E-government rolls on

The idea of e-government has been floating around since at least 1994. Today it is a hot topic in pretty well every country with internet infrastructure, and by 1999 even China was on board, declaring a *Year of Government Online*.

The Chinese Central Government's Official Web Portal is fairly typical in giving links to news, state and local government sites, official publications, laws and regulations, citizen services and (on the English language site) services for non-residents.[162]

However, concepts of e-government vary considerably according to each country's political system and internet coverage, and they are changing rapidly. The possibilities have multiplied with Web 2.0 technology, which brings various social and political repercussions. At the very least, e-government includes putting most government-to-citizen services online and integrating government services, leading to more efficiency and transparency. Some countries' visions for e-government emphasise citizen involvement and satisfaction, others the potential of e-government to reform government itself and reduce corruption in public service. Some countries see e-governance as a sub-set of IT development, or the driving force behind a new prosperity. Some focus on the digital divide, some on inclusiveness. Achieving so many goals takes time, and in that time, things change.

Way back in 2004, e-government developments were moving *from modernisation to transformation*, according to Paul Timmers, Head of Unit for eGovernment, European Commission.[163]

What does this mean for content writers? In your country, there won't be any confusion about what e-government means: simply read your own government's strategy. You will quickly see that some aspects of that strategy are directly relevant to you as you sit down to write documents bound for public sector web sites.

In the Australian e-government strategy a key concept is *connected and responsive government*.[164] The US E-Government Strategic Vision has a different slant:[165]

- Citizen-centered, not bureaucracy-centered;
- Results-oriented; and
- Market-based, actively promoting innovation.

Public service values: the writer's touchstone

All over the world, government agencies are expected to follow certain values. They are not the values of businesses or voluntary organisations. At times, distinctions blur, and some government agencies are expected to make a profit. Nevertheless, these values should distinguish public service sites from other sites.

As an example, let's look at New Zealand's e-government strategy and what it implies for writers.[166] There's no mistaking the public sector's obligations as stated in the strategy's key messages.

> **Key messages**
> - E-government affects everyone
> - E-government builds trust
> - E-government is collaborative
> - E-government delivers results
> - E-government engages people
> - E-government puts people first
>
>

New Zealand's values are not unusual. The e-government document explains their relevance to government web sites.

Equity means being fair and reasonable. People have no choice about where to go to get government services. Only one agency issues passports and one collects taxes. This places an onus on agencies to make their websites widely accessible. Public Service websites that disable users for whatever reason are not equitable.

Integrity means being whole and incorruptible. A website with integrity will be secure from interference, up to date, complete and authoritative. It will also be capable of being preserved as a complete record of what was available publicly at some point in time.

Trust and integrity go hand in hand. But trust goes further. For example, a site worthy of trust will provide appropriate authentication and security where personal information is accessed online, will not store cookies without explaining why and be free from errors (like spelling mistakes, wrong dates or incorrect information).

Economy means using public resources in a way that is efficient, effective and fiscally economical.

The main focus of the New Zealand standards is to ensure information and services are equally accessible to all users, are trustworthy, and reflect the core values of the public service. A glance at those values reminds us why standards are needed. There are practical, moral and fiscal reasons for the standards. There's an ideal. There's a payoff.
And the same is true for numerous other countries.

Guidelines and standards for government writers

Many countries have progressed beyond guidelines to standards for government sites. It's probably safe to say that these guidelines and standards are all based on those of W3C.[167] For countries using ABC languages, they don't vary hugely. Few governments look to increase or complicate the standard standards, though they are certainly free to select, omit, paraphrase and tinker.

On an official web site somewhere lie a handful of guidelines that apply to government writers in your country. They'll be jumbled up with others that concern designers, developers and content managers. Everything writers need to know matches the advice elsewhere in this book. It's just that for government writers, the 'advice' may be mandatory.

Which standards apply to content writers?

Your guidelines almost certainly list the minimum requirements for content: the documents that every government web site must include. Read and comply. At this stage, by the way, the risk of anything being left off a government web site is smaller than the risk of including thousands of redundant documents.

Let's look at a handful of standards that you'll find, in some form or other, in a typical e-government strategy document. No surprises here.[168]

- **Provide a text equivalent** for every non-text element (for example "alt", "longdesc", or in element content).
- **Use the clearest and simplest language** appropriate for a site's content. This includes writing clear and accurate headings and link descriptions; and writing link phrases that make sense when read out of context, alone or as part of a series of links.
- **Divide large blocks of information** into more manageable groups where natural and appropriate.
- **Place distinguishing information at the beginning** of headings, paragraphs, lists, etc.
- **Agency sites provide contact details** for specific policy or services.
- **Links to non-HTML documents** should indicate the document version, size and type, and any other aspect of the document that people should know about before deciding to download or access it.

The next guideline is a little unusual. It is sad that this needed saying. It's an acknowledgement that web sites tend to balloon with bad content. It's another way of stating the prime message of this book: *Web writing is business writing. Business writing is web writing.*

> A plan is expected to be in place to ensure material on the website is accurate and up-to-date.
>
> Online publishing must be fully integrated into the agency's information processes. For example, you have a workflow process for approving and publishing online material. This applies to any document intended to be posted on the web (principally for download purposes) as well as straight content.
>
> It is imperative that as much effort as possible be given to the management of style, quality and correctness of content on a par with any other medium (such as printed matter) an agency utilises for disseminating information.

Compliance with legislation

Staff writers risk forgetting that web content is not only visible to the whole world, but dreadfully durable. They have the difficult task of writing in a friendly, approachable way—and never transgressing the law. Fortunately, the legal staff of government agencies will give advice on request. All content writers, but especially public service employees, should be aware of relevant legislation in the following areas:

- official information
- human rights
- disability
- equal opportunity
- privacy
- public records
- freedom of information
- intellectual property and copyright
- consumer protection
- fair trading
- education
- and other areas.

Danger zones for government content writers

Don't get me wrong: there is a massive amount of extremely useful government web content out there. However, expectations rise even faster than the quality of web sites.

It's common, even healthy, to moan and groan about the public service—forgetting how privileged we are to even have such a thing. We are so quick to find fault, we forget how much progress has been made in e-government, and in such a short time.

All the same, I must point out the worst traps for government content writers, because bad habits breed bad habits. Check your own site: are you blind to its faults?

The most common disasters on public service sites are discussed below. They can all be fixed if writers are on the alert, and honest about what is under their noses.

Danger: forgetting about the web

If you're a government employee, you are doomed every time you write a work document without the web in mind. You're highly disadvantaged because you inherit a crushing culture of writing conventions that look ridiculous on a web site. A nifty mind-flip is required, well before you start typing.

So what have you been working on today? A report, perhaps? How will it look when somebody decides to put it on a web site? It's far too long, isn't it? And those boring generic headers may not make sense on the screen. And dear oh dear, look at those endless dot points within dot points within dot points. Luckily, web-proofing the report will be a small job—now that you've remembered.

A pretty typical government document is shown on the next page. Quite apart from the style, six obvious faults could have been fixed if the writer had just thought 'web' at the time of writing:[169]

- the non-informative heading *Introduction*
- *this booklet* repeated many times: this is not a booklet
- the long, long stretch between subheadings (535 words, more than one screen in a readable size font)
- footnotes using non-clickable superscript numbers instead of links; to find the footnotes we have to scroll down 17 (17!!!) screens
- *will be issued shortly*—ROT alert and credibility challenge: the foreword is dated 2002
- *Appendix*: this is an anomalous word to use on the web.

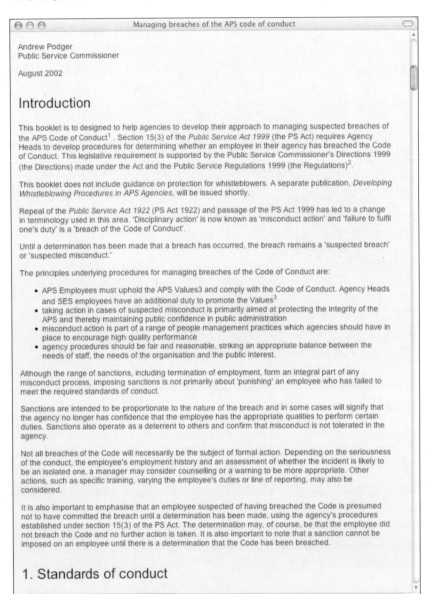

Danger: cold bureaucratic language

Remember, government sites are supposed to engage with the public. At its most primitive level, that means using the word *you*. But so often, it-language is used: snooty, abstract and hard to understand. The content in the next screenshot shows what I mean.[170] It certainly fails the *so-what?* test. And did I hear someone mention the word *equity*?

It's impossible to tell from the parsimonious heading *Accommodation* or from the menu that this page is supposed to help asylum seekers to claim support as they seek accommodation. These people are, by definition, under extreme psychological stress, displaced and poor. They may not be able to speak English well, either.

What destitute asylum seekers need is a way to contact someone who will help. But if you click the blue word at the top, *applying*, nothing happens: it's not a link.

The writer is certainly not relating to asylum seekers, the presumed audience. The content on this page is probably lifted from a manual for the staff of the Immigration and Nationality Directorate. It belongs on an intranet (or in a desk drawer), not a web site. It is highly inappropriate for the intended audience of destitute asylum seekers. In fact, for them, the language is more than unfriendly: it is cruel.

Danger: ghastly gobbledegook

The previous screenshot ended with the sentence *Further information is outlined in Policy bulletin 31*. This is the point at which pompousness becomes nonsense, as it tends to. I mean, you don't outline information: you either give information, or outline policy. This is the kind of gobbledegook that public servants slip into with horrifying ease.

Below is a nasty example of gobbledegook from the US Department of Justice.[171] Look at all the jargon and buzz words. The Flesch Reading Ease score for the first paragraph is 17. That's extremely low, when standard documents should score about 60 to 70.

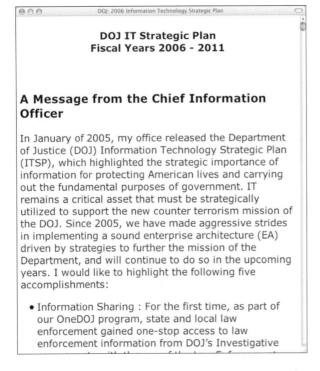

A public servant doubtless wrote or edited Governor Spitzer's first State of the State address, and in January 2007 there it was on the New York State home page.[172] Most of the speech was fine—but did Governor Spitzer himself understand the following sentence? I'm afraid I don't.

> As human capital emerges as the fulcrum of job creation, we must provide
> our schools with the necessary investment, reform and accountability to
> adapt to this new paradigm.

For some reason, education departments tend to be among the worst offenders with gobbledegook.[173]

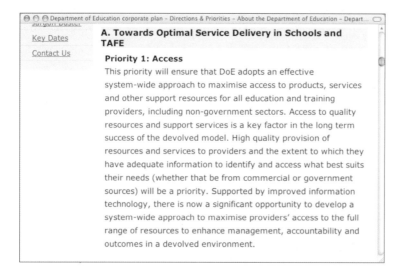

Readability statistics for the above paragraph are damning:
- Average words per sentence 31.2
- Flesch Reading Ease 18.00.

Notice certain classic errors of style that are typical of bad policy writing.
1. Verbs turned into nouns, so that a second or even third verb is necessary:
   adopts an effective system-wide approach to maximise = maximises.
2. Redundant words:
   there is now a significant opportunity to = we can now
3. Periodic sentences, i.e. sentences that make no sense until the full stop. The third sentence has a 35-word subject culminating in the anticlimactic verb phrase:
   will be a priority.
4. Meaningless words and weasel words: *effective, range of, enhance.*

Not surprisingly, this short passage even has a grammar mistake, namely a dangling modifier at the start of the last sentence. Why isn't that surprising? Because long sentences produce grammar mistakes: that's a given.

I suspect that fear of getting caught out or challenged is the reason for much bad government writing. Canada's Hazardous Materials Information Review Commission demonstrates this in the next screenshot.[174] They waste the first three paragraphs on wordy disclaimers, when the really interesting material is the table you can glimpse at the bottom. The killer is the second paragraph, which is a single 56-word, triple negative sentence: this writer was extremely nervous.

MSDS Violations

The WHMIS trade secret exemption mechanism administered by the Hazardous Materials Information Review Commission requires that the MSDS accompanying a claim be reviewed against the requirements of the *Hazardous Products Act* and *Controlled Products Regulations*. The statistical information shown below outlines the Commission's findings of MSDS non-compliance for the fiscal years 2003–2004, 2004–2005 and 2005–2006.

While the MSDSs reviewed by the Commission cannot be said to represent a random sample of all such documents in use in Canada (estimated to be in the order of some 750,000), there seems little reason to conclude that our findings should not be considered as broadly indicative of the state of MSDS compliance in general.

The term "violation occurrence" is used in the quantification of the Commission's MSDS review findings. For example, a missing acute lethality value for a hazardous ingredient counts as one violation occurrence. Similarly, if two such values associated with the same ingredient are undisclosed, or if a value has not been disclosed for two hazardous ingredients, there would be two violation occurrences counted in each case.

In general, it is important to note that the amount of information "available" for disclosure on a MSDS can vary substantially. For example, a LD_{50}(oral) value is more likely, compared to an LC_{50}(inhalation) value, to have been determined for a given hazardous ingredient.

Aggregate multi-year MSDS violation statistics have been published for several years in the Commission's Annual Report.

Violation Category	Number of Violation Occurrences		
	2005–2006	2004–2005	2003–2004
Hazardous ingredients (See Note 1)			
Chemical identity not disclosed	72	50	51
Chemical identity incorrectly disclosed	53	4	24
CAS registry number not disclosed	40	30	27
Concentration not disclosed	64	53	64

    If you are worried about being misinterpreted, just put an explicit link to a disclaimer elsewhere. You can cover your back without wrecking the page for readers.

    Guess what? The CEO of New Zealand's largest government agency, the Ministry of Social Development, uses plain language all the time, deliberately.[175] He says what he means. He means what he says. We understand what he means. I reckon if plain language is good enough for him, it's good enough for all government employees.

> **MSD Chief Executive condemns NZCCSS report**
>
> Ministry of Social Development Chief Executive Peter Hughes today challenged the New Zealand Council of Christian Social Services to use its influence constructively rather than destructively.
>
> "Their report released on care and protection does nothing to make a difference to the lives of New Zealand children. It is highly selective. It is unbalanced. It is unfair, " said Peter Hughes.
>
> "Every day, every week Child, Youth and Family staff do their very best for New Zealand's most vulnerable families. Despite the assertions made in their report, the NZCCSS does not have a monopoly on caring.
>
> "It is easy to sit on the sidelines and bag Child, Youth and Family. We would all get a lot further if the Council were to get behind the staff and back them to win.
>
> "I am staggered that despite the numeruous forums open to them, the Council has at no stage raised with me the concerns outlined in the report. Raising them in the media leaves me very cynicial about their motivation.
>
> "I am meeting with the council early next month. In the meantime I invite them to roll up their sleeves and support the Ministry and Child, Youth and Family in the very difficult work that we do," said Peter Hughes.
>
> For further information: Bronwyn Saunders, Chief Media Advisor, ph 04 916 3447 or 029 916 3887 or bronwyn.saunders002@msd.govt.nz

Danger: layout based on shoddy print conventions

A particular occupational hazard for government writers is amateurish formatting. Strange, ugly print documents are common in government circles, and nobody cares. But when the same klunky layout is replicated on web sites, that seriously interferes with usability. Among the problems are:

- tables used for text layout
- layout in nested lists instead of an F-pattern
- underlining for emphasis (not links)
- centred headlines
- headlines in block capital letters
- saggy-baggy, space-wasting content.

The first three problems were discussed in Chapter 8, *The feng shui of online content*. We have seen how centred headlines leave a hole in the F, and are literally not noticed by a significant number of online readers. It is well known that headlines presented in block capitals, whether in print or online, always slow readers down.

So let's look at the last factor, saggy-baggy content. This refers to content written as if scrolling were a non-issue. Saggy-baggy content often has multiple labels or headers jumbled at the top, and long skinny text. Consider the following page on *Working in the UK*.[176] Precious space is frittered away on a list of the countries whose citizens do *not* need a permit to work in the UK. People must scroll even to get to the end of the list, let alone read some useful content.

The Federal Transit Administration uses an ugly, saggy-baggy old template for inviting tenders online.[177] It duplicates certain lines and wastes heaps of space. Centred content breaks the sacred F-pattern and slows readers down.

And look at their numbering system: II.1.1). It just won't do. If you are producing content that looks like this, throw out those old templates and start afresh.

> Tenders or requests to participate must be sent to: As in above-mentioned contact point(s).
>
> I.2) MAIN ACTIVITY OR ACTIVITIES OF THE CONTRACTING ENTITY:
>
> **SECTION II: OBJECT OF THE CONTRACT**
>
> II.1) DESCRIPTION
>
> II.1.1) Title attributed to the contract by the contracting entity:
>
> Sourcing and logistical provision for security queue measurement for BAA Group Wide.
>
> II.1.2) Type of contract and location of works, place of delivery or of performance:

Saggy-baggy text is also created when writers explain what links are and invite them to click, instead of letting the link-text do the work. The following screenshots convey virtually the same amount of information. Two sag, the third one doesn't.

The US Inland Revenue Service, by contrast, packs useful information into the page from the very top.[178] F-readers can see at a glance that the page is well organised and rich in content, with generous white space to rest the eyes. It passes the serenity test with flying colours.

> **Tax Fraud Alerts**
>
>
>
> IRS Wants You to Know About Schemes, Scams and Cons
> "If it sounds too good to be true, it probably is!" Seek expert advice before you subscribe to any scheme that offers instant wealth or exemption from your obligation as a United States Citizen to pay taxes. Buying into a tax evasion scheme can be very costly.
>
> Corporate Fraud
> Criminal Investigation is involved in most of the regional corporate fraud task forces because of our financial investigative expertise. Also, corporate fraud frequently involves violations of the Internal Revenue Code (IRC) through falsification of corporate and individual tax returns and CI has exclusive investigatory jurisdiction over criminal violations of the IRC.
>
> Money Laundering
> Money laundering is a very complex crime involving intricate details, often involving numerous financial transactions and financial outlets throughout the world. Criminal Investigation has the financial investigators and expertise that is critical to "follow the money trail."
>
> General Tax Fraud
> The efforts of Criminal Investigation are directed at the portion of American taxpayers who willfully and intentionally violate their known legal duty of voluntarily filing income tax returns and/or paying the correct amount of income, employment, or excise taxes. These individuals pose a serious threat to tax administration and the American economy.
>
> Abusive Return Preparer
> Taxpayers should be very careful when choosing a tax preparer. You should be as careful as you would in choosing a doctor or a lawyer.
>
> Abusive Tax Schemes
> Abusive tax scheme originally took the structure of abusive domestic and foreign trust arrangements. However, these schemes have evolved into sophisticated arrangements that take advantage of the financial secrecy laws of some foreign jurisdictions and the availability of credit/debit cards issued from offshore financial institutions.

Danger: labels instead of headlines

You know this is bad. Government employees use endless templates with generic labels such as *Introduction, Background*, and *Conclusions*. I'm not suggesting you chuck these out, because they give documents a recognisable structure. But use an unobtrusive style for those labels and get into the habit of adding a proper headline, so that a skim-reader can make sense of the document—whether on paper or online.

Danger: the inhouse-outhouse syndrome

Lack of identity is a web-wide problem, but it is strangely common on government sites. The British are notoriously culpable. Site after site uses a cute logo with no clue that this is a government site, let alone a UK government site.

Why? Some government agencies live in a world of their own, and think the whole world knows who and where they are. Employees talk to each other cosily and everything happens inhouse. Or are government agencies coy about showing they are part of the public service, because of pressure to make a profit or an attempt to move with the times? Beats me. Trouble is, when documents are so inward-looking, they really belong in an outhouse. Ultimately, to withhold information that identifies the site owner is annoying at best, and can seem arrogant.

The UK's Rural Payments Agency is a classic example.[179] Apart from the gov.uk URL (which many people never notice—nor should they have to) only the footer *crown copyright* hints that the site originates in a country with a royal family. Bureaucratic jargon like *providing a range of services in support of the department's objectives* is another sign of an inward-looking page.

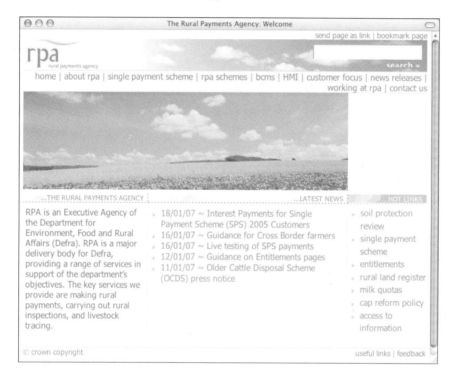

The next screenshot shows a simple page that is outward looking, useful and clear.[180] The readers' needs are central, as they should be. The page shows all current government consultations in Scotland 36 as at 17 January 2007. Links go to the full document and contact information. In the last column is the consultation period for each document, and—oh joy—this page is constantly updated.

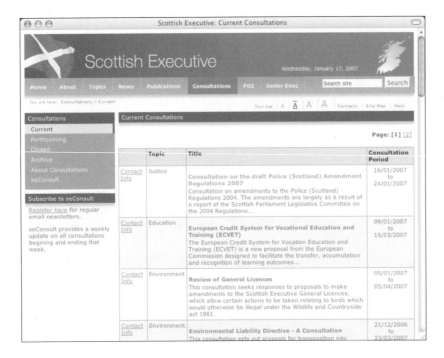

The bad examples cited in this chapter violate e-government standards left, right and centre. They most certainly do not use the clearest and simplest language appropriate for a site's content. They don't have clear and accurate headlines and link descriptions; they don't subdivide information into manageable groups... I'll stop there; it's too disheartening.

The bad examples also violate basic public sector values. Their communication style is unfair and unreasonable, lacks integrity, and extravagantly wastes public money. They don't engage people or build trust, and they certainly do not put people first.

The good examples show there is absolutely no need to fill government sites with pompous bureaucratese. When government writers consider the needs of the reader, standards are hardly necessary. Once writers have the basic skills of F-writing, simple commonsense and courtesy produce documents that satisfy both the public and legal requirements.

Here's to government web sites with simple, original, people-centred content. It's our money they're spending.

So how are we doing?

E-government has certainly moved ahead since its perilous beginnings, when many politicians thought it referred to political campaigning on the web. How far? A few facts follow from Brown University's 2006 annual review of state and federal e-government in the United States.[181]

- 54% of federal sites (up from 44% in 2005) and 43% of state sites (up from 40% in 2005) meet the World Wide Web Consortium (W3C) disability guidelines.
- 77% of state and federal sites have services that are fully executable online (73% in 2005).
- 82% of government sites give the public access to one or more databases.
- 1% of government sites are accessible through personal digital assistants, pagers, or mobile phones (no change from 2005).
- 64% of government sites are written at the 12th grade reading level: much too difficult for the average American, who reads at 8th grade level or lower.

Top-rated U.S. federal websites are Firstgov.gov, Department of Agriculture, and Department of Housing and Urban Development.

Different countries use different indicators to measure progress in e-government. For example, the U.K. excels in this indicator compared with other EU countries:[182]

- % basic public services for citizens fully available online

But the U.K. lags on these measures:

- % basic public services for enterprises fully available online
- % of population using e-Government services
- % of enterprises using e-Government services.

It's one thing to put services online. It's quite another to make them so efficient and usable that using e-government services becomes the norm.

This does happen, I'm happy to say. Many online services are heavily used: on government web sites we can file taxes, check refund status, renew drivers licences and vehicle registration, order hunting and fishing licenses, check the traffic, and search laws and pending legislation. There is every opportunity for online government services to multiply—and improve.

Everyone's blogging, why can't we?

That was the headline summarising a panel discussion on GOVIS 2007, New Zealand's public sector IT conference.[183] A sense of urgency came through: blogging by government mandarins was essential in order to attract keen young people into the public service. There should be no more hiding behind the office door. Young people expect direct messages from the top, and expect to be able to answer back. However, it hasn't happened yet!

> Attendees scratched their heads to think of any government agencies that have actually embraced blogging.

Discussing Web 2.0 for the public service, Jason Ryan is clear that blogs are just the inevitable way people will want to interact with government.[184] I think he should have the last word on the subject of e-government.

And, to be clear, this is **not** about technology: it is about developing solutions for social and governance challenges. The fact that it is happening on the web is just a reflection of the way that our culture is changing. In ten years time, most Kiwis will regard the Internet with the same sense of awe that they regard the television. The question we need to ask is, do we have to wait that long to deliver Govt2.0?

18.

Commercial content: trust me

The web was first perceived as a medium of communication. Sounds obvious? So for commercial sites, that meant a medium for communicating their marketing message. Gradually the nature of the web changed: for many businesses, web sites became the primary way of doing business—and in the 21st century the web has an infinite number of commercial uses. And along the way, a monumental change occurred in advertising, the most radical change in 50 years. It happened on the web, and it is the way of the web.

Here's how Rick Murray, PR expert and president of Edelman's Me2Revolution, puts it:

> The practice of (addiction to) top-down, center-out, one-way communications has been around since long before anyone reading this report was born. In its day, it was both efficient and influential. [...] The problem is that this approach ignores an unprecedented sense of empowerment among all audiences, particularly consumers and employees. [...] The traditional recipient of our messaging is now adding a whole new dimension by getting involved. They may lead the conversation; or they may jump-in on conversations others have started. Either way, they're in it for the long haul, and any corporation that ignores audience participation and leadership is [...] going to fall flat.[185]

Maybe that's over the top, but then again, Murray works in PR. Social software tools (including blogs, podcasts, social bookmarking sites, social networks, wikis, games and widgets) promote collaboration, involvement, and decentralisation of authority. Even the publishing tools associated with content management systems can be called social software: the job of writing and publishing online content is now shared by many staff, and central control of content has largely been relinquished. According to Michael Wiley, there's no escape:

> Most companies are still organized around a command-and-control structure in which consumers are talked to, not with. Today, only 8% of the Fortune 500 have an active business blog. While the vast majority of brands remain on the sidelines, likely overcome by fear of the unknown, a false belief that they still control their messages, or other forms of inertia, their advocates and detractors are discussing them and in many cases, launching their own forums for discussion.[186]

Overall, on commercial sites we have seen some deep and radical changes:
- from splash-Flash to information on the home page
- from cake-words to keywords
- from remoteness (remember when businesses didn't even give contact details?) to immediate, visible communication between experts and the public
- from mere branding to control by customers
- from passive customers to collaborators and advocates
- from product sales online to product development online.

This mind-shift has an impact on everyone who writes commercial content. Marketing copywriters have to face up to this brave new world. Everything they learned about persuasion 10 years ago is useless on the web. There's no future for the slightest hint of insincerity online. Unless they shift gear, their very job is on the line.

Adidas.com.uk has an old style home page: pure branding.

Reebok.com has a new style home page: brand plus content! Here's news, an auction for a good cause, product recall notice, link to careers, history… Audience participation is part of the deal.

Persuasion is not brainwashing

Amazon.com had the right idea from day one. Amazon doesn't just process orders; it persuades people to purchase more products. Amazon succeeded through brilliant strategy, technology, psychology and content. You won't find marketing hype on their site, but the features typical of persuasive technology:
- a dynamic site producing pages tailored to the user
- a huge, scalable, always up-to-date database behind the scenes
- non-invasive personalisation
- input from customers
- easily achieved goals
- purchase broken down into small steps
- a site where everything works perfectly.

Persuasive technology

All web sites exist to persuade, otherwise they have no point. In other words, they aim to change people's attitudes or behaviours or both, without coercion or deception.[187]

Businesses have a long, strong history of traditional advertising, which some find hard to turn their backs on. But to persuade web users, other methods are needed. For example, on eBay and TradeMe, buyers and sellers evaluate each other after completing a transaction. This motivates people to be honest, quick and polite in their interactions. In turn that generates trust.

One thing is sure: content was never more important than right now. High quality, accurate, fresh content is persuasive in itself: it persuades people that a company has expertise, and is to be trusted.

Staff writers need to know some basics about persuasive technology. To write persuasive web content, B.J. Fogg advises:
- reduce complex behaviour to simple tasks or steps
- guide people through a process
- offer suggestions at opportune moments
- let people know what point they have reached in a process
- offer praise and encouragement
- assume a role of authority.

Interaction on a web site provides a winning combination of anonymity and community. Writers should be aware that they are addressing one person at a time—and that those individuals combine to form their own virtual community. People can experiment with new behaviours and attitudes in the privacy of their own computers. However, they enjoy a sense of not being alone: they are more motivated to change if they can observe others doing the same, compare themselves with others, compete with others, cooperate with others, or be publicly recognised by others.

A form that persuades

The following form inspires confidence for many reasons. It persuaded me to continue with my purchase.

Naturally when ordering online, people expect to surrender personal details: it's a deal, and the purchaser gets something in return. Writers need to remember the balance is delicate: don't ask for more information than is obviously necessary. If some information is not essential, explain why you want it, or give people a choice. Nielsen Norman Group handles this aspect well, as we'd expect.

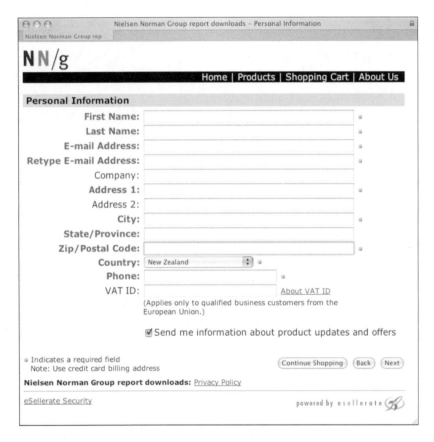

Some persuasive features on the above form are technical, some involve a content writer, and all were tested for usability no doubt. First let's consider the technological persuaders.

- The HTML page title (*Nielsen Norman Group report downloads– Personal Information*) confirms that I'm on the right page.
- The URL seems logical and is secure:

https://store6.esellerate.net/store/checkout/PersonalInfo.aspx
- The fields are perfectly aligned: the page passes the serenity test.
- *eSellerate security* reassures me about security.

A skilled form writer had a hand in the following persuasive factors in the content.
- The content is logically organised with fields in a natural sequence.
- There's a link to a Privacy Policy on every page of the transaction.
- I can immediately see that VAT ID doesn't apply to me, but information about VAT is available in the right place for those who need it.
- People can choose not to receive promotions.
- There's no superfluous information on the page.
- The purchase process is logically subdivided into discrete steps, one per page: ordering, personal information, billing information, purchase confirmation, and a printable purchase receipt.
- People can opt out or return to shopping at any point: they don't feel trapped.

You think it's easy to create a page like this? It should be, since there are excellent models around to copy. And yet bad forms abound, forms that frighten people away in mid-transaction.

Why people visit commercial sites

Before writing commercial content, writers need to ask some basic questions. Be sure you know why people are likely to visit the page you are about to write. They might visit to:
- comparison shop for prices and features
- get product information—facts, images, prices, sales outlets, reviews and tips
- get background information about the company.

Their goal may be even simpler, for example to:
- find a job
- meet people
- get expert advice on specific topics
- make bookings
- order products online
- play games
- download free stuff.

They don't visit commercial sites to be suckered by a cool brand or to witness a display of feathers.

Persuasive and non-persuasive pages

It's a funny thing, but the more a writer strains to persuade on the web, the less likely they are to succeed. Take a look at two web pages with similar purposes, and note just how many ways the writer can get things wrong—or right. It boils down to this question: is the writer addressing a reader or a reflection in the mirror?

In the example from Mercury Energy, the entire first screenful of content is wasted.[188] Below the banner, the writer squanders nine chances to get to the point. And apart from the URL, there's no sign of where this company operates.

9 ways to lose readers

1. First headline is just a label: Price Plans

2. Second headline ditto: Price Plan Rebate

3. First paragraph gives no information. (In fact it makes me feel nervous: so if I don't choose this special plan, you will overcharge me? Charming.)

   Our amazing new service will make sure that each year your Mercury Energy electricity bills are as small as they can be.

4. Second paragraph rephrases the identical marketing hype—and we're still none the wiser:

   Mercury Energy's new Price Plan Rebate service is designed to make sure you never pay more for your Mercury Energy residential electricity than you have to.

5. On the right a truism:

   AS YOUR LIFE CHANGES, YOUR ELECTRICITY USAGE CAN TOO.

6. Now an image of a 1960s light shade—what's the point? Words:

   Price Plan Rebate, only from Mercury Energy.

7. Now they invite us to stop and admire their 30-second TV advert. Why would we?

8. Not again! They invite us to view the 45-second version of the TV advert.

9. More hype (a claim that the plan is unique).

Finally, 14 cm from the top of my screen, some facts!

That page tells us *Mercury Energy is amazing* nine times before bothering to explain why. The more this is asserted, the less likely we are to care—let alone believe. Another problem with the page is that customers cannot compare two plans from the same supplier: instead, the plan is isolated on a separate page. And strangely, nowhere in the content can a reader click to start registering for this particular plan: no action is possible from this page, except getting information and registering for *My Account*. The underlying concept is that potential customers will passively read the company's self promotion, then initiate action without any help.

By contrast, the page from TXU Energy knows what potential customers need.[189] TXU strives to meet the reader's needs with plenty of facts and ample opportunity for action.

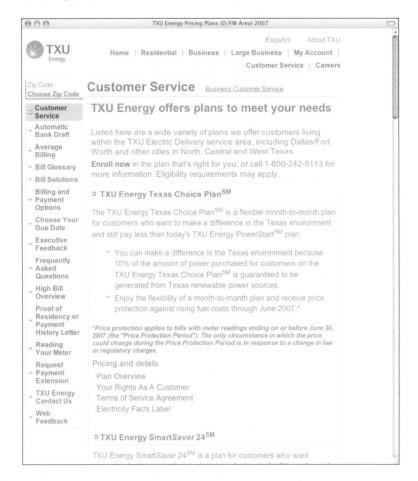

Many features serve to persuade, because the customer is in control.
- The page has a real headline: *TXU Energy offers plans to meet your needs*.
- A single page provides fact-packed summaries of eight plans, enabling comparisons.
- Comparisons between plans are actively encouraged.
- Facts are only lightly sprinkled with cake-words (for example, *enjoy*).
- Top of the page summarises the content and identifies the area the company serves.
- Top of the page offers a link enabling people to *Enroll now* in the plan of choice.
- Reassuring links to *Your Rights as a Customer* and *Terms of Service Agreement* are offered with every plan.
- The meaning of *Price protection* is explained.
- Links lead customers to the prices and other details of each plan.

Language and persuasion

The web has changed a core advertising belief in persuasive language. Yale's list of persuasive words was widely consulted, and for all I know still is—off the web. Even now, you can buy Ken McEvoy's e-book *Make Your Site Sell!* based on the old premise that some words are intrinsically, generically, globally persuasive.[190] Many of these are cake-words—counter-productive online, because keywords matter more. Don't believe a word of this:

> Use hot words (within the tolerance level of your target), especially in your headlines... free profit new now secret easy save guarantee today first how to amazing facts...

You can see McEvoy's approach is worlds away from the reality of current internet users. Would you search in Google using words like *new, now, secret, easy, today* or *amazing*? No? Then these are not keywords. Moreover, they are like red flags to any reader alert to scams.

Contrast Gerry McGovern's advice about language.[191]

> What's the number one mistake organizations make? (The bigger the organization, the more likely they are to make this mistake.) Thinking that what they care about is what their customers care about. Thinking that the words they like to use are the words their customers like to read.
>
> In the United States, over 80 times more people search for "cheap flights" than for "low fares." In the United Kingdom, 6,500 times more people search for "cheap flights" than for "low fares". No, that's not a typo. It is 6,500 times more! "Low fares" is what the airline industry likes to say. "Cheap flights" is customer language. This an extremely common mistake organizations make on the Web: assuming that their words are their customers' words. Never, ever assume that.

However, McEvoy's book does contain good advice for writers of commercial content.

> [...] and the hottest word of all...YOU! [...] The higher the "YOU" to "ME" ratio in your copy, the better; it should be 5:1.
>
> Make your copy one-to-one, conversational, friendly and personalized.
>
> Cut, chop, axe and prune. Chop every useless word. Then chop some more.

Overcoming distrust of commercial sites

Dot com! Dot com! Alarm! Alarm!

From the start, credibility studies have revealed that commercial sites are far less likely to be trusted than sites of non-profit organisations or government agencies. Just having a *.com* instead of an *.org* URL racks up suspicion. So commercial sites start from a disadvantage: they have to prove they are trustworthy.

Public faith in commercial sites is sure to wane and wax in sync with new scams and improved security measures. Credibility will always be a big deal. For example, in 2005, Princeton Survey Research Associates interviewed 1,501 adult US-based internet users.[192] An astonishing 90% had made changes to their behaviour due to fear of identity theft; of these, 54% had either stopped or cut back on buying things online.

B.J. Fogg and the Stanford Persuasive Technology Lab define credibility as a combination of trustworthiness and expertise. When people perceive a site as trustworthy (unbiased, fair and honest) and as expert (knowledgeable, experienced and intelligent), then they regard the site as credible. Only credible web sites can change people's attitudes and behaviours.

So at all costs, commercial sites need to establish credibility. This is increasingly tough in a world where:

> Global opinion leaders say their most credible source of information about a company is now "a person like me," which has risen dramatically to surpass doctors and academic experts for the first time, according to the seventh annual Edelman Trust Barometer, a survey of nearly 2,000 opinion leaders in 11 countries. In the U.S., trust in "a person like me" increased from 20% in 2003 to 68% today. Opinion leaders also consider rank-and-file employees more credible spokespersons than corporate CEOs (42% vs. 28% in the U.S.).

Whoah! That's scary. Quick, let's get back to B.J. Fogg and the Stanford Web Credibility Research team.[193] Their second major study, in 2002, found the basic requirements for credibility on the web to be largely commonsense. For a start, people trust web sites with professional (and appropriate) design, easy navigation, and perfect functionality. Those not are the responsibility of the writer.

On the other hand, among Stanford's ten guidelines for web credibility, the following are important for writers.[194]

- Make it easy to verify the accuracy of the information on your site. (Link to sources and support material.)
- Show there's a real organisation behind your site. (Provide street addresses, photos of real people and buildings, real people's names, email address etc.)
- Highlight the expertise in your organisation. (You are it!)
- Update content often.
- Avoid errors of all types, no matter how small. (Typos hurt credibility more than you realise.)

Consumer WebWatch has five guidelines for credibility.[195] They should all influence the way content is written.

1. Disclose identity clearly (includes physical location, contact details, ownership, purpose and mission).

2. Distinguish advertising (including sponsors and inhouse promotions) from news and information.
3. Disclose customer service fees and policies.
4. Correct false, misleading or incorrect information.
5. Display privacy policies.

Fogg distinguishes between presumed, reputed, surface and earned credibility. Earned credibility is the gold standard, and it depends on consistently accurate and unbiased content.

Note about corporate blogs

You have probably figured that strenuous blogging by a handful of the top thinkers in a business can seriously boost credibility. Such blogs can provide original, relevant, authoritative, and frequently updated content. What more could a commercial site want?

Well, an appropriate strategy, for starters. Goals. Constraints. Honesty. Talent. Writing ability. Clear expectations. Monitoring. A decent return on investment. With those in place, it's true: corporate blogs can become a tremendous asset.

In 2005, BackboneMedia questioned 97 corporate bloggers and interviewed six in depth.[196] Their verdict was that blogging can give both vast and tiny companies tangible benefits. Quick publishing brought immediate results in better search engine rankings and links. Longer term, bloggers got a more personal relationship with their audiences, more credibility, valuable feedback and stronger business relationships. The return on investment included increased sales, partnerships, business opportunities, and press coverage.

Companies tend to direct their bloggers to write only when there is something of value to say to customers. Often, that means writing about their products to the people who use the products.

For Macromedia (now Adobe), blogging has apparently brought customers into the loop of product development. The company began blogs to build a better community and get information out to customers quickly. Gradually they started using blogs to ask customers what they wanted changed in new versions of products. If the programmers were able to incorporate suggestions, they would then report back to customers. That's a big turnaround.

So, are you destined to be a corporate blogger? If so, study your company blogging policy and be crystal clear about what the company goals are for its bloggers. Sample plenty of blogs, good and bad. Get to know the difference: good writing, concise writing, genuine news, original ideas, and a passion for your topic. Be one of the good bloggers. And if you can't post at least once a week, think twice about starting.

The Adobe blogs page shows the latest posts from their developers.[197] Note how many blogs featured when I captured this page: 1303.

John Dowdell is one of the Adobe bloggers.[198]

Telling stories

People love stories. Storytelling is the age-old way of disseminating and preserving knowledge. It's a natural way to share enthusiasm, inspire others and impart moral concepts. Why do we forget this at work the moment we sit down at a computer?

Commercial content especially is often in dire need of humans. Dry facts and PR cannot compete human interest stories. Whenever writing documents about an organisation, ask yourself *What's the story here?* Then tell us the story. Don't force it through the seive of corporate language. Just tell us what happened to the people.

Story-telling is not always appropriate, of course, and it's never an excuse for wordiness. But it's surprising how often a story can convey facts more powerfully than a table.

One example of a company that used the power of storytelling to good purpose follows. They chose web TV for a crucial internal communications task.

Arcelor and Mittal were in the midst of a merger to form the 'largest steel company in the world'; no single intranet portal was available to all 110,000 employees in 60 countries. They needed to sing the same song and keep all staff informed about progress. So they created a pseudo TV soap opera.[199]

The TV soap opera was a familiar genre in all the relevant countries. The moment the genre is recognised, the audience is primed to sit back and enjoy the story—including the parody.

One problem with stories is their once-upon-a-time structure, which seems the opposite of F-writing. But look: Episode 1 starts with a summary! OK, it does have a hint of hype with that word *remarkable*, but nobody's perfect. What we see here is that storytelling and F-writing are compatible in the hands of a skilled writer.

Many ways of telling a story

The traditional way to *tell* a story is by using words. However, new technology makes it ever easier to manipulate images and sound, so smart people are finding interesting new ways to tell a story.

Documation, meaning animated documentary, is a word coined by the Simmonds Brothers.[200] This versatile tool works for corporate presentations, educational resources, music videos and training. Commercial documations cannot be shown, so let's look at a series of government training presentations on water quality, commissioned by New Zealand's Ministry of Health in 2006.

The usual approach would have been a scripted video or a slideshow.

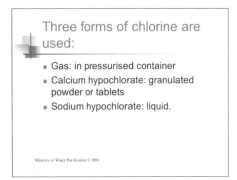

Instead, the Simmonds Brothers did it their way. They interviewed numerous people, edited the audiotapes, and created characters to speak the exact words spoken in the interviews. Suddenly, a presentation becomes a story. Using real interview material instead of actors working from a script brings the story alive in unexpected ways. Voices and style of expression vary greatly. Even the driest facts can come to life.

Test, test, test!

How do you know if your commercial web content is successful? Test it. Isn't it fantastic that you *can* test it, and improve it so easily if necessary?

19.

Academic content: practise what you preach

Another kind of online content is growing exponentially worldwide: academic content. Universities, polytechnics, senior colleges and community colleges[201] have web sites by the dozen. Besides that, lectures, course outlines, instructions for students, audio files and video files, reusable learning objects, e-textbooks—any aspect of teaching that used to happen in a school's classrooms and offices now happens on web sites and intranets too. Sheer economic pressure is forcing most universities to offer at least some of their courses online. A good deal of inhouse training happens on the intranet. The sale and purchase of e-learning (and its enabling software) is big business. Also, many universities put some of their course material online free, for the public.

Hold tight to the big four rules

As always, there is no escape: academic content desperately needs plain language, F-headlines, F-summaries and F-links. These rules apply to every conceivable type of online content, but for cultural reasons, certain teachers consider themselves exempt.

Some teachers are terrific at writing plain language, because they write the way they speak in the classroom. Nobody writes better than a confident, plain-speaking professor. And alas, nobody writes worse than a professor trying to impress other professors. Some tend to forget that a university web site is not an academic journal, and that a large proportion of readers are undergraduates, many of them ESL speakers.

Just like other on-the-job writers, teachers need to join the pilgrimage towards readable, usable, accessible online content.

Verdict on university web sites

University web sites have certain special problems, many of which impact on content writers.

For one thing, it's widely acknowledged that university web sites tend to fragment into sub-brands that can get right out of control. The word *chaos* recurs in discussions about the topic, as in Martine Booth's article *Chaos or collaboration? Web management in a decentralised university environment.*[202] When Shaun Nicholson investigated the web site management of 15 universities, he noted the cumulative problems caused by the universities' sheer size, complex systems, decentralisation, multiple campuses, and culture of high-minded, stroppy independence.[203] He says:

> Universities are a challenging environment for policy, which has led to a lack of distinction between policy, procedure, standard, guideline, and best practice.

Many university sites are so huge that staff lose sight of entire sub-sites. Naturally, ROT is endemic. When I searched for *current projects 2001 university* Google threw up 76,000,000 of these lost, lonely pages. Here is a typical one, long forgotten, many years out of date when I visited it. Believe it or not, I found it on the MIT site.[204]

Current Projects as of August 1999	
Current Projects as of June 2000, ending May 31, 2001	
Project Title	PI
Sources and Control	
Study of Fuel Rich Combustion Particulate Matter Formation	Cheng
PAH and Soot Formation Modeling using Detailed Kinetics and Experimental Data	Barton, Howard
Computer-Generated Kinetic Models for PAH Formation	Green
Numerical Tools for Large-Scale Kinetic Models	Barton, Green
Transport and Transformation	
Laboratory Studies of the Photochemistry of Organic Peroxides: Determination of the Photolysis Rate for Conditions Appropriate for Use in Urban and Regional Air Quality Models	Wennberg

The sub-sites on a university site are particularly prone to insularity: dozens or hundreds of individual departments, research institutes and other self-contained units publish their own content with no regard for what else their readers need. The sheer size of sites also makes errors in content more likely.

University sites have multiple purposes and audiences. They market the university to prospective students at home and abroad, and service current students and staff.

Usability specialist Dey Alexander of Monash University followed 39 prospective students as they visited 15 university sites to find a degree or diploma they were interested in, its cost, entry requirements, location and potential scholarships.[205] Here's how the students experienced the fragmentation of university sites.

> I wouldn't have a clue where to go... they should have a link.

> I'd expect it just to give me the advice straight away.

> When you want the answer to a question you don't want to be going from site to site to site.

They had plenty to say about the content, too.

What's the exact difference between programs and courses?

I don't know what coursework means... I guess I'll just go into one of the prospective things.

I've not been to uni before so I'm not right up with all this.

It says 'per 8 point subject'... I'm not quite sure what that means.

I don't know if it's some of the lingo they use on these kind of websites.

Too much detail for me to look at... I wouldn't waste my time on here trying to work it out for myself.

Oh god, I don't want to read through all this.

There's a lot of information here, that isn't necessarily a good thing all the time.

In 2004, Trent Mankelow assessed 7 New Zealand university web sites for usability.[206] At the time, he found they complied with only about half of the current best practice usability guidelines. General aspects on which the sites scored poorly included some that are the responsibility of content writers:

- basic mistakes with forms (non-scannable layout, scary and rude error messages, lack of examples and timely help)
- no sign of pages' location within the site
- non-skim-readable content, often due to inadequate headlines
- link-text that doesn't make sense when read out of context
- use of university jargon.

The use of jargon is disturbing. It's particularly unfortunate on university sites, because they are marketing to prospective students (including mature and international students) who don't even understand the concepts, let alone the jargon. And the jargon varies wildly between universities, and includes made-up names that mean nothing to outsiders.

> tertiary institution university polytechnic institute of technology programmes courses proctor Unipol majors minors endorsements qualifications PIMS points EFTs...

Consider the paragraph below.[207] The first five sentences are short, and there isn't a single passive verb. Unfortunately the last sentence—40 words long—wrecks any claim to plain language. And the main problem is the sheer density of university jargon.

> The University of Auckland has changed the structure of its academic qualifications. From 1 January 2006, a full time student will enrol in

courses carrying a total value of 120 points per year. This will apply to new and current students. New students will enrol under new qualification regulations. Current students will be able to complete their qualifications under Transition Regulations. The new points structure will align the University of Auckland qualifications with the majority of other tertiary qualifications offered in New Zealand and will facilitate credit transfer for students and provide increased flexibility for the content and structure of qualifications.

The writer then states:

The following pages provide information about transition for students, academic and general staff and the wider university community.

Transition? Academic staff may get the message, but don't assume that students will. Most likely the content on this page was written for academic staff as a policy paper, in which case the jargon presents no problem. University web sites are hard pressed for money and resources, and rewriting documents to fit the audience does take time. However, in this case a small investment of time would surely reduce students' confusion, errors and questions to staff.

To help prospective students who are struggling, the solution is certainly not adding more words. The Help page below is at least six times as long as necessary, and is spattered with non-skim-readable (and patronising) *Click here* links.[208] A simple index page of properly written, self-explanatory F-links would have been more useful.

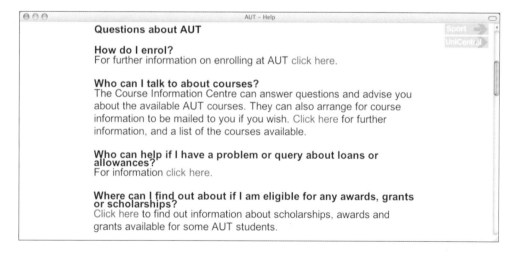

Naturally, Mankelow found much good content, and sees an interesting future for Web Me-Too functionality on university web sites. For example, readers might compare competing universities' courses (as e-commerce sites do with products), calculate fees, work out timetables, plan a degree, build a CV, and buy textbooks online. Sounds good to me.

Let's look at Alexander's findings. Some are the result of fragmented web sites, others of unskilled web writing.

University web site problem	What content writers can do
Students find the courses but can't find other information, because sub-sites only deliver 'their' information.	Think what other information your readers need, e.g. about fees and scholarships. Find it. Link to it.
Content with insufficient detail forces 72% of participants to wander around the site or to say they will contact the university.	See above.
Students overlook key links because of badly written link-text.	Write F-links as described in this book. Never take short-cuts with sloppy, too-brief or inaccurate links embedded in text.
Jargon confuses 72% of students. Most common and severe confusion: subjects/courses. Also: Programs/courses/units, graduate/postgraduate, sessions/semesters, and legal jargon.	A tricky one, as certain terms are mandatory, and must be used consistently. Explain the first time you use a confusing word on any web page. Provide a glossary too. Use plain language. A phrase in the summary or headlines, or a well constructed diagram can clarify meaning.
Content that is too long and wordy, or too dense, or contains irrelevant information.	Write plain language, F-headlines, F-summaries and F-links. Focus.
Unclear or misleading content.	Check accuracy, test content with real people, and update frequently. Write plain language, F-headlines, F-summaries and F-links.

But a wordy, badly structured page follows, exhibiting some of the worst aspects of university sites.[209] Some of the most important instructions, as far as students are concerned, are buried at the bottom of the page.

Final Exams

Last Day of Classes: Tuesday, May 15, 2007
1st Reading Day: Wednesday, May 16, 2007
Final Examinations Begin: Thursday, May 17, 2007
2nd Reading Day: Saturday, May 19, 2007
Final Examinations Resume: Monday, May 21, 2007
Last Day of Final Examinations: Thursday, May 24, 2007

Complete Final Exam Schedule

The Spring 2007 Final Exam Schedule for each department is available here. (This page is rather large. It may take a little while to load on slower connections.) The schedule indicates **start times only**; exams are two hours long unless otherwise noted. Times listed as 8:00 or 10:30 are AM; 1:30 or 4:00 are PM.

The link above will try to open a new window. If you see exams from a previous semester try refreshing the page or clearing your browser cache.

There is a chart of the building abbreviations used in the Final Exam Schedule available in the General Information area of our Web site.

Final Examination Policy

Final Examinations may be scheduled only during the final examination period. In classes in which no final examination or other class activity is scheduled during the final examination period, no examination should be scheduled during the final week of classes nor during the Reading Period. If an instructor in a course without a final examination wishes to give an hour examination to cover the material in the concluding section of the course, that hour examination shall be held during the final examination period, at the time that the final examination for the course would have been scheduled. Non-cumulative exams may be scheduled during the last week of classes only in classes in which an additional final exam is scheduled during the final examination period. Laboratory and studio courses that include a capstone experiment or a culminating presentation, respectively, during the last week of classes, are allowed to schedule a comprehensive final examination during the Final Examinations Week. This policy applies to both undergraduate and graduate courses.

University policy states that if a student is scheduled to take two final exams at the same time, the faculty member running the course with the higher final digit in the class number shall be required to offer a make-up exam. Further, if a student is scheduled to take three final examinations on the same day, the faculty member running the chronologically middle exam shall be required to offer a make-up exam. Proof of conflict shall be provided to the instructor by the student **at least two weeks prior** to the time the examination is scheduled. Proof may be obtained at the Registrar's Office, 213 Whitmore.

University policy and Massachusetts state law require faculty to offer make-up exams to students who are absent for religious observance. Students planning to be absent due to religious observance must notify their instructors **at least two weeks prior** to the time the examination is scheduled.

In the unlikely event of a delayed opening or official closing of the University during the final exam period, please refer to the Housing Services Cable News Network, the University Emergency Closing Web page, or a paper copy of the instructions titled "Rescheduling Of Final Exams On Official Snow Days" which is widely distributed several weeks before the final exam period.

Important Notes

Students enrolled in courses with conflicting scheduled exams or who have three or more exams scheduled in one calendar day should contact the Registrar's Office for assistance in resolving the problem.

When it becomes available, the full final exam schedule is published right here on the Registrar's Web site. Each student's own final exam schedule is also available to him/her through SPIRE. To view it, log in to SPIRE and select "For Students," then "Academic Summary," then "Exam Schedule."

The exam schedule occasionally has to be updated after publication to accommodate unique scheduling situations. In these cases, the Registrar's web site and SPIRE will be updated to reflect the most up to date information.

The edited version below is not half as daunting. It puts the students' immediate needs upfront, and summarises key points of policy that directly affect the students.

Final Exams Winter 2006 - University of Massachusetts, Amherst

Last day of classes: Wednesday, December 13, 2006
Final exams begin: Friday, December 15, 2006
Last day of final exams: Friday, December 22, 2006

Check your personal Winter 2006 exam schedule
Schedule may change: check again before exams
What to do if the university closes during final exams

Do you have two exams at the same time? Do you have three exams on one day? If so, at least two weeks before the exam report for help with rescheduling to:
Registrar's Office
213 Whitmore Street, Amherst
0900-111-111-111
registrar@umass.edu

The University's policy for scheduling final exams:

- includes procedures for dealing with schedule conflicts
- gives final exams priority over lesser exams
- advises what to do if the university is closed for official snow days or other reasons during final exams
- offers make-up exams for students who plan to be absent for religious observance.

Policy for scheduling final exams: your rights

Exam times (unless you are otherwise advised):
8am-10am
10.30am-12.30pm
1.30-3.30pm
4.00pm-6.00pm

Writing lectures for delivery online

Now we come to the nitty-gritty: issues for staff who prepare online courses. These are professional people, often with many years' experience in their work. They are teachers, not writers.

Teachers do much more online than write content—but this is a book about writing, not teaching. So I won't stray into certain areas, important though they are. I have no intention of telling teachers how to construct or teach a course. Also outside my brief are learning management systems, discussions, synchronous classroom sessions, and any other unscripted live teaching sessions.

Let's just look at the way teachers prepare content and communicate online with students, especially at senior college and university level.

If that's your role, you know exactly who your readers are, and exactly what you want to achieve. You want to convey information so that it sticks in the minds of your students. You want to persuade them to concentrate, to engage with the material and make it their own. You want them to learn in a questioning, positive, personal way. The goals are the same as when you are teaching in the classroom; you just need to adapt your skills to a different situation.

Online equivalents of your regular teaching skills

For example, in a physical lecture you must speak loudly and clearly enough for everyone to hear. The equivalent requirement online is that everyone can read and understand the lecture easily. This requires the big four rules (plain language, F-headlines, F-summaries and F-links).

Besides this, make an effort with layout: your professionalism is under scrutiny. Simple things make a huge difference. You have probably been using a font such as Times or Helvetica all your professional life, true? Now it is time to switch to a screen-friendly font. Only Verdana, Georgia and Trebuchet MS pass the test at the time of writing. And make sure your font is large enough to read on the screen, or can be enlarged. (Students are slow to upgrade their free Adobe Reader software, no matter how often they're told.)

In live lectures you use slides, images and video clips to illustrate your points and enliven the content: do the same in online lectures.

You put yourself on display when you lecture live: students respond to you as a person. In online content, boldly let your personality shine through. Some teachers freeze when they write. Maybe that's because spoken words fly through the air and are gone, whereas written words stay in the file to be read and analysed and criticised forever. But students respond more when you let yourself be human. Above all, show your enthusiasm; regardless of medium, this may be the teacher's greatest asset, even greater than knowledge. Don't muzzle your enthusiasm just because you are teaching on a web site.

The occasional short video can go a long way towards humanising the invisible teacher. Try it: all you need nowadays is a digital camera. And consider including your photo on each lecture. OK, this is a loathsome thought to most teachers, but you are not starting a personality cult—you are just trying to compensate for the fact that students can't see you.

In a real lecture, you get the students engaged by addressing them as *you*, stopping to ask questions, raising problems for them to solve, and referring to current events. Don't change that habit! However, remember your students may be of any age, living in any country. This will influence your choice of questions, examples and anecdotes.

Here's a tough one: in live lectures you notice non-verbal signals from the class: restlessness, chatter, nodding off. Smart teachers respond instantly to such messages. But how to do that online? It's helpful to read the students' contributions to discussions with a beady eye, especially their initial self-introductions. These reveal plenty, and reveal by concealing also. Sometimes the students who say the least are the ones that need encouragement: you won't see them frown, so you might want to question them. If you have the necessary technical support, little automated quizzes and polls are also excellent ways to check up on how much students have grasped. But the primary aim is to prevent misunderstandings by writing carefully.

In a live course, students' interaction with each other is a major component of learning. Sometimes you can organise students to work in pairs or groups, and discussion groups are a staple of most online courses. This enables students to express themselves in a friendly environment, as if in a live tutorial. When participation is mandatory and counts for part of the final grade, discussions go a long way to overcoming the isolation of distance education.

In a lecture room, students usually take notes. Online you might encourage them to keep a learning diary, and to use the discussion board freely for comments.

Structuring an online lecture

Structure is super-important for lectures delivered online.

In live lectures, you can pause, ad lib or gesticulate to indicate a shift of gear or a new development in your argument. You can't do that online.

Follow the usual basic structure: summarise the whole lecture at the beginning and the end. In other words, tell them what you're going to tell them, then tell them, then tell them what you told them. This immutable law applies even if your lecture begins with a question. In that case, you state the question at the beginning, relate every stage of the lecture to that question, and finally answer it at the end. An initial summary and clear F-headlines prepare students to listen or read actively.

A lecture in HTML or PDF can and should demonstrate its own structure. Once you have a good template, it is no effort to maintain a handsome, simple, highly readable look and feel for lectures, one where structure is obvious at a glance. Headline styles can be differentiated by colour as well as font size. No more pages of relentless tiny black type! Special styles—perhaps subtle changes of background colour—can signal special content types such as definitions or optional tasks. Be consistent, so it looks professional. In audio versions of lectures, a lack of summaries and sub-headlines is a catastrophe for the listener.

Give clear complete instructions the first time

A strange recurring problem on university web sites is that instructions are muddled up with other information. Instructions slither into policy or theory or chat. In fact, I'd say that instructions in general are delivered in a way that is messy, wordy, and unclear. This applies to instructions that are part of online classroom management, and instructions on the public web site.

My theory is that when teachers start writing web content, they revert to an approach they use in the classroom. This can be a fine thing for tone, because it means they speak rather than orate. But the collateral damage may be structure.

In a real classroom or lecture hall, the first messages teachers deliver usually have the structure of a jelly. Does it matter? No. The following text is based on videos of MIT lectures.[210] For the first minute or so, most professors hold forth something like this.

> Welcome everyone to Feline Terpsichorea 101. Does everybody here have the syllabus? Would you see me after class please? Over the semester we will cover the History of Feline Dance, Feline Anatomy, Physiotherapeutic Cat Dancing, Motivation and Psychology, Biomusicology, Preferred Ballroom Styles, and Pre-dance Exercises. Hello... there's a seat at the front here. The earliest written record of a cat dancing with a person dates from 1692 and evidence of the practice is clearly alluded to in the earliest versions of that rather strange nursery rhyme: Hey diddle diddle...No, you may not bring your cats to class. Yes, your question? The textbook is *Dancing with Cats*.[211]

You see what I mean: teachers naturally alternate between classroom management, course outline and actual teaching content, particularly at the beginning and end of each lecture. This occasional swiveling isn't necessarily a problem. On the contrary, when teachers notice puzzled faces in the audience they can immediately clarify matters, short-circuiting confusion. It's natural and it's fine, but it's something you must not do in an online lecture.

On a web site or intranet, making instructions crystal clear the first time is crucial. Every time you modify or re-explain an instruction online, you make things worse: students see multiple (and contradictory) versions of your instructions, all apparently of equal value. Which one should they believe? They see the instructions you wrote last month, unaware that a new directive has superseded them.

Mayhem arises from the fact that the things we say happen in a certain sequence, whereas web pages are not perceived as being published in sequence.

I recommend keeping the content for classroom management, curriculum and assignments completely separate from the course materials. Learning management systems are designed to make this separation straightforward, but it's all too easy to slip some instructions into a lecture and mess up. Keeping the files separate will help students to manage their learning. It will also save you a certain amount of grief from one semester to another, as you won't need to comb through lectures revising dates and details.

When students are figuring out the requirements for an assignment, it helps to provide a complete checklist right there in the course handbook. Then you just need to refer to the handbook instead of explaining the same thing again... and again... and again.

Avoid irony

The writing style of online teaching has a built-in paradox: it needs to be personal without being bland, conversational without being unstructured. You tread a fine line between the two extremes, which requires some sensitivity.

Above all, steer clear of irony! The students don't actually know you, and are likely to take your words literally. Trust can be destroyed with one ill-judged joke. Friends know you're joking; strangers don't.

You can see the same problem every day in newspapers' letters to the editor. People blithely assume all sensible readers share their views and know when they are being ironic. Well, we don't. Half the time, we read the whole letter without 'getting it'. The following letter is a typical example.

> Matthew Rawnsley claims our abortion laws are not being enforced properly and that the Government should give more money to women to prevent abortions; Prue Eckett claims CYF doesn't help desperate parents with delinquent children till the law becomes involved. Perhaps it should be illegal for women to give birth without a permit. Current worries concerning dysfunctional families would also be overcome.[212]

It's conceivable the writer offers his proposal in all seriousness. I honestly can't tell. Even the great satirist Jonathan Swift was taken literally by many when he proposed a totally outrageous solution in 1729 *for Preventing the Children of Poor People in Ireland from Being a Burden to Their Parents or Country, and for Making Them Beneficial to The Public*—he advised them to eat their own babies.[213] ESL students inevitably take jokes literally: that's a universal law until they are extremely fluent. The only safe course is to just say what we mean and mean what we say, and find other ways to lighten up.

How to write reusable learning objects (RLO)

What a horrible term. What a great idea.

So what is an RLO? It is a small, self-contained, reusable chunk of web-based learning content, tagged with metadata that make it easy to find. Teachers can search for them and use them in their own classes: what a bonus!

RLO standards for interoperability, accessibility and reusability are emerging, but no one set of standards is universally accepted as yet.[214]

Meanwhile, don't let the jargon put you off. Sure, an RLO can be an elaborate, hi-tech, interactive, online teaching session, but in practice, much of the time it's just an online lecture, scrupulously subdivided into topics, with proper metatagging. Just take a look at some RLOs and you will realise there's no mystery involved.[215]

National Science State University provides LabWrite, which is quite a sophisticated example.[216]

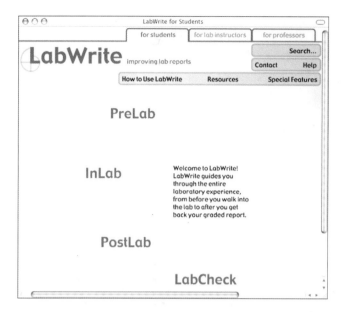

LabWrite's valuable resources include online guides and templates, and interactive applications.

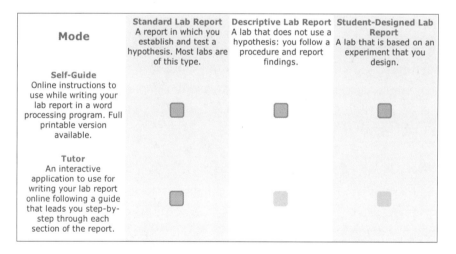

The next example, *Writing Skills for the Tax Professional*, has a simpler approach. Each lesson is a long (1300 words or more), low-tech, HTML page, accompanied by a number of self-tests.[217] The lessons don't have a professionally designed look and feel, and the site even uses the dreaded frames. (See the extra scrollbar on the left?) Nevertheless the course meets the standards for an RLO, and has been peer reviewed by MERLOT for quality of content, potential effectiveness as a teaching tool, and ease of use. It is doubtless useful, focused, and reusable by teachers anywhere.

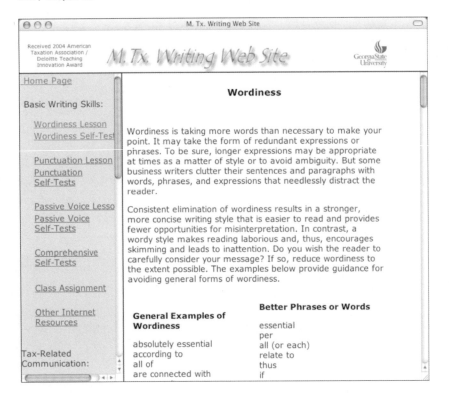

If you want to contribute to the store of high-quality free information available to teachers, do investigate the RLO phenomenon. If nothing else, it helps you to write focused content, and (depending where you send it) ought to ensure your content is peer reviewed. A good starting point is *Learning Objects 101: A Primer for Neophytes*.[218]

Online textbooks

These are another brilliant resource for teachers, thanks to the internet. E-books are usually PDFs, and are usually free or comparatively cheap. Any teacher can create an e-book and set it free in the wild. Open Source textbooks—in theory—go even further. They exist as web sites and are not only free, but open to contributions from readers.

The technology, infrastructure and business model for true wiki-based Open Source textbooks are by no means sorted. Keeping an online textbook up-to-date is a never-ending task. Meanwhile, author Robert H. Stewart takes the easy way out: he simply invites people to contribute new material to his book by email.[219] That leaves him free to select and edit contributions. Texas A&M University hosts and maintains the site.

Another valuable development is the textbook web site. Frequently a textbook has an accompanying site that supports teachers with quizzes, podcasts, blogs and updates.

Podcasts and audio files

Many universities provide podcasts (audio files freely available from a web site) of lectures, campus events, interviews, music, and even sports commentaries.

Podcasts are a godsend for e-learning. Students can listen to lectures as they skate, commute or walk the dog. Every second student seems to have an iPod, so access is just a matter of plug-and-go. Podcasts are ideal for students who like listening more than reading, and they're a handy way to revise course content.

For teachers, the technology is fairly straightforward, once you've got a microphone and some free software. You already have a script: it's your online lecture. Best not deviate from this, or some students may feel confused or cheated.

When listening, it is normal for attention to flicker on and off. Therefore, as you speak into the microphone, use all your ingenuity to re-engage listeners whose mind has strayed.

- Rehearse, and record your rehearsal, perhaps in sections. Follow the script, but try hard to sound as if you are thinking on your feet; discover each idea before uttering it.
- Start by stating your own name, the course title and lecture title.
- Then read the summary and the list of sub-topics.
- Before starting a new sub-topic, pause, and feel free to repeat its headline.

- Occasionally, invite listeners to think about a statement you have just made—then repeat the statement and pause for about 3-5 seconds. (They will seem as long as eternity.)
- If your own mind strays, stop and repeat the previous sentence thoughtfully. Good trick: it helps you and your listeners!

Using Video and Flash for teaching online

Some MIT OpenCourseWare courses include a complete set of videos showing a lecture in progress.[220] That's great for giving us a sense of what it's like to attend an MIT lecture. But who wants to watch for 15 hours, especially when all the teachers' slides are obscured? I can't see the point.

However, video and especially Flash do have value as online content. Each segment should be a few minutes at most. Flash can be great for demonstrating, illustrating, and interactive learning. Of course, this requires specialist knowledge outside our focus, which is writing. Step one is to explore examples and consider when and why you would use these media.

Some advantages of e-teaching

Online teaching has its problems, but it also has some advantages for the teacher. It's easy to:
- structure information in layers and link to sub-pages with more detailed, advanced, or easy information
- distribute supplementary lecture notes, examples and readings
- publish student work (with their permission) and get feedback from a wider audience
- provide links to free online teaching materials
- provide free-to-air material first broadcast on television or radio.

Many universities offer good advice on online teaching. For example, see La Trobe University's resources for their staff.[221]

Test, test, test

To get honest feedback from online students can be difficult. You can't see their frowns, and many are too insecure to say they don't understand something you have written. They think all the other students do understand. They think it's their fault if they don't understand. But the teacher needs to know!

All I can say is that ingenuity and vigilance are needed, plus the odd open-ended, comparative question. Maybe not 'Did you understand?' but 'Which idea in this lecture did you find the most obscure?'

20.

International content

Warning: this chapter contains coarse generalisations.

In May 2006 I went to a seminar on cross-cultural communication by Dr Carol Barnum of Southern Polytechnic in Georgia. I was shocked to notice that only a few of the audience were from mainstream organisations. Most had a professional stake in cross-cultural issues—for example, they worked with refugees or lectured in communications.

Why's that shocking? Because the topic is relevant to every web site, not just those for refugees or immigrants.

Maybe it's just been too hard to figure how to communicate successfully to a truly divergent audience. Yet commonly, a single site is intended for audiences from different cultures. This happens all the time. For instance, your local pizza outlet has customers who hail from Somalia and China as well as people born and bred in your city. Moreover, a fourth-generation local person may hold strong cultural values from a minority culture.

That's the problem web site owners want to run away from—but web sites are for everyone.

ACHOs and AFFLOs

In this chapter, I'll generalise coarsely, identifying cultures as either ACHO (achievement-oriented, individualistic, anyone-can-be-President, read-my-lips, includes USA, Germany and Australia) or AFFLO (affiliation-oriented, hierarchical, community-minded, formal, read-between-the-lines, includes most Asian cultures).

Say you come from an ACHO culture. You don't want to alienate AFFLO readers, but obviously, you don't want to lose your ACHO readers either. How far should we go to understand and meet the cultural and linguistic needs of other cultures? What can we do? Let's think about it.

By definition, the audience of most web sites is international. Cultural values are embedded in communication. By their very nature, these values are usually unrecognised. National values are inculcated from childhood, and taken for granted within the community. Yet cultures traditionally differ in the ways they perceive and value certain factors such as social ties and personal relations, authority and hierarchy, status, individuality, uncertainty and achievement.

Underlying all communication lie certain hidden assumptions, taken for granted by the person communicating. These assumptions might be something like *red is a lucky colour* or *everyone wants individual success*. That's no problem if the target audience shares the same deep values as the writer. But when writer and reader do not share the same cultural values, communication can go seriously awry.

On the web, problems lurk where content crosses cultures.

The western web

In the short time since its birth, the web has acquired its own conventions for display and navigation, just as books have done over the centuries. Conventions increase usability, and often evolve into standards. For example, we expect books to have a title page, a copyright page, a table of contents, chapters, a spine, a cover, a margins, and page numbers. Most books do, saving both readers and publishers a great deal of time. As conventions and standards are intrinsically useful, I'm not about to advocate right-to-left browsers.

However, we must note that Westerners have defined and shaped web technology because we had a head start on the web. 'My way or the highway,' that's the (typically Western) story. Most western countries use the ABC, and this alone was enough to influence the way browsers display content: text begins in the top left hand corner of the screen. If web content is too wide for a reader's screen, the starting point for scrolling sideways is at the left.

The West has already lost its dominance online. Any statistics I could quote would be phenomenally high, and out of date as soon as typed. How about *Asia has 364 million internet users*? *Chinese internet usage doubles every six months*? *Or nearly twice as many people speak Mandarin Chinese as English*? All out of date!

As more and more countries gain internet infrastructure, more ACHOs need and want to communicate across cultures. What can we do? Must we go back to square one, redesigning sites and software, and rewriting all our content? Hang on a minute, mate! Let's calmly consider the issues and the options.

- When creating web content, when should we consider changes to accommodate an audience from a different culture?
- What might confuse or alienate AFFLO readers?
- What aspects of Western web content must be retained?
- What can be easily adapted to suit a wide range of cultures?
- How about multiple sites in other languages?

I'd like to think it is rare for a Western organisation to create a web site for an exclusively AFFLO audience, without consulting that audience. If so, multinational companies need no advice: they'll get local expertise from local experts.

I'd like to think that such web sites all undergo rigorous usability testing, and that content is included in the testing.

However, if you don't have the resources for research and usability testing with your foreign audience, at least work through the suggestions in this chapter.

Issues around structure and thinking styles are tricky. Many cultures traditionally dislike getting straight to the point. For people from such cultures, explicit headlines and executive summaries may be anathema in general business dealings. However, the pressures towards skim-reading online content are extremely strong. If your main audience is in China, Japan, or Taiwan, or other countries with a spiral structure to communication, you have some challenges. Just don't use that as an excuse to burble and lose focus.

Style: meet in the middle

ACHO cultures tend to communicate in an informal, conversational style. The web, emails, and especially blogs have accelerated this trend. We were more formal when we wrote letters on paper, remember?

AFFLO communications often seem elaborate, flowery, abstract, or ceremonial to an ACHO person. You can almost see the lectern. Formality is valued.

The level of formality of your style need not be a problem: on most web sites, you can safely meet in the middle. On a company or government agency web sites, use plain English, be concise, but use correct grammar and avoid slang.

Feel free to carry on blogging! Blogs are blogs, with a style all their own, and hugely popular all around the world. Do make sure a personal blog is clearly distinguishable from other content.

Pronouns and photographs

AFFLO cultures are collective cultures, which value the group over the individual. Individuals subordinate their personal benefit from those of their family, village, company, or other group. They are self-effacing.

A simple and effective trick is to check the pronouns in your web content: such common little words, but they provide both problems and solutions. The wrong balance of pronouns can be a dead giveaway that you value individuals over groups, or you think of a certain group as outside of your own.

Beware of overusing the self-centred, individualistic pronoun *I*. Check your use of *they* and *them*: are you excluding certain people from a group identity? Even our beloved pronoun *you* can ruffle feathers, if it obviously addresses a single person rather than an indeterminate number of readers. AFFLO readers will generally be more comfortable with *we* and *us*.

When using photos on web pages, consider using a group of people instead of individuals. A change that trivial can make an AFFLO person feel more at home, whereas an ACHO person probably won't care either way.

Tweak your *About Us* content

For a brief moment, when the web was new, people commonly believed they could and should mask their identity online. Self-employed people pretended they were companies. Small companies tried to give the impression they were large.

Today, web users are canny, and research has proven that credibility is a very big deal. If I don't know who you are, I won't trust you. And if I don't trust you, I won't do business with you. Therefore, whatever your culture, you benefit from providing detailed information about your company or organisation. At the very least, you should provide a street address, contact details, names of key staff members, and a brief background of the organisation. Commonly, you will list the outstanding achievements of a company.

Now that is all excellent content for your international audience. But you could go still further. Consider some values shared by many AFFLO cultures.

- Authority: feature your top executives, itemising their degrees, university background, and status; if your organisation is established or supported by government, say so. Provide more than a profile: provide a pedigree.
- Affiliation: mention affiliation with partners, other professional organisations, government agencies, and key clients.
- The long-term view: state the number of years you have been operating, and the history of your organisation.
- Social ties: feature the work of groups instead of individuals.

Adding such factual details to a web site is quite a simple matter, and makes the site more acceptable to people in AFFLO cultures. At the same time, it doesn't offend ACHO people.

On the other hand, some ACHO web sites blow their own trumpets, boasting about achievements which may in fact be quite modest. (I am putting this as politely as I can.) Inflating personal achievements is not an appropriate way to communicate online, and in particular, it may alienate AFFLO people.

Structure: no compromise

It is in the structure of web content that the clash between technological and cultural demands is loudest.

The structure of communication in AFFLO cultures tends to be circuitous. A typical letter or email will begin with an introduction, then develop the theme, then signal a transition to the real message, and finally—bingo, the business or action point comes last.

This is the exact opposite of good practice in the west, where all teachers of business communication skills advise starting documents with a summary or the main point. (Exceptions include specific situations such as delivering bad news.) We perceive the classic inverted pyramid structure as a mark of respect for readers: it prepares them for our message, and avoids wasting their time.

In an AFFLO culture, direct, clear, first-things-first documents may be interpreted as aggressive. In a meeting, getting straight down to business can lose the contract: bonding comes first. Actual meaning should not be too obvious, as many AFFLO cultures traditionally dislike getting straight to the point. An explicit headline and executive summary can cause surprise. In letters and meetings, it is normal to circle slowly towards the point of doing business. The onus is on the reader to read between the lines and figure what the writer is hinting at. Writing is subtle, readers are patient, and communication depends heavily on non-verbal cues.

So when communicating in person with a specific AFFLO individual or group, it is occasionally necessary to adjust—or completely upend—the inverted pyramid, the western structure of communication. (Note the word *occasionally*. More and more AFFLO people in business, government and education are accustomed to our communication methods.)

But as for the structure of web content, stick to the western way. Make no concessions over structure, because you'll lose more than you gain. Carry on F-writing, even though there is no *F* in Mandarin or Hindi. Write a clear, comprehensive, front-loaded headline, as always. Write a short summary of the page next, as always. Provide plenty of sub-headlines, as always. Write clear link-text and align it to the left hand margin, as always.

The pressures towards skim-reading online are extremely strong. Whatever the reader's nationality, they are unlikely to read a web page with the same dedication as a printed document. And if all readers must scroll to find the main point, you'll annoy and lose at least some of them—possibly most of them.

Am I being arrogant, to deliver such an ultimatum? Never! This is a pragmatic acknowledgement that the web is the web, where technology demands the main message be placed at the top of the page. There are at least three big reasons to apply this rule consistently.

1. Web users, both ACHO and AFFLO, expect the convention of a meaningful headline and summary at the top of the page. Breaking the convention creates confusion.
2. Anyone reading in an ABC language reads in an F-pattern first. The first headline and paragraph are almost certain to get some attention. A message lower down on the page is likely to be completely ignored unless the headline and summary have already met with approval.
3. Many sites recycle the page headline and summary in other places, for example on the home page and in the search results of an internal search engine. If the writer attempts to be subtle or places the main point elsewhere, this would seriously affect usability.

How about multilingual sites?

It goes without saying that any organisation targeting a particular country will need to provide a site in that country's language. In some territories, it is mandatory to provide at least some government content in several languages, for example in EU countries.

Multilingual sites have some notorious problems, all of which should be considered in advance. Then the solutions can be planned. Non-English content:

- is not a one-off development, but requires ongoing time and personnel
- must be updated as often as the English content
- must match the English content, because people dislike feeling excluded
- must not be a word for word translation but adjusted for cultural differences
- should not be linked to by a flag, but by the word for the language in that very language, as in the following screenshots:

Details of style: global English

Truly foolproof international communication is hard to achieve, but a few editorial tweaks will greatly improve your chances of success.

I suggest you just write content normally, and where necessary, convert your text to global English at the copy-editing stage.

First and foremost, meticulously follow the rules of plain language. Short sentences are a fantastic start. Negative language is particularly dangerous, both culturally and linguistically. And words that are unusual, ambiguous, metaphorical, or more than three syllables, can cause a heap of misunderstanding.

On the other hand, you may be surprised to hear that mini-words (of 3 letters or fewer) also cause trouble to speakers of English as a second language. Naturally we can't write without using mini-words such as *a, the, of* and *to*. But sentences with a heavy load of mini-words tend to be difficult for non-English speaking readers. Some mini-words, such as *get*, have many meanings, so they are hard to decipher from a bi-lingual dictionary. Other mini-words, such as *to*, have no meaning, or have no grammatical equivalent in other languages. Mini-words cluster in certain expressions that confuse international readers:

- wordy phrases, for example *in a position to*
- colloquial expressions, for example *it is all over*
- clichés, for example *at the end of the day*
- phrasal verbs, for example *get on, get off, get on to it*.

In speech, it is almost impossible to avoid using clichés, colloquialisms, and idiomatic phrases. Try to avoid them, because they cause puzzlement in non-native speakers of English. Those readers tend to either interpret the expressions literally, or be further confused when they consult a dictionary.

Numbers, dates, currencies, and measurements all need to be spelled out clearly when your web site audience is international. At least be aware of variations in the way large numbers and decimal points are written around the world. Spell out the month, because *2/7/2002* is ambiguous. Spell out the dollar—US, Australian, Singapore, Samoan? Does your target audience use miles or kilometres? Because of international differences, web sites need to be meticulous about consistency in numbers.

The F in other languages

The advice in this book is intended for sites with content in any language using the ABC, such as English, French or Spanish. But cultural and linguistic differences mean the advice is not applicable to every site in the world.

In some languages, including Chinese and Japanese, optional arrangements of text are theoretically possible. Text has traditionally been able to flow horizontally or vertically, and horizontal text may begin on the right or the left. However, both Chinese and Japanese web sites are far more likely to use the Western way, with text flowing horizontally from left to right. This has been mandatory for Taiwan government web sites since 1 January 2005.

I can see why left-alignment is a sensible decision for web sites in such languages. First, with right alignment, people with small screens or small windows might need to do the dreaded horizontal scrolling. Second, the same people may also be viewing web sites in English. It is easier for users if all web sites follow the same convention, so that people used to skim-reading in the F-pattern don't have to change their ways.

If a web site needs to be provided both in English and Arabic, designers have a particular challenge. I have read no eye-tracking research for Arabic sites, but I imagine readers' glances forming a mirror image of the F-pattern. In Arabic, text is right aligned, beginning in the top-right corner. (To complicate matters, numbers are read from left to right.) Letters in Arabic are cursive and asymmetrical, creating another challenge for online readers. Hala Memayssi mentioned other issues for the designer:[222]

> Some words simply don't translate literally but must be described in a longer, more conceptual way. Arabic does not have the concept of acronyms, and many technical terms caused translation challenges. [...] Compared to English, Arabic words occupy more space horizontally and are set, with the chosen typeface, four points larger than the English font.

Conciseness gains a new urgency in this situation. If writing for translation, the writer needs to be fully aware of these kinds of factors. A consistent grammatical structure is also a great help to the translator.

21.

Culture change: getting contented

So, you've pretty well read this book, or at least skipped through it. That may have a considerable impact on your own business writing and web content, which is terrific.

But if you are on a web management team, that's not the point, is it? You'll be thinking about how to raise the overall quality of content throughout your organisation's web sites and intranets.

For content to improve overall, the organisation itself has to change. It needs to become one where good writing is the norm, online content is usable, and all documents are web-proofed in advance. All documents will be written in plain language and most will be structured so that they can be published online without further editing. You could say the organisation becomes *contented* with all its business writing.

Web managers are contented because most documents produced by the organisation are fit to go on a web site or intranet. Writers are contented because they know their writing will pass the test. Readers are contented because the organisation's paper documents, web pages and intranet pages alike are user-friendly and easy to find. They serve the purpose. They are great!

I admit, this is a huge change. After all, plain language has been around for 50 years or more, and it still has an uphill battle. Why would a change to web-worthy business documents be any easier?

Physics is explanation enough for the barriers: the greater the mass, the more difficult it is to speed up, slow down or change direction. Individuals (even overweight individuals) can change their approach to writing easily, but large organisations are like an ocean liner steaming ahead on a predetermined course. Changing direction takes time and effort.

Well, you may already have a plan in action. I'd like to share my thoughts, and hope they may be helpful. Here's a shortlist of what I think you need for the big campaign.

1. At least one key person in top management convinced that investing in quality content is necessary and will pay off. (If the CEO is a believer, it will happen.)
2. Widespread, genuine involvement of staff in the change.
3. A comprehensive, usable style guide that covers all documents from glossy publications to email.

4. Ongoing training for writers.
5. Usability testing of content.

Top management convinced

With the best will in the world, a handful of individuals can rarely fast-forward a change of this magnitude. At least three departments have a stake: HR, IT and Corp Comms. But only top management has control of the rudder. When someone at the top 'gets it', seeing the massive implications for data quality, financial benefits and public relations, they can often turn the ship in a new direction.

Without support from above, middle managers can still chip away at the problem of bad, blinkered business writing. Professional development in web writing can be fostered within the normal training budget. However, the budget for an internal communications campaign, a web-proof style guide, and routine usability testing of content will probably be constrained.

Widespread, genuine involvement of staff

The typical content writer is knowledgeable in a certain field, with experience in a relevant type of writing.

So for a small cadre to create and impose all the rules and regulations for content from above is probably not a good move. These intelligent people should be invited to get involved and contribute right from the start.

The struggle is to convince staff that everyday business writing is, de facto, web writing. Content writers need to be wooed and won, but not in a way that implicitly differentiates web writing from other business writing. As we know, the principles of online writing (concise, skim-readable, objective) are relevant to all business writing.

The company style guide is a logical place where staff can contribute ideas and innovations. The benefits are many.

- Contributions from staff will definitely improve the style guide.
- Staff understand more about the issues surrounding web content because they have been involved.
- Staff feel more committed to the resulting style guide because they have been involved.

In the end, an editor smoothes over the cracks of any jointly written document, including a style guide. But many valuable points can be sorted out together first.

A comprehensive style guide

What's needed is a style guide that covers every kind of document, whether paper-based or electronic. All staff writers need all this information.

- Most organisations have both a regular (paper-writing) style guide and a set of technical guidelines for web team—and never the twain shall meet.
- Sooner or later every organisation needs to radically overhaul its existing style guide to accommodate online content.
- The web team still needs its technical guidelines, which are not relevant for regular on-the-job writers.

Style guide issues spotlight the folly of treating web content writers as part of the technical web team. Writers rarely attempt to read a web guidelines document, where they will encounter language like this:[223]

> Use "alt" for the IMG, INPUT, and APPLET elements, or provide a text equivalent in the content of the OBJECT and APPLET elements.
>
> For complex content (e.g., a chart) where the "alt" text does not provide a complete text equivalent, provide an additional description using, for example, "longdesc" with IMG or FRAME, a link inside an OBJECT element, or a description link.
>
> For image maps, either use the "alt" attribute with AREA, or use the MAP element with A elements (and other text) as content.

Now come on! What policy writer or HR writer is going plough through a document like that in search of writing guidelines? Yet at present, that's where the good stuff is buried, the few facts that they actually need to know about writing great web content.

That's why the regular company style guide should include guidelines for web content, and not just as an add-on.

The aim is to change the company style guide's content, structure and design so that it explains and demonstrates good practice for both paper and online documents. Web style should be the default style. After all, if every document starts with a clear descriptive headline and summary, is skim-readable and written in plain language, then the document is not only well written but also virtually web-proofed.

Be warned: I have never seen a style guide that truly blends web content and general writing guidelines, and practises what it preaches. So you are unlikely to find an ideal model—you will be pioneering here.

A usable style guide: choosing a format

Most style guides are ignored by all but Corp Comms, with good reason. Usually they look boring and they are boring. They are often hard to follow, with woolly, meandering prose. They are often impossible to skim-read—yet nobody reads a style guide from cover to cover! People consult style guides under pressure, seeking clarification for just one point. No wonder company style guides get conveniently lost. Usability is their weakest point.

Style guides are often written and published as if they were literature—yet they are help tools. So watch out for the bugbear of style guides: they should walk the walk.

Your new style guide should:
- be easy to find on the intranet
- look inviting, clear, accessible
- be very concise
- be searchable
- be easy to skim-read.

It's dangerous to create a printed version of a style guide. Just say no! A printed style guide risks going out of date within weeks. Things change. Organisations change. Technology changes every time you blink. You can update an online style guide with a few keystrokes, but an out-of-date printed style guide will hang around misinforming staff forever.

Don't even think about publishing the style guide as a PDF. For a document like this, PDFs are awkward, inaccessible, begging to be printed and lost.

Consider creating a small web site for your style guide and other resources for writers. It is possible to produce a style guide that is built on a database and functions like a familiar help tool (such as MS Word Help). I love this idea. Don't you?

Some people will still want to print part of the style guide, and that should be made possible. However, printing can skew version control. So I know you'll make sure every printed page carries a last-updated note, plus the URL of the only authoritative version.

Updating the style guide: the process

A comprehensive style guide won't be created in the flick of a paper dart. It takes time, and several stages. Corp Comms are the logical group to manage the development of a style guide.

To involve staff in the development of a style guide, best set up a wiki. The wiki might simply be an expandable alphabetical list of guidelines. I suggest throwing it wide open to all staff so that everyone with interest or knowledge can get involved. Naturally, a style guide must have a single authoritative version—but interested parties can continue to contribute to a working version, and the editor can update the authoritative version whenever appropriate.

Where a wiki isn't possible, other methods of honest consultation with staff can be used instead.

Style guide content

The purpose of a style guide is to ensure all corporate documents including web sites have the approved look and feel and writing style, to control use of brands, and to make sure all important documents have a consistent style and standard.

People want a style guide to show them what to do: they are not looking for policy but practical instructions and models. However, there's also a place for policy and many other relevant resources. Consider including at least three levels of information: one or two pages giving the bigger picture; a scalable, searchable database of topics; and a short list of standards.

Work on the assumption that a comprehensive style guide will have many guidelines and few standards. Make sure people know the difference: standards are mandatory.

When drawing up comprehensive guidelines for all staff writers, be aware of cross-media issues with tables, images, graphs, glossaries, procedures, ROT, metadata, links and long documents. The style guide should contain templates (or screenshots of templates that are part of a publishing tool), and a few good examples of web content and other documents. Guidelines for corporate blogging must be included. Staff writers may also need guidance on using other media, such as email, slide presentations, and podcasts.

And remember, any style guide is a moving target. Constant vigilance is needed to keep it up to date. Hence the sense of an open-ended wiki.

Examples of style guides

The world is full of information about what should, could and must go into a company style guide and into a web style guide. It just needs integrating, that's all. Studying other style guides is one place to start.

The style guides mentioned below are a small sample of many, listed in no particular order. They were produced by particular organisations for use by their own staff. Judge them by their usability: notice which web style guides are skim-readable and searchable.

Many universities and organizations have a short web style guide for staff. Monash University's Web Style Guide is a good model.[224]

1. The outstanding winner is The Yahoo! Style Guide. It's magnificent, and lives up to its subtitle: The ultimate sourcebook for writing, editing, and creating content for the digital world. Ideally, buy the complete style guide as a regular book.

2. The Sun Microsystems' web writing style guide, first published in 1998, is widely used and of historic interest.

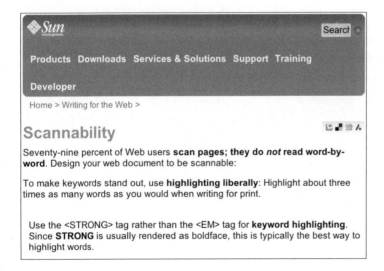

3. A List Apart puts a short style guide on a single page.[225] It begins with writing tips, and progresses to more technical details.

4. IBM publishes its style guidelines on the web as a PDF displayed in a browser, which I find inconvenient and inaccessible.[226] It barely mentions web content. But I like the simple alphabetical table of contents.

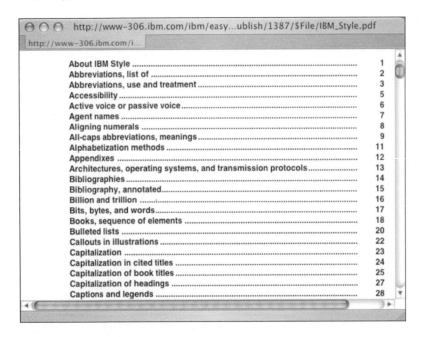

5. For government sites, first port of call should be your own country's e-government guidelines and standards.

6. Usability.gov guidelines are all supported by research.[227] When last I looked, they were available only in PDF format and heavy with screenshots.

7. Finally, the Economist Style Guide is widely used by journalists.[228]

Training writers

Writing is *a ticket to work—or a ticket out*, which makes it a make-or-break skill professionally.[229]

For an individual, training as a web content writer is not a problem nowadays. Anyone wishing to improve their skills has a choice of face-to-face, 1- or 2-day group courses, university or college courses, and online courses. In many cases the employer pays for tuition as a normal part of career development. Naturally I recommend my own short online course at CONTENTED.com![230]

But when it comes to raising the standard of all documents that are posted on web sites and intranets, things are not so simple.

First of all, staff training is an ongoing commitment. The organisation cannot just train one bunch of writers and never bother again. Producing usable online content is not a project—it's a core skill for all staff who write as part of their job.

Inhouse workshops on web content writing are often valuable, for example, at the start of a new project or for specialist staff. Trouble is, face-to-face workshops present problems of logistics and budget, so that only a minority of staff writers can be trained this way. If trained writers are in the minority, their skills can be neutralised by untrained colleagues, managers and editors. And staff turnover is a fact of life: train 100 people this way, and within weeks some have left and some have changed jobs.

Of course, you can start by training a core group who will then launch an organisation-wide communication and training campaign for the remaining staff writers. This requires full-scale planning, as well as considerable energy, people, and funds.

A different, easier, more cost-effective training solution can be found to supplement the core training.

Remember, the ultimate organisational goal is for the majority of salaried workers to write and structure all documents in a web-friendly way. This is a huge change, a culture change. And the time-honoured way that organisations change is for a significant proportion of people to make one little wee change in their behaviour.

For example, if 60% of staff writers merely gave every document an F-headline—nothing more—you would find:
- company documents would become far more user-friendly
- document management systems would work better
- search results would improve
- the usability of the intranet would rocket
- good models would start to predominate, and F-headlines become the norm.

Teach 4 people 96 skills, and you have 4 experts (until they leave). Teach 96 people 4 key skills, and business writing improves across the board. And the key skills are, of course:
- plain language
- F-headlines
- F-summaries
- F-links.

One logical approach to mass training is to make self-study, self-tested tutorials available online for any employee to visit at any time.[231] The advantages include:
- no seminar rooms, tutors or workbooks
- learn by lunch-time (just in time)
- lower costs
- no limit on numbers who can study.

A commitment to make training continuously available to all staff reflects systemic thinking, which is oriented to holistic, long-term goals. Systemic thinking is one mark of a learning organisation, according to Peter Senge.[232] Indeed, I have found that fragmented thinking is one of the main barriers for organisations seeking a solution to the horrible problem of bad online content. Departmental budgets and systems and priorities clash, so everything takes longer.

Ideally, all parties will cooperate to study the big picture, set goals, and plan training and support for all on-the-job writers. Frankly, for this to happen, somebody powerful has to push.

Luckily, behind the scenes, individual training carries on. This creates a less dramatic scenario for change. One by one, staff writers are quietly acquiring the 4 essential web writing skills. Numbers build, until they eventually create a tipping point. No grand plan. Just lots of people writing better, and understanding how to web-proof everyday documents.

How a CMS helps writers

A content management system (CMS) is virtually a necessity for large web sites and intranets. Many schools and universities could hardly function without their special educational software. A CMS smoothes the path between work writer and online publication. More staff are able (and obliged) to upload their own documents.

Built in to a CMS should be a workflow process that ensures all pages are checked by an editor or manager before being published. This is a protection for content writers, and an automated reminder system can do much to prevent ROT.

A CMS can assist content writers with templates that are highly structured, breaking content down into headlines, blocks or chunks of text, lists of links, and metadata. This makes the structure and destination of online documents more obvious to the writer. Using a CMS can help writers analyse the purpose and audience of their pages. Needless to say, staff need training to use templates properly.

Proprietary CMSs like to invent their own unique terminology. Writers naturally get confused if CMS terms are at odds with the terms used in training. Web publishing templates can be customised so that they closely reflect the required behaviour of content writers. The main thing is to study and rationalise the terminology of your own CMS.

- Use *Headline*: not *Teaser* (because writers should not tease); nor *Title*, (because there are so many *Titles* in the code and metadata); nor *Header* (because headers are too short).
- Use *Summary*: not *Abstract* (an academic term), nor *Description* (which some CMSs use to mean page type, for example, *homepage*).

Support for all staff writers

Doubtless you are keen to totally transform all your web and intranet content, eliminate bad content, stop ROT in its tracks, web-proof all future paper-based documents, and ensure that all new content is usable, accessible, and findable?

That's a big ask, and staff will need all the support they can get.

Even on a small budget, you can celebrate small successes on the intranet. Involve and consult. Showcase good new content. Give credit for improvement. Publicise savings of time and money. Highlight paper documents that work well both on the web or intranet.

The University of Melbourne's Web Centre offers an excellent model of professional development for staff involved in web sites.[233] It provides information, tools, guidelines, templates, and plenty of tips. It includes training courses, a web forum by email, a regular 'web cuppa' and brownbag lunch seminars.

But no matter how brilliant, the University of Melbourne's site still puts staff writers into a techie web ghetto. To avoid this, consider creating a similar resource for all on-the-job writers—not just those who consider themselves web content writers. This could do a lot to change the toxic perception that web writing is special, different, and super-technical.

Testing the usability of content

Usability testing of web sites is, thank heaven, becoming much more common. But the testing of new web content—and especially intranet content—is not so common.

One rule applies equally to the usability of an entire site and a single page: you don't know whether it is usable until you observe a few people using it. *People*, in this case, don't include the writer. In fact, the writers are the very people who cannot test their own content. (Writers can't understand why anyone would fail to grasp their meaning.)

Luckily, potential testers are everywhere.

Originally, it was thought that usability testing should be done by typical target readers. But it turns out that almost anyone will do. Steve Krug, in his tremendously popular book *Don't Make Me Think*, reckons *the importance of recruiting representative users is overrated.*[234] He gives commonsense advice on how to do your own testing on a shoestring, and points out that testing one user is 100% better than testing none. Here's how.

1. Write the content of a page.
2. Grab someone nearby and ask them to read your page.
3. As they read, watch. Do they frown, do their eyes backtrack, do they look puzzled? Where?
4. Don't explain, guide or help the user. Ask them a few simple questions, for example:
   - What's the page about? What's it for?
   - Do you get it?
   - Is this what you need? Is it what you expected?
   - What would you do next?
5. Fix the page.
6. Repeat with other colleagues until someone gets it.

Your colleagues don't have to solve the problem: they just have to stumble over the problem.

Nothing beats hands-on testing of content. But in addition, you can deliberately invite feedback for intranet content. You might want to ask on intranet pages, *Is this page clear? Is it useful?* and providing an email link for replies. Fortunately, your colleagues will let you know instantly if you get something wrong on the intranet. A general feedback page is also useful.

End of story, start of story

As I finish this final chapter, let me thank you for reading, and wish you the best of luck.

If your job includes writing web content, I hope you have learned at least 4 and possibly 96 useful tricks. I imagine you are full of new ideas, triggered by something you have read here. I know you will raise the usability of your own business writing and write terrific web content. My wish is that you will succeed in generating content that makes people happy—yourself, your customers, your client, your boss, and above all, your readers.

If you manage web content, I hope this book has thrown light on some of the difficult issues that you juggle and struggle with in your work. I'd like to think you are burning with enthusiasm to help transform the quality of business writing in your organisation, online and off. I wish you all the best as you fight the hydra-headed beast of business writing on the web.

And I leave you with this mantra:
Web writing is business writing.
Business writing is web writing.
Web writing
is business writing
is web writing
is business writing.

Keep in touch with Contented

Contented specialises in short, scalable, web-based courses on writing skills for the digital world. Train your staff to write usable, findable content, from micro-blogging to business reports, from standard intranet content to high-level policy. These are gorgeous courses for clever people, and highly cost-effective for groups.

Web site: Contented.com
E-mail: content@contented.com
(That was an advertisement. I'm sure you noticed.)

Endnotes

Complete URLs are not supplied for references, because many pages will have disappeared or moved by the time you read this book. Sometimes you can find the exact page from the home page, for which URLs are provided. Sometimes Google will find the page you want.

Chapter 1. 21st century business writing

[1] Malcolm Gladwell (2000). *The tipping point.* London: UK. Little Brown.

[2] Gerry McGovern (2007). *The problem of dirty data.* New Thinking. Retrieved 22 April 2007 from http://giraffeforum.com

[3] Richard Maven. *Web launch delays blamed on lack of content.* Retrieved 2 February 2007 from http://www.e-consultancy.com

[4] James Robertson (2006). Retrieved 3 February 2007 from http://www.e-consultancy.com

[5] You may wonder why I write *10* and *3* in digits instead of *ten* and *three*. It's because this book will be read on a screen as well as on paper. More about this in Chapter 8, *The feng shui of onscreen content.*

[6] John Morkes & Jakob Nielsen (1998). *Applying writing guidelines to web pages.* Retrieved 15 February 2007 from http://www.useit.com

[7] Jakob Nielsen (2006). *F-shaped pattern for reading web content.* Retrieved 24 May 2007 from http://www.useit.com

Chapter 2. Why the dream seems impossible

[8] Kara Pernice Coyne, Mathew Schwartz & Jakob Nielsen. *Intranet Design Annual 2007* (2007). Retrieved 16 January 2007 from http://www.nngroup.com

[9] Bob Boiko. Retrieved 2 February 2007 from http://www.steptwo.com.au

[10] MIT. Retrieved 2 February 2007 from http://mit.edu

[11] Gerry McGovern. (2006). *Is your content a waste of time and money?* Retrieved 18 December 2006 from http://www.gerrymcgovern.com

[12] National Commission on Writing (2004). *Writing: a ticket to work... or a ticket out. A survey of business leaders.* Retrieved 17 December 2006 from http://www.writingcommission.org

[13] National Commission on Writing. Same.
[14] National Commission on Writing (2005). *Writing: a powerful message from state government*. Retrieved 17 December 2006 from http://www.writingcommission.org
[15] National Commission on Writing (2006). *Writing and school reform*. Retrieved 17 December 2006 from http://www.writingcommission.org
[16] New Zealand Ministry of Education (2006). *Student outcome overview 2001-2005: Research findings on student achievement in reading, writing and mathematics in New Zealand schools*. Retrieved 17 December 2006 from http://www.educationcounts.edcentre.govt.nz

Chapter 3. Not your usual reader

[17] Ann Holland (2005). *Top five eye-tracking laboratory test results*. Retrieved 6 May 2006 from http://chiefmarketer.com
[18] Center for Education. Retrieved 14 February 2007 from http://ce.com
[19] Malcolm Gladwell (2005). *Blink. The power of thinking without thinking*. London: Penguin.

Chapter 4. Plain language online

[20] Lisa Kunde, Communications Manager of Virgin Blue (2006). Discussion forum, GDID 701, Christchurch Polytechnic Institute of Technology. Retrieved October 2006 from http://www.cpit.ac.nz
[21] Jakob Nielsen (2005). *Lower-literacy users*. Retrieved 15 February 2006 from http://www.useit.com
[22] Capitalised phrases count as single words. So the *Ministry of Silly Walks* is perceived as one word. That gives you a bit more room to manoeuvre.
[23] Jakob Nielsen (2003). *Information pollution*. Viewed 9 May 2006 on www.useit.com
[24] B.J. Fogg (2002). *Stanford guidelines for web credibility*. Stanford Persuasive Technology Lab. Retrieved 9 May 2006 from http://www.webcredibility.org
[25] LexisNexis. Retrieved 15 February 2007 from http://www.lexisnexis.com
[26] Kathy Sierra (2005). *Writing kicks formal writing's ass*. Retrieved 15 February 2007 from http://headrush.typepad.com
[27] 37signals. Retrieved 15 February 2007 from http://www.37signals.com
[28] There's more about writing objectively in Chapter 11, and about persuasion in Chapter 18.

[29] Stephen J. Pyne (1986). *The ice.* London: Orion (2004 ed.).

Chapter 5. F-headlines: flying the flag

[30] Jakob Nielsen (1999). *Intranet portals: The corporate information infrastructure.* Retrieved 20 March 2007 from http://www.useit.com

[31] John Morkes (2000). Usability Week. Sydney, Australia. (Oral statement).

[32] Stanford University and Poynter Institute (2000). *Poynter-Stanford online eyetrack study.* Retrieved 6 May 2007 from http://www.poynterextra.org

[33] State of California. Retrieved May 2006 from http://www.ca.gov

[34] Page titles are discussed in Chapter 12. Page titles are not headlines.

Chapter 6. F-summaries: do or die

[35] See Chapter 13 for more details and examples.

Chapter 7. F-links and cuff-links

[36] Jared M. Spool, Christine Perfetti, and David Brittan (2004). *Designing for the scent of information.* North Andover, MA: User Interface Engineering. Retrieved 9 March 2007 from http://www.uie.com

[37] Belize National Emergency Management Organization (NEMO). Retrieved 28 January 2007 from http://www.nemo.org.bz

[38] OurBrisbane.com. Retrieved 28 January 2007 from http://www.ourbrisbane.com

[39] Gunnar Anziger. Retrieved 28 January 2007 from http://www.gksoft.com

[40] State of Illinois Business Portal. Retrieved 28 January 2007 from http://business.illinois.gov

[41] PandemicFlu.gov. Retrieved 28 January 2007 from http://www.pandemicflu.gov

[42] Right-aligned links in Urdu and Arabic. Retrieved 28 January 2007 from http://www.kuwait-info.com and http://www.ksu.edu.sa

[43] OurBrisbane.com. Same.

[44] Spyridakis, J.H. (2000). *Guidelines for authoring comprehensible web pages and evaluating their success.* Technical Communication, 47(3), 359-382.

[45] Jared M. Spool, Christine Perfetti, and David Brittan. Same.

[46] USA.gov. Retrieved 28 January 2007 from http://www.usa.gov

[47] Hamilton County Tennessee Services. Retrieved 29 January 2007 from http://www.hamiltontn.gov

[48] Jakob Nielsen (2005). *The top ten design mistakes in web logs.*

Retrieved 28 January 2007 from http://www.useit.com

49 Tom Coates. Retrieved 23 January 2007 from http://www.plasticbag.org

Chapter 8. The feng shui of online content

50 Jared M. Spool, Christine Perfetti, and David Brittan. Same.

51 Usability.gov (2006). *Research-based web design & usability guidelines.* Retrieved 15 January 2007 from http://www.usability.gov

52 Asian Development Bank. Retrieved 11 January 2007 from http://adb.org

53 Energy Star. Retrieved 12 January 2007 from http://www.energystar.govt.nz

54 Snooks & Co. (Ed). *Style manual* (6th ed, 2002). Brisbane, Australia: Wiley.

Chapter 9. Function and dysfunction

55 Dennis Matthies (2001). *Question driven writing.* Stanford, CA: Stanford University.

56 Jakob Nielsen (2006). *Digital divide: the three stages*. Retrieved 29 December 2006 from http://www.useit.com

57 Vodafone. Retrieved 28 December 2006 from http://www.vodafone.co.nz

58 Levi's. Retrieved 29 December 2006 from http://www.us.levi.com

59 Inland Revenue Department, New Zealand. Retrieved 30 December 2006 from http://www.ird.govt.nz

Chapter 10. Focused, freestanding content

60 Asian Development Bank. Retrieved 3 January 2007 from http://adb.org

61 Department of Social and Family Affairs. Retrieved 8 January 2007 from http://www.welfare.ie

62 Department for Education and Skills, U.K. Retrieved 8 January 2007 from http://www.dfes.gov.uk

63 Treasury Board of Canada Secretariat. Retrieved 13 May 2007 from http://www.tbs-sct.gc.ca

64 FFTW (Fastest Fourier Transform in the West). Retrieved 10 January 2007 from http://www.fftw.org

65 Metal Finishing Industry. Retrieved 11 May 2007 from http://www.p2pays.org

66 FAO. Retrieved 10 January 2007 from http://www.fao.org

67 AGIMO. Retrieved 10 January 2007 from http://www.agimo.gov.au

Chapter 11. Fresh and factual content

[68] Belize Coastal Zone Management Authority and Institute. Retrieved 28 January 2007 from http://www.coastalzonebelize.org

[69] The Library, University of California, Berkeley. Retrieved 28 January 2007 from http://www.lib.berkeley.edu

[70] Palomar College. Retrieved 12 January 2007 from http://daphne.palomar.edu

[71] Boston University. Retrieved 11 January 2007 from http://www.bu.edu

[72] South Canterbury District Health Board. Retrieved 12 January 2007 from http://www.scdhb.co.nz

Chapter 12. Photos, figs, Flash and audio

[73] Jakob Nielsen and Kara Pernice Coyne (2006). *Eyetracking Web Usability* (Manual for Usability Week, Sydney 2006). NN Group.

[74] Accu-tel Call Centre and Emrill Call Centre. Retrieved 14 May 2007 from http://www.accutel-callcentre.com and http://www.emrill.com

[75] This page does not exist. It's a mock-up using photos © Ashley Wood.

[76] National Statistics. Retrieved 14 January 2007 from http://www.statistics.gov.uk

[77] The two images with unsuitable fonts were retrieved 14 January 2007 from http://www.bbc.co.uk and http://ftp.sas.com respectively.

[78] Sine Patterns. Retrieved 14 January 2007 from http://www.sinepatterns.com

[79] NASA. Retrieved 14 January 2007 from http://www.heasarc.nasa.gov

[80] Atuleirus. Retrieved 14 January 2007 from http://www.atuleirus.weblog.com.pt

[81] University of Puget Sound. Retrieved 14 January 2007 from http://www2.ups.edu

[82] Parliament of Australia. Retrieved 14 January 2007 from http://www.aph.gov.au

[83] Microbe of the Month (April 2006). Retrieved 14 January 2007 from http://www.peacockshock.com

[84] Better Living Through Design. Retrieved 1 November 2006 from http://betterlivingthroughdesign.com

[85] Hans Rosling (2007). *Debunking third-world myths with the best stats you've ever seen.* TED. Retrieved 26 May 2007 from http://www.ted.com.

Chapter 13. Findable content

[86] The image is a SERP from Google, as if you needed telling. Retrieved 3 January 2007 from http://google.com

[87] MSN Career Builder. *Four jobs on the cutting edge*. Retrieved 2006 from http://msn.careerbuilder.com

[88] Search Engine College. Retrieved 28 May 2007 from http://www.searchenginecollege.com

[89] Online Web Training. Retrieved 3 January 2007 from http://www.onlinewebtraining.com

[90] Agriculture and Agri-Food Canada. Retrieved 19 March 2006 from http://www.agr.gc.ca

[91] Agriculture and Agri-Food Canada. Same.

[92] Commonwealth of Virginia. Retrieved 14 May 2007 from http://www.dhrm.state.va.us

[93] Australian Universities Teaching Committee. Retrieved 4 January 2007 from http://www.autc.gov.au

[94] Royal Australian Navy. Retrieved 4 January 2007 from http://www.navy.gov.au

[95] Study in Australia. Retrieved 4 January 2007 from http://studyinaustralia.gov.au

[96] World Wide Web Consortium (W3). Retrieved 14 May 2007 from http://www.w3.org

[97] Google. Retrieved 4 January 2007 from http://google.com

[98] Yahoo! Retrieved 4 January 2007 from http://help.yahoo.com

[99] OneStat.com reported in July 2006 that in the USA, only 6.19% of searchers typed single words into the search box. More people used 6- or 7-word phrases than single words. Results: 3-words used by 28.83%, 4-words 22.28%, 2-words 20.43%, 5-words 11.97%, 1-word 6.19%, 6-words 5.76%, 7-word phrases 2.59%. Retrieved 4 January 2007 from http://www.onestat.com

[100] Insurance Technology Solutions. Retrieved 14 May 2007 from http://www.ascendantone.com

[101] Linbeck. Retrieved 4 January 2007 from http://www.linbeck.com

[102] Most government metadata are based, directly or indirectly, on the Dublin Core (DC) group's metadata. Other groups are also working on metadata standards. For historical reasons, web sites may use several kinds of metadata, not just those prescribed by their government.

[103] To see the metadata of a Word document, select the document and check File: Get Info. You can add metadata when in Word by selecting File: Properties.

[104] U.S. Government Printing Office. Retrieved 4 January 2007 from http://www.gpo.gov

[105] Gerry McGovern (2007). Retrieved 10 January 2007 from http://www.gerrymcgovern.com

Chapter 14. Web Me-Too and what else is new

[106] Time Magazine (2006). *Person of the year: You*. Time Inc.

[107] Rosner, Bob. *Working wounded: Time's person of the year*. ABC News. Retrieved 21 December 2006 from http://abcnews.go.com

[108] O'Reilly, Tim. *What is Web 2.0?* Retrieved 21 December 2006 from http://www.oreillynet.com

[109] IBM developerWorks blogs. Retrieved 20 December 2006 from http://www-03.ibm.com

[110] James Snell (2005). *IBM blogging policy and guidelines*. Retrieved 21 December 2006 from http://www-03.ibm.com

[111] Dominion Post (14 May 2007). Wellington, New Zealand. Retrieved 14 May 2007 from http://www.stuff.co.nz.

[112] Jerry Bowles (2006). *Top 10 management fears about enterprise Web 2.0*. Fastforward. Retrieved 19 December 2006 from http://fastforwardblog.com

[113] Sydney Morning Herald (14 June 2006). Retrieved 20 December 2006 from http://www.smh.com.au

[114] Amanda Lenhart & Susannah Fox (2006). *Bloggers. A portrait of the internet's new storytellers*. Pew Internet. Retrieved 16 May 2007 from http://www.pewinternet.com

[115] Nielsen, Jakob (2006). *Participation inequality: Encouraging more users to contribute*. Useit.com. Retrieved 17 December 2006 from http://www.useit.com

[116] Dorje McKinnon (2005). OnlineGroups.net. Retrieved 29 December 2006 from http://onlinegroups.net

[117] BBSCR. This web site has been substantially changed. Retrieved November 2003 from http://www.bbsrc.ac.uk

[118] UNDP. Retrieved 20 December 2006 from http://europeandcis.undp.org

[119] McLuhan, M. (1964). *Understanding media: The extensions of man*. Columbus, OH: McGraw-Hill.

[120] Time Inc. Retrieved 16 May 2007 from http://www.time.com

[121] My Story. Retrieved 16 May 2007 from http://www.watchmystory.tv

[122] Mary Madden (2006). *Podcast downloading.* Pew Internet & American Life Project. Retrieved 16 May 2007 from http://www.pewinternet.org

Chapter 15. Standard pages need a brain

[123] Jakob Nielsen & Hoa Loranger (2006). *Prioritizing web usability.* Berkeley, CA: Peachpit.

[124] Mitsui & Co. (USA). Retrieved 18 May 2007 from http://www.mitsui.com

[125] Fonterra. Retrieved 18 May 2007 from http://www.fonterra.com

[126] University of Sydney. Retrieved 18 May 2007 from http://www.usyd.edu.au

[127] University of Southampton. Retrieved 1 January 2007 from http://www.soton.ac.uk

[128] Internal Revenue Service. Retrieved 1 January 2007 from http://www.irs.gov

[129] Cochise College. Retrieved 18 May 2007 from http://www.cochise.edu

[130] WorkSmart. Retrieved 1 January 2007 from http://www.worksmart.org.uk

[131] Clinton County Health Department. Retrieved 19 May from http://www.co.clinton.ny.us

[132] Philip Morris International. Retrieved 1 January 2007 from http://www.philipmorrisinternational.com

[133] Toyota. Retrieved 1 January 2007 from http://www.toyota.com

[134] Princeton University. Retrieved 1 January 2007 from http://www.princeton.edu

[135] Wellington City Council. Retrieved 1 January 2007 from http://www.wellington.govt.nz

[136] Agency for Healthcare Research and Quality, United States Department of Health & Human Services. Retrieved 19 May 2007 from http://www.ahrq.gov

[137] Microsoft. Retrieved 19 May 2007 from http://www.microsoft.com

[138] Microsoft. Same.

[139] Mitsubishi USA. Retrieved 2 January 2007 from http://www.micusa.com

[140] Philip Morris USA. Retrieved 1 January 2007 from http://www.philipmorrisusa.com

[141] Philip Morris USA. Same.

[142] For example, editors may require Verdana font, a lead paragraph saying who did what where when and why, writer's 24-hour contact details on every page, photo format, and photo opportunities.

[143] Indiana University Media Relations. Retrieved 2 January 2007 from http://newsinfo.iu.edu

[144] Indiana University Media Relations. Same.

[145] ThinkGeek. Retrieved 19 May 2007 from http://www.thinkgeek.com

[146] Morkes, John (2006). *Content usability 1.* Nielsen Norman Group.

Chapter 16. The secret life of intranets

[147] NetStrategyJMC. *"Global intranet strategies today & tomorrow" Survey*. 2006. Retrieved 4 October 2006 from www.netjmc.com

[148] Kara Pernice Coyne, Mathew Schwartz & Jakob Nielsen (2007). *Intranet Design Annual 2007*. Nielsen Norman Group. Retrieved 16 January 2007 from http://www.nngroup.com

[149] Toby Ward (2007). *The end of internal communications.* Intranet Blog. Retrieved 2 February 2007 from http://intranetblog.blogware.com

[150] Mike Theaker (2006). *Web earns central role in hr service delivery*. Equity Skills News and Views. Retrieved 4 February 2007 from http://www.workinfo.com

[151] Mike Theaker. Same.

[152] Peter Tiersma. *Plain English laws*. LANGUAGE and LAW.org. Retrieved 20 May 2007 from http://www.languageandlaw.org

[153] Retrieved 10 January 2007 from http://hrnt.jhu.edu

[154] Retrieved 10 January 2007 from http://www.dhrm.state.va.us

[155] University of Otago. Retrieved 20 May 2007 from http://www.otago.ac.nz

[156] Usability.gov. *Research-based web design and usability guidelines*. Retrieved 5 February 2007 from http://www.usability.gov

[157] Sullivan University. Retrieved 5 February 2007 from http://library.sullivan.edu

[158] Accident Compensation Corporation (ACC). The page no longer exists in this form. Retrieved 2003 from www.acc.co.nz

[159] New Zealand Post. Retrieved 20 February 2007 from http://www.nzpost.co.nz

[160] Toby Ward, 14 February 2007. Retrieved 21 February 2007 from http://intranetblog.blogware.com

[161] NetStrategyJMC. Same.

Chapter 17. E-government: because you must

[162] The Central People's Government of the People's Republic of China. Retrieved 18 January 2007 from http://www.gov.cn

[163] Paul Timmers (2004). EU eGovernment Policy—Vision, Actions, Challenges. United Nations Online Network in Public Administration and Finance. Retrieved 18 January 2007 from http://unpan1.un.org

[164] The Australian Government Information Management Office (AGIMO). Retrieved

18 January 2007 from http://www.agimo.gov.au

[165] USA.gov. Retrieved 18 January 2007 from http://www.usa.gov

[166] E-government New Zealand. Retrieved 18 January 2007 from http://www.e.govt.nz

[167] W3C. Retrieved 18 January 2007 from http://w3c.org

[168] E-government New Zealand. Same.

[169] Australian Public Service Commission. Retrieved 19 January 2007 from http://www.apsc.gov.au

[170] Home Office. Retrieved 19 January 2007 from http://www.ind.homeoffice.gov.uk

[171] U.S. Department of Justice. Retrieved 19 January 2007 from http://www.usdoj.gov

[172] New York State Web Portal. Retrieved 18 January 2007 from http://www.ny.gov

[173] Department of Education, Victoria. Retrieved 18 January 2007 from http://www.education.vic.au

[174] Hazardous Materials Information Review Commission, Canada. Retrieved 18 January 2007 from http://www.hmirc-ccrmd.gc.ca

[175] Ministry of Social Development, New Zealand. Retrieved 18 January 2007 from http://www.msd.govt.nz

[176] Working in the U.K. Retrieved 18 January 2007 from http://www.workingintheuk.gov.uk

[177] Federal Transit Administration. Retrieved 18 January 2007 from http://www.fta.dot.gov

[178] Internal Revenue Service. Retrieved 18 January 2007 from http://www.irs.gov

[179] Rural Payments Agency. Retrieved 18 January 2007 from http://www.rpa.gov.uk

[180] Scottish Executive. Retrieved 17 January 2007 from http://www.scotland.gov.uk

[181] Darrell M. West. *State and federal e-government in the United States, 2006*. Taubman Center for Public Policy, Brown University. Retrieved 20 May 2007 from http://www.InsidePolitics.org

[182] Europe's Information Society (2007). i2010 Annual Report 2007. Retrieved 20 May 2007 from http://ec.europa.eu

[183] Dominion Post (14 May 2007). Wellington, New Zealand.

[184] Jason Ryan. *5 principles for Govt2.0*. Network of Public Service Communicators. 29 April 2007. Retrieved 15 May 2007 from http://www.psnetwork.org.nz

Chapter 18. Commercial content: trust me

[185] Edelman (2006). *A corporate guide to the global blogosphere*. Downloaded 15 January 2007 from http://www.edelman.com

[186] Edelman. Same.

[187] B.J. Fogg is the father of persuasive technology, and he gives the full picture in *Persuasive technology* (2003). San Francisco, CA: Morgan Kaufmann.

[188] Mercury Energy. Let's hope this page has changed by the time you check it out. Retrieved 16 January 2007 from http://www.mercuryenergy.co.nz

[189] TXU Energy. Retrieved 16 January 2007 from http://www.txu.com

[190] Ken McEvoy (2002). *Make your site sell!* Retrieved 3 January 2007 from www.sitesell.com

[191] Gerry McGovern (2006). *Do you know what's in your long neck?* Retrieved 17 January 2007 from http://www.gerrymcgovern.com

[192] Princeton Survey Research Associates International (2005). *Leap of faith: using the internet despite the dangers*. Consumer Reports WebWatch. Retrieved 17 January 2007 from http://www.consumerwebwatch.org

[193] The Web Credibility Project. credibility.stanford.edu

[194] The Web Credibility Project (2002). *Stanford guidelines for web credibility*. Retrieved 17 January 2007 from http://www.webcredibility.org

[195] Consumer WebWatch. *Consumer reports webwatch guidelines*. Retrieved 17 January 2007 from http://consumerwebwatch.org

[196] Backbonemedia (2005). *Corporate blogging: Is it worth the hype?* Retrieved 14 January 2007 from http://www.backbonemedia.com

[197] Adobe XML News Aggregator. Retrieved 20 May 2007 from http://weblogs.macromedia.com

[198] John Dowdell. JD on EP. Retrieved 16 January 2007 from http://weblogs.macromedia.com

[199] Arcelor Mittal TV. Retrieved 26 January 2007 from http://www.arcelormittal.tv

[200] Simmonds Brothers. www.simmondsbrothers.com

Chapter 19. Academic content: practise what you preach

[201] For the rest of this chapter I'm just going to call these upper level educational institutions *universities*. Instant promotion for some.

[202] Martine Booth (2005). *Chaos or collaboration? Web management in a*

[203] *decentralised university environment* University of Melbourne. Retrieved 21 January 2007 from http://ausweb.scu.edu.au

[203] Shaun Nicholson (2003). *An investigation into the management of a university web site.* Retrieved November 2003 from http://webteam.waikato.ac.nz

[204] Massachusetts Institute of Technology (MIT). Retrieved 21 May from http://web.mit.edu

[205] Dey Alexander (2005). *How usable are university websites?* Monash University. Retrieved 21 January 2007 from http://ausweb.scu.edu.au

[206] Trent Mankelow (2004). *A usability assessment of New Zealand university websites.* Wellington, New Zealand: Optimal Usability. Retrieved 26 January 2007 from http://www.optimalusability.com

[207] University of Auckland. Retrieved 26 January 2007 from http://www.auckland.ac.nz

[208] AUT University. Retrieved 26 January 2007 from http://www.aut.ac.nz

[209] University of Massachusetts, Amherst. Retrieved 21 May 2007 from http://www.umass.edu

[210] Massachusetts Institute of Technology (MIT) Open Courseware. ocw.mit.edu

[211] This nonsense was inspired by *Dancing with cats*. Retrieved 22 January 2007 from http://www.monpa.com

[212] Neil Woodbury (25 January 2007). Wellington, New Zealand: Dominion Post

[213] Jonathan Swift (1729). *A modest proposal.*

[214] One influential set of standards for RLOs at present is SCORM: Sharable Content Object Reference Model. Visit Advanced Distributed Learning for details and content examples, but don't let it scare you: ask the technical experts in your university to guide you. Retrieved 22 January 2007 from http://www.adlnet.gov

[215] The University of Wisconsin in Milwaukee has a long list of sites with collections of learning objects. www.uwm.edu

[216] LabWrite. Retrieved 22 January 2007 from http://labwrite.ncsu.edu

[217] Georgia State University. Retrieved 22 January 2007 from http://www2.gsu.edu

[218] Glenn Millar. *Learning objects 101: A primer for neophytes.* British Columbia Institute of Technology Learning and Teaching Centre. Retrieved 22 January 2007 from http://online.bcit.ca

[219] Robert H. Stewart (2005). *Introduction to physical oceanography.* Texas A&M University. Retrieved 27 January 2007 from http://oceanworld.tamu.edu

[220] Massachusetts Institute of Technology (MIT) Open Courseware. Same.

[221] La Trobe University (2004). *Online learning*. Retrieved 22 January 2007 from http://www.latrobe.edu.au

Chapter 20. International content

[222] Hala Memayssi et al. (2006) *Designing an Arabic user interface.* User Experience Vol 5, Issue 1, 2006. Usability Professionals Association. Retrieved 16 May 2006 from www.usabilityprofessionals.org.

Chapter 21. Culture change: getting contented

[223] World Wide Web Consortium (W3C). Retrieved 3 May 2007 from http://www.w3.org

[224] Monash University. Retrieved 30 January 2007 from http://www.monash.edu.au

[225] A List Apart. Retrieved 31 January 2007 from http://www.alistapart.com

[226] IBM Style Guidelines. Retrieved 30 January 2007 from http://www-03.IBM.com

[227] Retrieved 31 January 2007 from http://www.usability.gov

[228] The Economist. Retrieved 4 May 2007 from http://www.economist.com

[229] National Commission on Writing (2004). *Writing: A ticket to work... or a ticket out. a survey of business leaders.* Retrieved 3 February 2007 from http://www.writingcommission.org

[230] Contented, a short online professional development course, focuses on the 4 essential skills for web and intranet content writers. www.Contented.com

[231] Contented is valuable training for web-proofing all business documents. Same.

[232] Peter Senge (1990). *The fifth discipline. The art and practice of the learning organisation*. London: Random House.

[233] University of Melbourne. Retrieved 30 January 2007 from http://www.unimelb.edu.au

[234] Steve Krug (2000). *Don't make me think*. Indianapolis, IN: New Riders.

Index

96:4 rule, 9, 264–265

A

About Us, 60, 160–161, 169–173, 248

Academic content, 14, 31, 39, 50, 69, 133, 160–163, 230–244, 263

Accessibility, 7, 19, 23, 72, 112–125

Alignment, 35, 56, 58, 64, 69, 74, 94, 219, 251

ALT-text, 112–115, 120, 136

Audience, 19–25, 27, 29–30, 41–42, 80, 203, 237–238

Audio. See Podcasts

B

Blogs, 144, 147–148, 195, 213–214, 226–227

Budget, 8, 17–18, 136

Bullet points. See Lists

Business writing, 1, 10–12, 14–17, 253, 261, 265

C

Cake-words, 39, 107

Captions, 111, 116–118

Cell phones, 153–154

Charts. See Graphs

CMS, 45, 46, 666, 262

Commercial content, 147–148, 157–179, 215–229

Conciseness, 29, 107–109, 180–182, 190, 205, 209, 220–221, 233

Consultation, 149–151

Contact, 165–168

Credibility, 7, 21, 66, 166, 169–173, 174–175

Cross-cultural communication, 245–252

D

Data, 45, 86–88

Dates, 103–105

Description, 48, 140

Design, 20, 30, 34–35, 58, 66–75, 116

Documation, 228–229

Dot points. See Lists

E

E-books, 155–156

E-government, 89–93, 95, 140-144, 196–214, 260

E-learning, 124

Error messages, 178–179

Executive summary, 47–49, 248–249

Explanations, 29, 50–51

Eye-tracking, 9–10, 21, 111, 252

F

F-language. See F-writing

F-links, 54–65, 136, 230, 234

Flash, 124–125, 27, 244

Focus, 88-90

Forms, 81–84, 166, 179, 218–219

F-reading, 7, 9–10, 23–25, 33–35, 38, 56, 58–59, 67–70, 95–98, 207, 209, 249, 251–252

Front-loading, 37–39, 53

Function. See Purpose

F-writing, 9–10, 136–137 See also F-reading

G

Global English, 250–251

Google, 4, 24, 39, 51, 52–53, 86, 90, 102–102, 126–144, 223, 231

Government sites. See E-government

Grammar, 17, 22, 26, 30, 205

Graphs, 115–124, 125

Guidelines, 7–8, 198–199, 211–213, 255–260

H

Handheld computers, 153–154

Headings, 34, 36
Headlines, 33–43, 210, 249, 262
Heatmaps. See Eye-tracking
Help, 41, 178–179
Home page , 157–159, 216, 367

I

Identity, 7, 91-93, 105, 182–183, 210–211
Images, 111–125, 247
Index pages, 57, 159–165
Instructions. See Procedures
Interaction, 22, 41, 55, 81, 145–151, 180–181, 215, 217–219, 254
International communication, 245–252
Intranets, 13, 15, 125, 130, 180–195
Introductions, 29, 46, 50–51, 201–202, 210, 248
Inverted pyramid, 7, 53, 107, 248–249

K

Key message, 7, 47
Keywords, 38, 53, 107, 136, 138–140, 142–144

L

Label pages, 165
Languages, 23, 58, 198, 251–252
Layout, 207–210
Lectures, 236–237
Legal issues, 193, 200
Link-text. See F-links
Lists, 74, 95–96, 121, 188, 201
Long documents, 41, 93–98

M

Management, 3–5, 230–231, 253–265
Marketing, 166–167, 169–173, 216, 220–222
Media releases, 175—177

Memos, 193–194

Metadata, 140–144

MS Word, 79

Multifunctional texts, 42–43

N

News stories, 41, 175–177

Newspapers, 35–36, 37

Numbers, 74

O

Objective writing, 9, 102, 107, 157–159, 163-164, 169–173

Our People, 173

P

Paper documents, 65, 79, 99–100, 115–116, 126, 140, 183–184, 200–203, 253, 261

PDFs, 98–99, 140, 259

Persuasion, 32, 217–215

Photos. See Images

Plain language, 7, 26–32, 137, 178–179, 181–182, 185–186, 201–207, 223, 230, 232, 240, 247

Podcasts, 125–127, 154–155, 215, 243–244, 257

Policy, 41, 149–151, 184–190

Positive language, 42, 205

Procedures, 41, 188, 190–193, 238–240

Pronouns, 7, 24, 32, 174, 202, 223, 247

Publishing tool. See CMS

Purpose, 7, 20–21, 22, 76–84, 88-90, 173, 219

Q

Questions, 78–81

R

Readability, 29, 102, 204–205, 232–233

Readers. See Audience

Reading, 26

Reusable Learning Objects, 240–242

ROI, 8, 26, 225, 254, 261

ROT, 80, 102–106, 193, 201

S

Saggy-baggy content, 189, 190, 207–209,

Scanning. See F-reading

Screen-reading software, 72, 111, 155

Search engines, 24, 126—144

Search results, 52–53, 66, 102, 128–144, 182, 249,

Sentences, 28, 47, 75, 121, 177, 232,

SEO, 128-130,

SERPs, 66, 130—138

Shovelware, 183–184

Skim-reading. See F-reading

Spelling. See Grammar

Standard pages, 157–179

Standards. See Guidelines

Storytelling, 174–175, 226–229

Strategy, 1–2, 8–9, 13–18, 76–78, 81, 104, 129, 215–218, 225, 253–265

Structure, 7, 29, 44–45, 50–51, 53, 85–86, 205, 235–236, 238–239 248–250

Style, 30–32, 250

Style guide, 66, 69, 74, 255–260

Sub-headlines, 39–40

Subject metadata, 142–144

Summaries, 7, 44–53, 134–136, 140, 230, 249, 262

T

Tables, 70–73, 191–192

Teaser, 34, 37

Technology, 23, 51, 151–152

Testing, 7–8, 9, 27, 54, 82, 100–101, 102, 122–123, 127, 144, 179, 229, 232, 234, 244, 246, 254, 264

Textbooks, 242–243

Tips , 41, 178–179

Titles, HTML page, 132–134

Titles, other, 115, 140

Training, 4–5, 9, 17, 230, 260–262, 263

Translation, 250, 252

Trust. See Credibility

U

Universities. See Academic content

Usability. See Testing

Use of page, 49, 81

V

Video. See Flash

W

W3C, 72, 112, 135–136, 198–199, 213

Web 2.0, 145–156, 197, 213–214

White space, 28, 74–75, 209

Wikis, 146–148, 181, 194–195, 215, 242, 256

Words, 27, 67

Writers, 2, 11, 15, 18, 77, 263

X

XML, 45, 79

Y

Yahoo!, 24, 137

You. See Pronouns